16-95 / 9

D0495131

The joke's on us

Morwenna Banks was born in Cornwall. After studying English at Cambridge University, she toured Britain and Australia with the Cambridge Footlights, returning to Australia with 'The Radio Active Revue Group'. She now works as a performer/writer for theatre, radio and television. Her credits include *Weekending*, *Bodgers, Banks and Sparkes* and *Radio Active* for Radio 4; *Saturday Live*, *The Lenny Henry Show* and *French and Saunders* for television. She is currently working as a scriptwriter on *Alas Smith and Jones* and *Hello Mum* for the BBC. This is her first book.

Amanda Swift studied Modern Languages at Oxford University; since then her performing work has ranged from repertory to women's, community and children's theatres. She has worked at the Bristol Old Vic and Derby Playhouse and with *Inter-Action* and *Little Women*. She is currently touring in the double act, Gorham and Swift. Her radio work includes *Cabaret Upstairs*, *Aspects of the Fringe* and *Pirate Radio 4*; she has appeared on television in *Cabaret* and *Lift Off!* Amanda Swift has researched several books and was Assistant Editor of *The Good Hotel Guide*. Her reviews and articles have appeared in *Time Out* and *Women's Review*. *The Joke's On Us* is her first book.

The joke's on us

Women in comedy
from music hall
to the present day

Morwenna Banks
and *Amanda Swift*

London

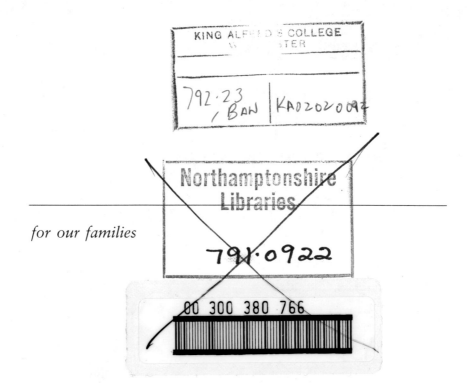
for our families

First published in 1987 by
Pandora Press (Routledge & Kegan Paul Ltd)
11 New Fetter Lane, London EC4P 4EE

Set in Sabon and Rockwell Light
by Columns of Reading
and printed in Great Britain
by Richard Clay Ltd, Bungay, Suffolk

© *Morwenna Banks and Amanda Swift 1987*

British Library CIP Data

Banks, Morwenna
The joke's on us : women in comedy from music
hall to the present day.
1. Women comedians—History
I. Title II. Swift, Amanda
791'.092'2   PN1590.W64

ISBN 0-86358-196-X (c)
*   0-86358-119-6 (p)*

Contents

Acknowledgments   vi
Introduction   vii

Stand-up – music hall, clubs and cabaret   1

Male/female humour: is there a difference?   50

Radio   52

   On looks, glamour and image   86

Character actors, monologuists and women's theatre   88

   Should there be more women in comedy?   128

Film   130

   How would you like things to change for women in comedy?   176

Writers and revue   178

Who or what makes you laugh?   224

Television   226

Conclusion   261

Historical chart   263
List of interviews   274
Photographic credits   275
Extract credits   277
Useful addresses   279
Bibliography   281
Index   286

Acknowledgments

With special thanks to David Tyler who first brought us together with the idea for a project on women in comedy; to Cathy Livesey for her invaluable research; to Simon Wilson for thoughts, words and deeds; to John Docherty and Moray Hunter for sharing the office, and to Bill Thomas and Chris Whittingham for lending and mending the word processor.

Additional thanks to: Actorum, Andy Aliffe, Dolores Banks, Vivienne Clore, Louise Clover, Angus Deayton, Chris England, Carl Gorham, Abi Grant, David Grant, Dr Peter Holland, Jonathan James Moore, Dr Lisa Jardine, Anne Ling, Neil Mullarkey, Alan Nixon, Imogen Parker, Geoffrey Perkins, Roger Planer, Dr Harry Porter, Diane Scally, Jo Scanlan, Leah Schmidt, Cathy Shipton, Fiona Shivas, Carol Smith, Godfrey and Mary Smith, Ted Taylor, Frances Tott, Teresa Watkins.

British Theatre Association Library, British Film Institute, Fawcett Library, Feminist Library at Hungerford House, Mander and Mitchenson Theatre Collection, Westminster City Libraries, Women in Entertainment, WRPM.

We should like to thank Ken Powles and the Northern Ireland Tourist Board for sponsoring our trip to Belfast.

Introduction

Women in comedy? That'll be a very short book.
(BBC Light Entertainment Producer)

Why write a book about women in comedy? The question has often
been asked of us, and at times we have even asked it of ourselves.
However, each time it has arisen, we have returned to the original
impulse that led us to approach Pandora Press with the idea for a
book on the subject. Working in the field of comedy and 'light
entertainment', as it is deceptively known, we are often struck by
the assumptions of employers, writers, the media and the general
public, that women, on the whole, are not funny. These assumptions
are frequently borne out by the popular press who have recently
published a spate of articles on contemporary women comedians
with such headlines as 'Funny Girls' and 'Bold, Bawdy and
Beautiful'. These articles claim to have 'discovered' Britain's women
comedians. They are written as if a funny woman is some sort of
oddity. Women are nearly always discussed in terms of being 'the
next' someone or other, 'The next Pamela Stephenson', 'The next
Tracey Ullman' – titles which suggest that there is only room for
one at a time, and that once 'the next' has arrived, 'the original'
must bow out gracefully. This leads to the perception of
professionally funny women as exceptions to a rule, a novel
minority. From the number of women we have met and seen
perform in all areas of comedy, we are prepared to argue that the
vestigial idea that women are generically unfunny is nonsense.
That's why we decided to write a book.

In writing this book, we wanted to unearth and expose funny
women not just in the emancipated 1980s, but to go a little further
back into history, to before film, radio and television began to
shape their image. We chose the 1880s, the heyday of the music
hall, as our starting point, a time when a woman could top the bill
and pull as many crowds as a man, and when perhaps the greatest
star of the British halls, Marie Lloyd, was at the peak of her

popularity. We believe that an historical approach is important as it provides an essential perspective on the subject, and often proffers gems of surprising information about women who, in the past, have made people laugh. To consider the past can help to inform us about the present and future.

When we started out on this venture, we had hopes that the book would do full justice to every women who has been professionally funny since 1880. We hoped to discover and assimilate patterns and trends, and from them to draw comprehensive conclusions about women working in comedy – why they've done it, and why more haven't. However, we have been unable to present a completely comprehensive study for a number of reasons, some of them practical. The scale of a preliminary enquiry like this made it impossible to follow up the minutest lead which may have led us to a forgotten heroine. We have based much of the book on live interviews with women working in comedy, but there remain essential people who, for various reasons, we were unable to interview. We regret these omissions, but have tried to cover the major facts about these women. One of the main reasons for any gaps in historical consistency is the lack of documentation about women in comedy. Music hall histories often consist of fond but inaccurate memories of acts, which all too frequently gloss over the female contributors. Despite this, music hall is one of the better-documented areas. A more recent history of comedy, John Fisher's *Funny Way To Be a Hero* contains a chapter entitled 'Are Women Funny?' Whether he thinks they are or not, only one chapter is devoted to the subject. Other books on comedy and on comedians of our time have actually omitted women altogether. This has not made our job easy. So our historical overview has been a matter of piecing together relevant extracts from records, tapes, films, videos, books, periodicals and live interviews. It is as accurate and as full as we can make it, but we do not claim it is exhaustive.

There are few things more destructive to comedy than analysing it. We have tried to steer clear of any tedious dissection of the various genres under discussion, whilst at the same time, we have tried to provide an insight into different styles and methods of performance, without deadening them for the reader. We have had to describe acts and shows which we would have preferred the reader to see, but alas, practical criticism must suffice. We have been unable to print live interviews in full, but the extracts we have chosen have been edited as little as possible, so that individual character remains. In doing the interviews, we have been taught to expect the unexpected. We have found the conflicting opinions and observations of many women, as well as the many similar strands and recurring themes, continuously striking. We have not tried to force the conflicting ideas into a single conclusion, we have tried rather to give them space. Performer Miriam Margolyes said of women in comedy: 'We all know each other but we have no corporate voice.' Our aim in this book has been simply to provide a voice.

It cannot be denied that the recording of historical fact has for centuries mainly been done by men, and has inevitably represented history from a male viewpoint. Thus it is not surprising that women have played a minor part in historical consciousness. We have no desire to dwell overlong on male oppression but rather to celebrate the lost and undervalued comic women of the past one hundred years.

The book has six main chapters, divided by genre, each of which could have been the subject of a book in itself. We have added an historical chart of events from 1880 to the present day, so that readers can relate developments in comedy to social changes. We have used the term 'comedian' to mean any woman who works through comedy in the fields of theatre, television, film, radio and stand-up comedy. The differences in performance styles are taken into account in the appropriate chapters. By encompassing all types of comic performer, we have gathered information on the differences between the various fields from those who know most about them.

Finally, we hope we have gone a little way to putting the notion that 'women aren't funny' to rest. We have tried to do this by offering a celebration of past and present successes, and by bringing to attention some of the funny women of the future. We hope that the book will encourage people to reconsider the idea of the funny woman, and that it will act as support to anyone who is considering being one for a living. Many will argue that there is no problem, that they have never considered that a woman might not be funny simply because she is a woman, or that there is be any difference between male and female humour. And perhaps this is the case. So most of all we hope that it is a good read and that you like the pictures.

MORWENNA BANKS
AMANDA SWIFT

Stand-up – music hall, clubs and cabaret

... it's the loneliest, hardest job in the world
(Beryl Reid)

Think 'comedian' and what do you see? A man at a microphone telling jokes. Although it's not the only way of being a comedian, it's seen as the epitome. The modern image is the tortured persona of Richard Pryor, or the dour offensiveness of Bernard Manning, the incisive wit of Billy Connolly or the political aggression of Ben Elton. Women stand-ups do not spring easily to mind.
It is commonly thought female comedians are performers who use 'tamer' forms and work as monologuists, character actors or satirists: Joyce Grenfell, Beryl Reid and Eleanor Bron are obvious examples. Whereas stand-up comedy is seen as a male domain: aggressive, dangerous and obscene. Yet women have worked in various areas of stand-up for the last hundred years and this chapter highlights and analyses that work. Whether in music hall, working-men's clubs or alternative cabaret, stand-up has two important characteristics which, if well-used, are a huge asset to women performers and, by inference, women in general: it is very public and it is highly dependent upon personality.
It's often said that women write novels and poetry rather than plays because they traditionally function in a domestic world and are more adept at presenting the psychological than the political, the private than the public. But in stand-up you are centre stage and you are the only protagonist; there is no play, no set, no character. You do not have the shield of a theatrical character; you are, in theory, presenting yourself.
Women who take up the challenge and are accepted as skilled stand-ups are making crucial progress. We're getting used to women as public figures in all kinds of professions – politicians, bankers, lawyers, doctors and so on – but the work demands that we see only a part of the women's life: the professional image. Whereas when a stand-up comedian is at work, we become aware

of her preoccupations, her imagination, her sense of self-worth, her relationships, her sexuality. If we respond we are responding to a personality. As current trends increasingly show, the influence of personalities, whether a Bob Geldof or an Anita Dobson (who plays Angie Watts in the BBC's soap, *Eastenders*), is enormously strong.

Personalities may wish to be politically influential but they achieve this end by gaining the public's approval. The politician or political activist has her supporters' approval, but she is forced to challenge the opposition and function in an aggressive, combative environment. Some political theatre functions similarly, and challenges assumptions by attacking its audience. For most performers, however, the public's approval is essential and the success of the performance takes priority over the ideas of the piece.

Actors are therefore dependent on the audience's preconceptions of what they should be. In the case of women, the preconception is that female actors are sexually attractive and if they are comic actors, the options are limited to being a sexy stooge, as in Benny Hill's shows, or an eccentric frump. It's often assumed, not just by audiences but also by performers, that a woman cannot be both attractive and funny.

It's true that many comedians have not been conventionally attractive or have chosen to play down their looks, but there are significant exceptions. British music hall boasted a number of female stars. Stand-up comedy as we know it did not exist in the music hall; comic performers presented a mixture of songs, patter and gags. There were female double or triple acts who did a mixed turn with singing and dancing, although the majority of women in music hall were dancers and chorus girls. Women comedians were outnumbered by men but they were a significant minority.

Marie Lloyd and the male impersonator Vesta Tilley are the most famous among the music hall women, but there were many other female music hall stars who displayed various skills and styles, including impressionists (Cissie Loftus and Florence Desmond),

---

Florrie Forde (1876-1940)

A famous singer of music hall chorus songs and a great pantomime artiste. Busby's illustrated *Who's Who* of music hall states that 'she was the darling of the old school which considered that from bosom to thigh, principal boys couldn't be too massive'. Among her hits were, 'Hold your Hand out, Naughty Boy', 'Down at the Old Bull and Bush' and wartime favourites: 'It's a Long Way to Tipperary' and 'Pack up your Troubles'.

Stand-up – music hall, clubs and cabaret

Florrie Forde

Jenny Hill

womens
careers

Victoria Wood.

male impersonators (Nelly Power and Ella Shields) and male-female double acts (Mr and Mrs Howard Paul).

There is a current concern that women, though now relatively numerous in comedy careers, are not having an impact upon the industry or public at large because they populate the lower echelons of the career ladder and do not break through to the top of the profession. One of the reasons why comedian Victoria Wood is so remarkable is that she is enormously successful on a national scale. Marie Lloyd's national fame was obviously limited by Victorian travel and communications, but she nevertheless had a phenomenal impact.

Max Beerbohm included Marie Lloyd with Queen Victoria and Florence Nightingale as the three most memorable women of the age (Farson). From an impoverished East End background, Marie Lloyd made her stage debut in 1885, aged 15; by the time she was 17 she was earning £100 a week. In 1886 she bought a house in the south-east London suburbs, a pony and trap and hired a governess

---

Jenny Hill (1850-1896)

'If I were asked who, in my opinion, was the greatest artiste we ever had on the Variety stage, I would unhesitatingly plump for Miss Jenny Hill.'
(*Recollections of Vesta Tilley*)

'The Vital Spark', as she was nicknamed, was a high energy, quick-witted 'low' comedian whose stage persona was down-trodden but defiant. She particularly appealed to women in the audience:

'Her act centred upon a body of material related to the lives of women, and especially the women likely to be in her audience: working class wives and mothers, working girls in London trades, in shops, in service, or in the lower reaches of the entertainment business.'
(*Music Hall: Performance + Style*)

Sadly few of her songs have survived partly because they were blue and Victorian music publishers would not print them. This is one of the few surviving lyrics:

He's out on the fuddle with lots of his pals,
Out on the fuddle, along with other gals;
He's always on the fuddle
While I'm in such a muddle –
But I mean to have a legal separation.

precise
delivery
confidence

for her brothers and sisters; she eventually graduated to a detached house in Lewisham. By the time she was forty she had earnt £100,000 and, though she lost a lot of money in later years, she was extraordinarily wealthy, particularly for a Victorian woman of working-class origin. Her success cannot be quantified solely in terms of wealth; far more important is the extent of her popularity. When she died, 100,000 people followed her coffin and the taps in the bars round Leicester Square were draped in black crêpe.

Pinpointing the secret of Marie Lloyd's success is a tempting and fascinating business. Surviving film clips and recordings are rare and poor in quality, but Daniel Farson, one of Marie Lloyd's biographers, has used them, along with contemporary memories, to assess 'The Magic of Marie'. An essential ingredient was her expertise: 'Her delivery is precise and determined and she gives the impression of knowing exactly what she's doing' (Farson). This, combined with a relaxed manner, huge vitality and a unique rapport with the audience, made for a confident stage presence. Marie Lloyd's performance was assertive and celebratory, as Don Ross, one of the last impresarios of the music hall, recalls in Farson's biography:

> Marie's number goes up at either side of the proscenium, immediately there is a hum of excitement, a chuckle of merriment, and her music starts. And so, as the excitement grew, up would swing the house-tabs on to a full stage, possibly a palace set or a drawing-room set and up on the right hand corner the limes were all focused and then a moment of sheer magic – she would appear.

Marie Lloyd (1870-1922)

The music hall, I loved, as a child. We went every Friday to the Met – that was the big, lovely place in the Edgware Road. The comedians used to go three times; I think they had a cab waiting for them, and then they went from one to the other. Marie Lloyd did, I remember.
(Irene Handl)

All my life people kept coming up to me and saying: 'You really are like Marie.' So when I got the chance to play her, it was unbelievable. And she took me over. I used to have all the people who'd come with sheets of music – that's what they used to do with her. She was wonderful, she had a great sense of humour, a really kind lady.
(Barbara Windsor)

Marie Lloyd

*fun' risque
 Victorian
 era.*

> Always with a lovely smile, looking full of good humour and almost saying with her expression 'Now we're going to have some fun', she would walk with a nice, brisk, swinging gait down to the footlights.

Her charisma and comedy were obviously closely bound up with her looks and sexuality. She had two chief styles, as Colin MacInnes describes in his history of pop song (1840-1920), *Sweet Saturday Night*:

> She wore, according to Marie Kendall, 'a white lace dress with pink and blue ribbons and her golden hair right down there, natural . . . and her big blue eyes and her tiny baby's cap of lace. And she came with a hoop, and looked like a toy doll.' As she grew older she became rather 'grand' in this style and, so Ella Retford tells us, 'wore a fabulous gown that was slashed up to the waist and showed pink silk tights . . . with a wonderful diamond garter. And she had the smallest little hat over one eye – the one she used to wink – and the largest paradise I have ever seen – pink. And don't forget the stick. A long, long cane, all studded with diamonds.' Marie was 5′ 2″ ('semi-petite with beautiful limbs' says Marie Kendall), her teeth were 'beautiful and rather prominent' and Ella Retford speaks of 'the way she handled her beads . . . and rubbed them across her teeth with that saucy look and that wonderful smile.

Marie Lloyd was no innocent and her sexual suggestiveness did not find favour with genteel Victorians who believed that women should be decorous and naive. The music hall audiences, however, loved her and she did not offend them, partly because the sexual connotations of her act were never explicitly stated but, through innuendo, were strongly implied. The suggestive wink is famous; her ad lib and patter are notorious. The stories of Marie Lloyd's ad libs may well be apocryphal but they're too good not to repeat. Daniel Farson:

sexual connotations

> One story describes her arriving with an umbrella, waving it in front of her to the point of embarrassment until it opened – 'Thank God! I haven't had it up for months.'

Another time she made a production of picking a banana skin off the stage – with the aside to the audience – 'If the man who threw this wants to get his skin back he can come to my dressing room afterwards.'

Marie Lloyd managed to be both risqué and hugely popular.

Colin MacInnes points rather patronisingly to what might have been the secret of her success:

> My own guess is that she personified, for Londoners in her day, the good-bad girl that most women would like to be, and every man would like to have: the girl who is flighty, alluring and physically attractive, yet wise, understanding and basically reliable.

The neat equation of the 'good-bad girl' can hardly be a paradigm for 'most women', whether Victorian or modern, yet it works as a comic formula: the comedian who is rude but never obscene, sexual but not seedy, clever but not undermining. Most modern comedians do not function in the way that Marie Lloyd did but there are notable exceptions.

The pervasiveness of television means that modern audiences are saturated with sketch shows, situation comedy and variety, unaware of a significant group of comedians who perform in working-men's clubs, community centres and village halls across the country. This type of work is undeniably threatened by television, cinema, video and disco, and men have always outnumbered women comedians within it. *Showcall* is a directory of commercial club and cabaret acts; its 1986 index lists 111 male and 14 female comedians; female club comedians are rare.

Ellie Laine is one of the few. At 22, she has notched up 13 'O' levels and 5 'A' levels, a stint as a topless model and six years of working as a stand-up comic in clubs. Most of her work is in front of live audiences, but she's made some guest appearances on television, including Noel Edmond's *Late Late Breakfast Show* and *Good Morning Britain*. With headlines like 'Not on your Ellie!' (*Daily Mirror*) and 'Miss Ellie — Britain's own Joan Rivers' (*Sunday People*) Ellie Laine is heralded as unprintably rude and a devastating combination of page 3 looks and Mae West wit.

Hungry to see this phenomenon for ourselves, we raced down the A23 to catch the Ellie Laine show in a village club near Gatwick airport. After two hours of tacky warm-up acts, the audience was well tanked and warmed up and Ellie was announced. She dashed on to the stage in the skimpiest of dresses and launched into a 60-minute act of jokes, patter and song which had the audience in hysterics throughout. Her jokes are mainly about sex, and invariably put down men in the audience and men as a gender. It's a refreshing role reversal, but not one which alienates men, because Ellie alleviates the potential aggression in her act by making jokes about women as well and generally exposing sex, in graphic and earthy detail, as a laughable activity.

9

Ellie Laine

He said: 'If I'd've known you were a virgin I'd've taken more time.'
I said: 'If I'd've known you had more time I'd've taken my tights off.'

Stand-up – music hall, clubs and cabaret

Her concentration and energy never flag; her patter takes her into the heart of the audience where she picks out individuals, remembers their names and cleverly returns to the banter at intervals. 'Whose is this? Who does this one belong to?' she exclaims over a particularly feeble man and, to a young boy, 'Hello darling, why aren't you out stuffing some bird like any normal lad?' Ellie Laine diffuses potential shock at her gags by laughing herself and making comments: 'She knows what I mean, don't you darling?' and 'It's murder, innit?' Though the act is blue it's refreshing to hear a woman openly joking about subjects that are generally taboo.

Comedian Marti Caine, who has also worked in the clubs, defended what she called 'dirty comedy':

> I love it, 'cos it makes me laugh, and if it makes me laugh it's a tonic, and I don't care, 'cos I'm not prudish and I'm not narrow-minded, and anything that pertains to life has got to be funny . . . it's a natural cleansing process – bringing sex out into the open. Words are just words, they don't mean anything if there's no venom behind them.

With this bawdy atmosphere, the clubs are the natural descen- dants of the music halls which, particularly in the early years, were a tough arena for any performer, let alone for women. The roots of music hall go back as far as the scratch entertainments at the courts of ancient Egypt, but are more recently traced to the ancient fairs such as London's St Bartholomews, which took place at Smithfield. Music hall emerged properly after the 1843 Theatres Act which divided the Lord Chamberlain's and the magistrates licence for entertainment, legally inventing music hall, where drink could be served, but no plays could be performed. The halls expanded in the 1860s; during the 1870s and 1880s the music hall style was developed and tradition established. Money was poured into the music hall industry which led to the syndicated halls, and put the stamp of respectability on the music hall by the first decade of the twentieth century. Nineteenth-century venues varied in respecta- bility. At the lower end of the market, were the penny gaffs (unlicensed places of entertainment) – converted shops or stables where for 1d. you could watch an hour's show of comedy, tragedy, farce, singing and dancing. At the other end, the song and supper rooms served hot food and drinks and presented relatively sophisticated entertainment. The standard of other music hall forerunners – the pleasure gardens, taverns and music rooms – fell between these two extremes. Despite the variations, the early music hall provided popular working-class entertainment.

Pauline Daniels

The atmosphere was undeniably rough; the audience sat on wooden tables and chairs; they ate, drank, smoked, heckled and threw things on to the stage. This atmosphere prevailed until the last years of the nineteenth century, when music hall gained respectability and men eventually brought their wives and families. Until then, Marie Lloyd and her colleagues worked with chorus girls, dancers, and prostitutes, whose business thrived in the ribald milieu of the halls.

It's hardly surprising that this sort of atmosphere has, over the years, made it hard for women to prove that they are witty and skilled, and not simply decorative and sexually available. Most of the time Ellie Laine manages to prove that she's sexy and funny, but at times the preconceptions of male audiences make it an uphill task. Ellie Laine once played to 1,500 paralytic bikers and her combination of wit and humour was beyond them. She topped the bill after four strippers and a stag comic; despite the cries of 'get 'em off' and a few proferred penises from the balcony, she finished her set.

Marti Caine is famous for her television shows and recent situation comedy. It's easy to forget that her early experience was not dissimilar to Ellie Laine's. She served her apprenticeship in the clubs, where for seventeen years she did a stand-up act; she started when she was 19, her husband was earning £4.10 a week and they needed extra money. She described a night in the clubs:

> The workers were a rough school, a really rough school. You had stag dos, hen dos, as well as ordinary mixed, and there's kids running about, they're drunk most of the time, there's bingo coming up, there's pretty waitresses or pretty women flitting about, so you've got to go out and attack straight away . . . it's like a dog, if you show it fear it'll bite you.

Pauline Daniels

> I asked him to make love to me in the kitchen.
> He said 'what for?'
> I said: 'I wanna time an egg.'

humiliating mens sexual performance

A stand-up comedian from Liverpool, Pauline Daniels was involved in the 1986 Liverpool Festival of Comedy. The festival held a series of workshops for women comedians who then performed in the Festival's competition, Slaughterhouse. Pauline Daniels told us that the women comedians fared extremely well and on the night that she compered Slaughterhouse, one of the group won.

audience prejudice)

For Marti Caine, aggression in stand-up is essential; Victoria Wood, another successful comedian who worked as a stand-up, disagrees:

> I don't believe you have to be aggressive to do stand-up but you have to get them on your side, in a way. I suppose you just choose the way you feel is best. You certainly have to dominate them, but that's a technical thing. Any performer has to make contact with the audience and be in charge. But that doesn't mean going on like Bernard Manning.

She admits, however, that performance style cannot solely be the result of personal choice, but is dictated by venue:

> I think that you have to be in the right venue. I could still not work the clubs or the cabaret circuit because the material would be inappropriate, and I don't think they would like me, whereas if I were a man, I could possibly get away with it. I think that certain audiences have certain expectations and so possibly in these areas there might be prejudices.

Women cannot create roles and performance styles in a vacuum. If club audiences expect a level of aggression in a performer, then it is foolish not to conform. This may hinder women's exploration of a more personal comic style, but it does allow them to demonstrate that they can be more than a match for male aggression. Marti Caine:

> I did a stag do once in Newcastle and it was a lunchtime, all men; for a start, they drink different beers in different areas and it affects them differently and Newcastle Brown is the strongest and most corruptive, it sort of melts the brain, and they'd all been on Newcastle Brown, and there were four strippers who'd been on before me, all with huge breasts, and I followed. There were all these heaving drunken rugby players, mashed potatoes all over the walls, I walked on, there was a stunned silence and one of them lurched to his feet and shouted 'we want tits', and they all fell about, as is their wont. My retort, God knows where it came from, was: 'You'd look bright with tits'.

Before embarking on theatre and film work, actor Barbara Windsor worked as a singer and comedian in West End night clubs and, despite the relatively sophisticated atmosphere, had to cope with heckling: 'You're working with people who are four parts cut, so you've got to be on the ball all the time'. But she excelled in the situation because: 'I've always had too much to say for myself'.

14

The sharp comeback is not only the prerogative of twentieth-century women. Bessie Bellwood was a bawdy comic in the Marie Lloyd vein, whose splendid put-down at the Star of Bermondsey was recorded by Jerome K. Jerome in the *Idler Magazine* in 1892:

Introduced by the Star's Chairman as 'The World's Famous Zither Player Signorina Ballantino', she was at once heckled by a hefty-looking coalheaver who made it clear that he had no intention of allowing his drinking to be disturbed. A slanging match ensued with Bessie declaring her intention of 'wiping down the bloomin' 'all with him and making it respectable.' For over five minutes she let fly, leaving him gasping, dazed and speechless. At the end, she gathered herself together for one supreme effort, and hurled at him an insult so bitter with scorn, so sharp with insight into his career and character, so heavy with prophetic curse, that strong men drew and held their breath while it passed over them, and women hid their faces and shivered. Then she folded her arms and stood silent, and the house, from floor to ceiling, rose and cheered her until there was no more breath left in its lungs.

Heckling is a hazard and a challenge for comedians in a wide variety of venues and the modern alternative cabarets are no exception. Some performers thrive on it, even base their act around it; others dread it. The female double act, French and Saunders, performed in the early alternative venues, the Comic Strip and Comedy Store, and did not relish the prospect of heckling. If they sensed that it was imminent they would try to prevent interruption by doing the act very fast (they once got through a 20 minute set in 5 minutes). Sometimes, however, they would respond. Dawn French was affected by her day-time teaching role and replied, not with a tirade or a series of crushing one-liners, but with a teacher's ticking off:

Excuse me, you, prickhead there, now come on! If you don't think it's funny then leave, but I'm not going to have this talking . . .

The skill and guts it takes to be a good club comedian should never be underestimated. The unique way that the personality is exposed and pressurized on stage has been examined in two recent plays: Catherine Hayes' *Not Waving* is about a female club comedian whose life crisis is expressed by the harrowing interaction of public and private when she breaks down during her act.

15

Victoria wood.

Book.

Stand-up — music hall, clubs and cabaret

Comedian Kate in Terry Johnson's *Unsuitable for Adults* tries to use the stand-up's monologue as an expression of her anger about women's oppression and particularly about violence against women. The painful interaction of her personal experience and her political opinions is reflected in the spiralling intensity of her set, until she desperately tries to wrest the audience from their passive acceptance by an act of self-destruction.

Victoria Wood described her early fears of stand-up:

> I could only go on if I had a fag and a bar of chocolate, and I would only stand in the crook of the piano, I didn't want to stand on stage . . .

As she gained experience, her terror diminished:

> It's all right now, but I don't think anybody does it right to start with. I don't think anybody for years gets anywhere near it. That's why the best ones are the old ones.

The long apprenticeship of the clubs is invaluable and the opportunities of television, though inviting for young performers, can be destructive because they bring fame and exposure too early. Beryl Reid:

Wd

> The terrible thing now is that there is nowhere to learn. There's nowhere to serve your apprenticeship and to be a comical person and to be liked, it's a long, long apprenticeship. It's the longest.

Beryl Reid served her apprenticeship in variety; it gave her the opportunity to develop from a performer who needed a 'coat-hanger' to a stand-up comic who could be herself:

> If you're a comic you've got to find a coat-hanger for your particular type of comedy and I hadn't got that, of course, when I started. I knew I wanted to do something funny but I did

---

Bessie Bellwood (1857-1896)

One of the most humorous and certainly one of the sauciest serios ever seen in the saucy halls of our time, was Bessie Bellwood. Although lacking the versatility and character-acting genius of her great rivals, Marie Lloyd and Jenny Hill, Bessie was a real artist of the brainiest, most alert kind.
(*Recollections Of Vesta Tilley*)

16

Bessie Bellwood

French and Saunders

French and Saunders: *Friendly advice*

Saunders: You know contraception?

French: Yes.

Saunders: What is it then?

French: Well if you're asking me what contraception is, it must mean you're going to do it then. You're gonna have it off aren't you?

Saunders: How do you know when you're having it off then?

French: God, you don't know anything, do you? Well, have you ever seen a man's toilet parts? Well a man, right, has got three dangly toilet parts and the middle one is the important one and when the man wants to 'have it off' the middle one stands up and it's a bit like a sort of cactus and it's got all spikes coming off the top of it and he calls it his todger, and when his todger's all sticking up, you know it's time to have it off, so you get on the bed and open your legs and wait for the eggs to come, stupid. Now the egg starts to come and it's trying to get out, but it can't because there's a bit of skin a bit like a sort of trampoline at the bottom that's called your hymen and the egg keeps bouncing back and it can't get out. So the man gets on top of you and tries to break the hymen; eventually it breaks and a lot of green slime comes out. It's true. And that's when you know you're having an organism. And then the egg drops out, and you just wrap the egg in a towel and put it in the toilet. You'll never believe what happens next, I didn't believe it myself when I heard it. The man stands up, and he says 'Oh God', and the top of the todger opens up and five thousand million fish come jumping out the top – and they go off the ceiling, off the walls, all over the floor, everywhere. And you've got to scrape them all up into a towel and put it in the toilet because, you see, if you let the fish get near the egg that's how you get pregnant, you see.

Saunders: The fish just die then, do they?

French: Well, most of them die but if there's any left on the floor sort of 'flapping', you just grab their tails and get a mallet or a book and you just bash 'em on the head, scrape them into a towel and put them in the bin. Then you have to smoke.

Saunders: I see.

French: A very pleasurable experience.

impersonations because I hadn't really got anything of my own . . . but now, because I've done a lot of work, for a long time, I can now just talk as myself, I don't need the coat-hanger so much now.

In 1977, Beryl Reid performed at the National Theatre in Edward Albee's *Counting the Ways*. At one point in the play the house lights came up and a sign with the words 'identify yourselves' appeared on stage. The actors were then expected to improvise out of character, as themselves. Beryl Reid's experience of stand-up allowed her to improvise happily for five minutes, but it terrified her colleague: 'That was easy for me, but it was terrifying for an actor who hadn't addressed an audience – ever.'

It's clear that with opportunities and experience women can and do work as stand-ups but to what extent do women in this environment have to adopt the same performance techniques as men? The aggression and confidence are comparable, but Marti Caine was categorical about certain restrictions on the scope of women comedians:

> There are several things that a woman can't mention, no matter how crude she gets, and in working-men's clubs you have to get crude. Farting is out for a woman and she can say anything else: she can use any of the four-letter expletives. She can do anything except she cannot mention tampax or anything to do with the menstrual cycle and she can't mention fart, for some reason.
> You're allowed to talk about sex as long as you put it in someone else's mouth: '. . . and he said' or 'my kid said' not 'I said' – it can't be you, you must be repeating a conversation – then you can get away with anything.

These restrictions tie in with Colin MacInnes's 'good-bad girl' theory about Marie Lloyd: it's obviously acceptable for a woman to go so far but she cannot be as crude as a man.

Another distinction for women comedians is their relationship with women in the audience. This is not traditionally the male comic's concern. His jokes uphold the status quo, he does not feel threatened by the women in the audience, nor is he particularly concerned to please them as well as the men. This is not the case for women comics: an attractive woman telling jokes is a potential threat to women in the audience and it's in the stand-up's interest to undermine herself in order to get the women's approval. Marti Caine:

> It's all psychology, if you've got any sense at all. It's like knocking myself: if you are under 16 stone and under 90, you're

20

immediately classed as competition to the women and the men will not laugh if the women don't laugh, and if a man laughs at you, his wife'll really hate it, strangely enough. So the first thing you've got to do, in my case anyway, is knock yourself so that they start defending you. Then they think: 'She's not that bad' or 'Well at least she knows she's a mess' and then it confirms in their mind that you're not as hot as you look. Then you're all right.

Ellie Laine uses a similar technique, not simply to diffuse antagonism but because she's genuinely interested in establishing a rapport with women and using it to ridicule men:

I'm not here to talk to the men, I'm here to talk to the women, 'cos us girls have got to stick together – all right girls?

She explains:

I warm them to me so that I get to the stage where we're mates and it's between girls and we can say anything we like and the men have got to laugh because the wife's laughing. There's nothing they can be outraged about anyway, because if a man comic said some of the things that we discuss they would be very offended in front of the wife, but if the wife's laughing and talking back to me, the man's got to laugh anyway.

Women like Ellie Laine and Marti Caine, though few and working in a far from radical field, are nevertheless contributing to changing the way that women are perceived. Humour, often seen as escapist entertainment, can be considered apolitical. This is not necessarily the case. As Norma J. Gravely points out in her essay (Winegarten, 1978), 'Sexist humour as a form of social control – or – unfortunately – the joke is usually on us' humour is a social mechanism and one of the functions of joke telling and appreciation is social control. She quotes La Fave:

A joke is often humorous to the extent that it enhances an object of affection and/or disparages an object of repulsion, unhumorous to the extent that it does the opposite.

Thus, a social group, and in the case of comedians, usually white heterosexual men, proves its superiority to a group it considers inferior, due to sex, sexuality, status or race, by telling a joke. One theory is that this group needs to dominate the 'inferior' group by the social mechanism of the joke because it knows that its sense of superiority is unfounded and unjustifiable.

. . . men could perceive women, or the autonomy of women as a

21

threat to their basic security – their power, 'rightness', importance and position. It could be quite threatening to those in power to foresee competition or possible overthrow from a group – quite obviously equal in capability, intelligence strength and energy – that had been maintained in subordination by methods of social control. The motivation would be strong enough to counteract any tendency towards assertiveness, independence and autonomy with even stronger controls . . . (Gravely)

For a woman to break out of this kind of control, to refuse to be the butt of the joke and make her own jokes directed at her own victims, as the music hall performers did and club comedians do today, is a radical departure, as Norma J. Gravely points out:

> For women, the butt of the sexist jokes, it's a 'damned if you do and damned if you don't' situation. If we stay in our 'assigned' roles we are devalued with humour, and if we move outside those roles we are put down with jokes. Since we can't win that war anyway, why not stage a counter-revolution – write our own jokes . . . and fight back!

Many women comedians turn the tables in this way, but it is simplistic to argue that women's retaliation against sexist humour should merely take the form of role-reversing traditional jokes. This is an important initial stage but not an unquestionable direction to take: Ellie Laine's anti-male jokes are interspersed with racist and homophobic jokes. She has been heralded as a female match for Bernard Manning – not necessarily an ideal role model for women comedians. But the politics of humour is not the concern of all female comedians.

Pauline Melville

'It's so radical here I could faint. I mean there's nothing bourgeois in sight; I wouldn't be here if there was. I've just come from the thrush workshop for women in Room 14. I don't see why you laugh – it's about time radical ornithologists got together.

I've made some terrible mistakes, you know, before I got, you know, "well adjusted". I'll never forget my first study group . . . it's imprinted on my collective unconscious – they were discussing whether the Albanian leadership had the correct political position in 1952 or not – well, some people said they did, some people said they didn't – I said "look why don't you phone up the Daily Telegraph Information bureau". . .'

Pauline Melville

Christine Pilgrim

By contrast, the London 'alternative' cabaret circuit was started by a group of performers, which included Alexei Sayle, Jim Barclay, Tony Allen and Keith Allen, all of whom rejected mainstream humour because they felt it reinforced stereotypes and encapsulated reactionary politics. They had also become frustrated with the limitations of political fringe theatre.

They were overtly radical in their performance and were loosely described as 'alternative', although many of them do not ascribe to the title. Much alternative humour has now become popular in the mainstream and the present-day cabaret circuit, increasingly apolitical, is still dubbed 'alternative'. We are therefore using the term throughout this book as a convenient, rather than an accurate, description. Pauline Melville, the only woman in the group, described its origins: '. . . it was obvious that there was some new energy about, it needed somewhere to come out and it just popped out, quite independently.'

At first, in 1978-9, they performed in London clubs and fringe theatres, but within eighteen months they were invited to perform to an audience of 900 at Leeds City Variety:

> The place was packed . . . there was a kind of need for it . . . when we first started nobody – *nobody* was getting up on stage and making a joke about Michael Heseltine or Tebbit. It was really stunning and savage: jokes about the SAS, jokes about the police, it was completely new . . . .
> (Pauline Melville)

The material was political but the emphasis, partly because Pauline Melville was the only woman, was on socialist rather then feminist issues. Pauline wanted to satirize the 'brown rice boom' and chose a comic character, Eedie, who was immersed in every

---

Christine Pilgrim

Christine Pilgrim has her own one-woman music hall show, *Pilgrims*, and is the only known music hall chairwoman in history. Discontented with the apolitical style of much modern music hall, she spices her act with relevant comments and in doing so is probably much more in keeping with traditional music hall than her more reverent colleagues:

> 'Maggie the Snatcher, I call her, Attila the Hen, the Finchley Führer. I don't know what's the matter with her police force. There's two of 'em standing guard outside number ten – twenty-four hours a day – she still gets out.'

Stand-up – music hall, clubs and cabaret

alternative philosophy under the sun – the orange people, macrobiotics, yin and yang, and so on – but thought and dressed like a conservative and malaproped and misunderstood abundantly: 'I was bursting to take the mickey out of mysticism.' Apart from a pressure from male colleagues to do stand-up rather than character material and the dominance of aggressive male stand-up techniques, Pauline Melville doesn't feel that sexism towards women comedians was a major issue in the early days of alternative comedy.

But despite the relatively political nature of alternative comedy, female comedians are no more numerous in this area than they are in the clubs. Maria Kempinska, who runs London's biggest and most popular cabaret, Jongleurs, estimates that only 10-15 per cent of comedians that regularly perform there are women. Maggie Steed and French and Saunders were early performers on the circuit, followed by Jenny Lecoat, Helen Lederer and Maggie Fox. One might expect a greater acceptance of women comics in alternative comedy than in the mainstream, but it appears that prejudice runs deep. Maggie Fox, who now works in the comedy duo, Lip Service:

Jenny Lecoat

You woke one night at 2 a.m.
You touched my hand, said: 'Darlin', are you sleepin'?'
And I said: 'what, at 2 a.m.?
of course not, I was taking in the washing.'
You looked at me with soulful eyes,
And told me that your willy, it was freezing
You asked me if I'd find a warmer place for it,
And Darling, I said 'yes'.

CHORUS
And now your willy's boiling in the kitchen
Boilin' up with the kidney beans real fast
And with the chilli I put in
It should only take a day
Till you become your true consistency at last.
from *The Willy Song*

and from her new act:

I'm obsessed with my weight, because when I was twelve years old I used to read *Jackie* magazine. Remember those articles? 'Feeling fat girls? Try this simple test. Just slip yourself down between the wall and the radiator . . . if you can't do it, you're a fat bitch.'

26

Jenny Lecoat

> If two men get up and do a comic act, the audience relax because that's normal, but when two women get up they're immediately uneasy and think 'Oh my God, are they going to make fools of themselves?'

The feminist face of Ellie Laine's manbashing appeared on the alternative circuit. Jenny Lecoat was a leading exponent who sang songs and developed wry patter about the struggles of the enlightened feminist. Her early work aimed to enlighten as well as entertain. She appealed to those women in the audience whose preoccupations, particularly in the area of sex and relationships, had not been expressed by male comedians. The effect on men in the audience was varied, ranging from taking offence to enjoying the criticism, with the characteristic masochism of a certain breed of left-wing man. Her appearance was in keeping with the style of the act, though it has developed:

> When I first started, it was really cropped hair, bovver boots. It was really heavy stuff. Then it softened down a bit. A woman called Eileen Pollock said: 'You're giving too much away when you come on. As soon as people look at you they know what they're going to get. Have you thought about confusing them a bit? If you came on in something quite feminine and quite pretty, it'd much more interesting.' So then I would look like, potentially, somebody's wife, somebody's girlfriend, somebody's sister. So that men in the audience would not just be able to dismiss me as some stroppy lesbian.

It is interesting to note that many women in alternative cabaret have chosen to dress like their male counterparts. Although women who worked in music hall as male impersonators adopted more precise and deliberate male dress than modern stand-ups for whom, of course, dress is less gender specific than for the Victorians, a comparison of the two styles is interesting. Modern alternative stand-ups have used 'male' clothes to deflate their sexual appeal and address feminist issues, whereas in the music hall male impersonators achieved a potent sexual ambiguity for both sexes which was attractive and successful, but did not necessarily challenge gender assumptions in the way that modern stand-ups frequently do. The politics of male impersonation is discussed in Sara Maitland's book *Vesta Tilley*.

Vesta Tilley was one of the greatest stars of music hall and certainly the most famous male impersonator of her time. At her final professional appearance (in 1920) she 'received a forty-minute

28

Vesta Tilley

limitations of female roles

ovation, and Ellen Terry, the most popular serious actress of the time, came on stage to embrace Vesta Tilley and make a short speech. Nearly two million individuals had signed "The People's Tribute", which was presented in bound volumes . . .' (*Vesta Tilley*)

Vesta Tilley first adopted male drag because she was bored with the limitations of female roles:

> Young as I was, I had, in song, run through the whole gamut of female characters, from baby songs to old maid's ditties, and I concluded that female costume was rather a drag. I felt that I could express myself better if I were dressed as a boy.
> (*Recollections of Vesta Tilley*)

Vesta Tilley's male impersonation increased her scope. She appealed to men as a woman: for a Victorian man to see a woman's legs in tightfitting clothes was extremely attractive, but men also admired her meticulous male appearance. By the 1890s she was setting men's fashions and Vesta Tilley souvenirs included largely male items, such as the 'Vesta Tilley Vest (waistcoat), Vesta Tilley Cigars and Vesta Tilley Socks' (*Vesta Tilley*).

Vesta Tilley did not interpret this sexual ambiguity as subversive. She married a Conservative politician, became, as Lady de Frece, firmly rooted in the establishment, sang patriotic songs, and saw herself, as distinct from Marie Lloyd, as the respectable face of music hall.

While Vesta Tilley focussed solely on her appeal, Jenny Lecoat sought both to appeal and disturb. However, she grew frustrated with the limitations of her act and decided it was time for a change. After a year away from the circuit – presenting *Watch the Woman* for Channel 4 and playing the lead, a stand-up comedian, in *Unsuitable for Adults* at Liverpool Playhouse – she has returned to the cabaret with a new act:

> I now want to say: 'I'm a comedian first, not a manbasher.' I have strong politics and they will always be there but I also felt it was dishonest – I'm a heterosexual and I have lots of men friends and I thought, 'this has got to stop.' What I was doing was quite justified at the time but it's a question of moving on. The new set is going to be stuff that I've wanted to write about for a long time. I'm trying to tread a fine line now between not leaving behind the audience I've got but trying to move on and cover new areas. One of the things I've always wanted to do but didn't feel sure enough to do is to talk about women and the contradictions within modern women's lives: being 'right on' and actually being completely fucked up, being a right on feminist and reading the

how the joke is made; limiting yourself

right books and crying because you've put on five pounds. This material is more dangerous because I can see myself falling into all sorts of 'sell out' traps, but it's something that I've got to do. (Jenny Lecoat)

Jenny Lecoat's misgivings point to a crucial problem for women comedians: while rejecting stereotypes that society imposes, they may be creating stereotypes of their own. The feminist comic, the woman comedian who talks about the issues of womanhood, can become a limiting role.

The term 'stereotype' is used widely and loosely in discussions on humour and on women's representation in particular. It is often seen as negative, but the fact that feminist comedians, and not just women in mainstream humour, feel stereotyped shows that the term is more complex than at first appears.

The crucial distinction is between type and stereotype. Humour functions on recognisable characteristics and behaviour patterns: the comic reveals something about herself, members of the audience recognise that they have the same characteristics and the joke is made. In this interchange the audience form a group, they are the 'type' of person to laugh at the 'type' of observation made. When, however, humour is no longer a discovery but a prediction, and a woman comes on stage and is immediately *expected* to make feminist jokes, the freshness of the exchange is lost and the comic is placed in a fixed role which has the limitation of the stereotype. Trevor Griffiths, in his play *Comedians*, argues the case against stereotyping. Eddie Waters, a reputed but controversial club comedian, lectures on his ideals to a class of budding comedians (all men):

It's not the jokes. It's not the jokes. It's what lies behind 'em. It's the attitude. A real comedian – that's a daring man. He *dares* to see what his listeners only shy away from, fear to express. And what he sees is a sort of truth, about people, about their situation, about what hurts or terrifies them, about what's hard, above all, about what they *want* . . . there's very little won't take a joke. But when a joke bases itself upon a distortion – a 'stereotype' perhaps – and gives the lie to the truth so as to win a laugh and stay in favour, we've moved away from comic art and into the world of entertainment and slick success.

Women comedians have learnt that an awareness of the specific problems women performers face is necessary, but it doesn't necessarily strengthen performance.

Helen Lederer found that the trend for political statement spoilt the spontaneity of her early performance:

31

It was real euphoria to start with, then it got absolutely abysmal. The circuit changed, it got larger, and people became more demanding of what you stood for. And in a way it became more limiting. By that I mean, we were under the impression, rightly or wrongly, that we had to have a message, and that is the beginning of the end. That made us self-conscious. At the beginning we were not self-conscious, we had that kind of energy and love of what we were doing.

Though Helen Lederer is aware and articulate about the role of women comedians, she's decided that analysis doesn't improve performance:

I used to present myself as an oddity. In fact I was just presenting myself as a woman, but I wasn't used to it. What will help them [the audience] become used to it is if we [women comedians] are completely at ease with it. I think the battle is not focussing on the difference but trying to get into being female and being as funny as we can. If we don't focus on the problems we'll discover all sorts of wonderful things about humour.

Helen Lederer says of her unusual, very personal stand-up style:

I personally, humourwise, find a fascination with neuroses and what would initially be seen as a weakness, not strength. And I actually explore weakness, for myself, because that's really my starting point, that's not where I'd like to end, but that's how I started.

and in her act:

'I got asked to a party a couple of months ago, it was a theme party, um – being middle class, sorry to say that – no I am – you tend to get theme parties, stupid really – anyway, the invitation said "Henrietta invites Helen" to a "leave your partner at home" party – anyway – I was a little bit worried whether I was eligible – not having a partner at home – so I phoned up Henrietta and explained the problem; I said "look I can arrange for my cousin to stay in the flat for the duration of the party, like you know, leave the phone number, he can phone, accuse me of having a good time, that kind of thing" – so she said, "No, this is just the modern way of reducing the stigma of being single" – no, again, you're right not to laugh because it's not a joke.'

Helen Lederer

The rejection of a feminist stereotype is distinct from the rejection of a sexist stereotype because with the latter there's no doubt that the image is limiting whereas with the former there's always the doubt that in rejecting an overt statement, you're rejecting the politics to boot. But political forms are as prey to taste and fashion as any other. Pauline Melville explained the fervour and frustration of political theatre:

> There's a time when you can use certain forms to say certain things and in the early seventies political theatre was absolutely vibrant and refreshing and wasn't being done and was a joy. It became dogmatic, stiff, complacent, conceited. By the mid-seventies it had faded . . . I'd been with 7:84 which is really 'right on', I'd been round the factories, I'd been in all that patronising shit . . . I'd had enough of coming on stage and saying 'I'll take you to the shop steward.'

There's the same weariness about unimaginative feminist performance:

> In 1986 there is no point any more in going on stage and saying 'Women are oppressed, women have a hard time, women are chained to the kitchen sink.' I mean, please! We've heard it all before.
> (Jenny Lecoat)

This is a common view among performers who work largely in London where audiences are the first to demand new directions; elsewhere feminist performance may not have to meet the same demands. In general, however, women are breaking away from the direct feminist statement because it can become limited and because the form, along with a lot of 1970s political performance, has become outmoded. This desire for a more individual performance should not necessarily be seen as a reactionary trend.

Germaine Greer is illuminating on this point in her study of women painters, *The Obstacle Race*. She suggests that it is the role of the feminist critic and not of the artist to discover and discuss the politics of art:

> Feminism cannot supply the answer for an artist, for her truth cannot be political. She cannot abandon the rhetoric of one group for the rhetoric of another, or substitute acceptability to one group for acceptability to another. It is for feminist critics to puzzle their brains about whether there is female imagery or not, to examine in depth the relation between male and female artists to decide whether the characteristics of masculine art are the

Rebecca Stevens

A founder and long-term member of Cliff Hanger Theatre Company,
Rebecca Stevens performs as a solo stand-up:

> 'Girls seldom make passes at men with big arses – my last
> boyfriend had one of those arses where you can see the crack at
> the top of the trousers – I used it as an ashtray.'

Jenny Eclair

One of the well-established alternative cabaret performers, Jenny Eclair has toured the circuit for four years. *Time Out* described her act as 'wildly engaging comic confessions':

> 'Whenever my mother sees me she says to me "Jenny, Jenny, why aren't you wearing a petticoat?"
> "Mother, it's because I've got jeans on." '

Kit Hollerbach

An American comedian who's performed in London for the last two years, Kit Hollerbach has helped to introduce American improvisation techniques to London performers: she runs workshops and performances at the Comedy Store:

> 'I was in a cab the other day. The driver was going on and on about how Americans get into this weird violence.
> I wanted to knife the bastard.'

---

characteristics of all good art and the like. The painter cannot expend her precious energy in polemic, and in fact very few women artists of importance do.

Any artist should have the luxury of expressing his or her individuality: 'For all artists the problem is of finding one's own authenticity, of speaking in a language or imagery that is essentially one's own . . .' (*The Obstacle Race*)

Claire Dowie

Alternative stand-up comedian:

Question: 'When did you start performing on your own?'
Claire Dowie: 'When I came out of the womb, I think.'

We should encourage the idea that the art that women produce can become great art and not just great women's art. We need feminism to make women's experience visible, but having done that, we must then accept that a woman artist may choose her material – which may emphasise being a woman, or may not.

However, some performers do not see their acts as representing an evolving and 'artistic' form; they are intent on carving a successful media career and do not wish to question the confrontational nature of stand-up.

There are alternatives: stand-up can be gentle, non-confrontational and warmly appreciated. This is rare, particularly in the commercial, urban, media-minded world of the clubs and cabarets. Lilla Miller, who lives and performs in Cornwall, is the gentlest stand-up imaginable. She's a rotund pixie of a woman who first wrote and performed a double act for a WI function, then went solo and has been in huge demand all over Cornwall ever since. Her stage persona is Mrs Rosewarne, an eccentrically dressed woman, who tells 'stories' about local people, customs and carry-ons in the home, village and church. Lilla Miller insists that her 'stories' are not jokes, and indeed half the pleasure of her act is her natural delivery of the Cornish accent, language and local interest. Lilla Miller is positively opposed to climbing the career ladder: she's performed on local radio and made two cassettes (though she would deny it, she's something of a local celebrity) but she draws the line at television. She feels the fuss and exposure would be excessive. In fact she's slightly weary at having to perform as much as she does, but she accepts the bookings, partly because a lot of them are in aid of charity.

We caught Mrs Rosewarne's act at the monthly meeting of the Arthritics' club at Redruth hospital. The audience of 20-30 was mainly elderly and disabled. After Barbershop and Cornish nationalist folk songs (it was Trevithick Day), Mrs Rosewarne topped the bill with a string of her 'stories', including requests for favourites. Lilla Miller illustrates the importance of context and venue in comic performance: her character, delivery and observations create a warmth and community feeling in Cornwall that would be lost in the boxing ring of urban clubs and cabaret.

Marjorie Rea is a Northern counterpart to Lilla Miller. Similar in age and appeal, she lives in Belfast, is semi-professional and has been performing, initially as a singer and increasingly as a stand-up, since she was a teenager. Like Lilla Miller, she's modest about her work, but is obviously in demand, travelling all over the province to do her act. We saw her in a large, undecorative hall in Newtonards outside Belfast. The show was in aid of the Church restoration fund and after a juve genius had demonstrated his wondrous ripples on the electric organ and the Spinnersesque band, Bakerloo Junction, had delighted us with hot numbers like *Streets of London*, Marjorie Rea shimmered onto the stage in a glittering blue evening dress and eye make-up to match.

She is gloriously portly and unselfconscious about it, cracking jokes about her weight and diet, as well as her husband, her driving and her Ulster accent. She looks as if she enjoys being on stage and intersperses her jokes with a magnificent wheezing cackle. Again, this is not avant-garde or high-tension stand-up; it works in a community with shared experiences, among people who are relaxed and prepared to show their appreciation.

While Lilla Miller and Marjorie Rea appeal to the rural community who now attend live performances on the lines of music hall, Marie Lloyd's urban impact was similar. T.S. Eliot desribes this appeal:

> . . . no other comedian succeeded so well in giving expression to the life of that audience, in raising it to a kind of art. It was, I think, this capacity for expressing the soul of the people that made Marie Lloyd unique, and that made her audiences, even when they joined in the chorus, not so much hilarious as happy. . . . I consider her superiority over other performers to be in a way a moral superiority: it was her understanding of the people and sympathy with them, and the people's recognition of the fact

---

Lilla Miller

'It does seem to me that farming is appealing a lot to these city boys now. This boy from Birmingham was sent down to do some practical work on a farm in Cornwall. The first morning he was there the farmer put him to manure a patch of ground. Well of course the boy wanted to do the right thing so he didn't use very much manure. So when farmer came out he said "Oh my dear boy, thee s'have to put more than that there. I'm gon'ta put tatas in this ground and they're some hungry things." Well the boy didn't quite understand what he meant but he did what he said and put on more manure. About one o'clock, farmer's wife came out and said "Now come on in dear, wash your hands and have your dinner." Well there was a lovely pasty on the plate so he took a bite or two and he looked at her. He said "I know now what master meant when has said that tatas are hungry things." She said "You do?" "Yes," he said, "they've been here and ate all the meat in this pasty." '

Lilla Miller

Marjorie Rea

'I was on a beach last Summer, on a lovely beach sunbathing and one of those life guards came up and he said to me "Madam, you'll have to move – the tide wants to come in." '

that she embodied the virtues which they genuinely most respected in private life, that raised her to the position she occupied at her death. And her death is itself a significant moment in English history. I have called her the expressive figure of the lower classes.
(*Selected Essays*)

Commentators like Eliot accepted the significance of class in cultural expression, but appeared to be totally oblivious to the significance of gender. At a time when women didn't even have the vote, were barely represented in the professions and rarely financially independent, Marie Lloyd was a remarkably rich and successful woman. Her songs reflected women's experience – in love, work and marriage – and must have appealed to the growing number of women in the music hall audience who were hardly emancipated, but had found a relatively independent life in the city, where there was a greater variety of work and a wider choice of husband than their predecessors had in isolated, rural, pre-Industrial Revolution communities.

Marie Lloyd, although she may have been oblivious to her political influence, was a pioneer. In our more politically sensitive age, we need more performers who reflect the true social make-up of society, and this is why women, as well as performers who are black or gay or members of other minorities, should be welcome participants in the arts.

Cultural expression which reflects minority positions cannot immediately expect, however, to have mass appeal. Inevitably, the most exciting and controversial performance will be marginalised, because it challenges the status quo. Alternative comics are not allowed to be as explicit or as radical on television as they are on stage and as a result, their performances can become anaesthetised and insipid. Pauline Melville feels strongly about this:

The really clever thing, and I think this is what's happened but it's just a theory and I might be wrong; the really clever thing is that you can make a fuck of a lot of money now at being absolutely radical, you can make such a fortune that your jokes become pointless. They've actually bought it off, radicalism and all. I know there's something wrong when Michael Heseltine can go on *Wogan* and say that *Spitting Image* is one of his favourite programmes.

Television obviously didn't exist for Marie Lloyd, but her story is comparable. Though she was enormously popular, Marie Lloyd was always controversial and never gained the respectability outside the music hall that other women, such as Vesta Tilley, achieved. Her act was too risqué ever to please the establishment. During the nineteenth century, music hall gained respectability; the wooden tables gave way to plush red velvet seats, the focus moved away from working-class south and east London to the West End where impresarios such as Oswold Stoll and Edward Moss built music hall palaces including the Hippodrome and the Coliseum.

As the music hall's respectability grew, narrow-mindedness descended. Mrs Ormiston Chant, the Mrs Whitehouse of her day, objected vehemently to music hall, claiming that it 'catered for

---

Beverley Bell is a young impressionist, currently receiving press and public attention. She performs in clubs, theatres, hotels, cabarets and on television (including *The 6 O'Clock Show*, *Good Morning Britain*, *Black on Black* and *The Bandung File*). Her act has become a clever, and politically interesting melange of styles. As well as impressions which include Margaret Thatcher, Princess Diana, Tessa Sanderson and Deirdre Barlow, Beverley Bell has created West Indian and African characters. She has developed satirical material – Thatcher talking about her trip to Brixton – which she intersperses with her own comic patter. This sketch features Marcia, the West Indian who's always trying to cover up for her family's downfalls; she meets her inquisitive friend Eunice in Brixton market:

> Eunice: Marcia, A me Eunice. You still living?
> Marcia: Yes me dear. Me heart still de pang pang. Thanks to the Lord.
> Eunice: So wait, How is you husband? Him still pan de bus dem?
> Marcia: Yes an him still lazy and watless an good fe not'n. But him alright.
> Eunice: That's nice (sarcastically). So how is you daughter? How much pitney she have now?
> Marcia: She's doing fine you know.
> Eunice: Oh. She studying?
> Marcia: No. She's too busy breeding me dear. She have about six pitney now. Is one ting about that girl. She likes to keep it small. I wish the others were like her.
> Eunice: (Hurriedly, after hearing the gossip) Well my dear. I can't stop fe tell you about my life. Cause me have me wrestling fe watch, an a Saturday. Soup fe boil. Chicken fe season up fe tomorrow. God bless you my dear. Me we see you. Bye.

Beverley Bell

Karen Parker and Debby Klein

Karen Parker and Debby Klein formed Parker and Klein in 1984 with the aim of making lesbian theatre commercially successful. *City Limits* magazine voted them one of the top three cabaret acts of 1986.

> Parker: Our first production, DEVILRY, was an outrageous fantasy.
> Klein: Based on the Faustian legend.
> Parker: . . . A piece of experimental theatre . . .
> Klein: . . . A sort of camp cabaret . . .
> Parker: . . . A musical comedy . . .
> Klein: Whatever it was it inspired us to hit the cabaret circuit.
> Parker: Which at the time wasn't exactly teeming with lesbian acts.
> Klein: We decided that our image should be chic and glamorous . . .
> Parker: Within the limits of our budget . . .
> Klein: In order to confound the stereotypes created by a heterosexist culture . . .
> Parker: Actually we just love dressing up. We're naturally glamorous people.
> Klein: Even though we were once billed as a drag act.
> Parker: People do have odd ideas about us. The *Sunday Express* said the mums and dads love us.
> Klein: I wonder if they were referring to the castration sketch?
> Parker: Or the right on feminist chatting up the stripper?
> Klein: We're a very cosmopolitan act.
> Parker: Oh yes . . . West Norwood . . . Brockley . . . Luton . . . remember Luton?
> Klein: Squeezed in between the under 10's ballet displays . . .
> Parker: They didn't know what had hit them.
> Klein: Mind you our cult following thinks we use subversive humour to challenge our audience's preconceptions . . .
> Parker: But she always says the right thing if we buy her a drink.
> Klein: We are totally without prejudice, we don't mind performing to heterosexual audiences.
> Parker: In fact we'll perform anywhere . . .
> Klein: Except Luton . . .

Karen Parker and Debby Klein

people who had a small proportion of brains' (Farson). She was chairman of the Purity Party and opposed the renewal of the music hall's licences at the Magistrates' sessions. She objected to the 'Ladies of the Promenade' and in 1894 summoned her supporters at the London County Council to purge the Empire of them. The young Winston Churchill was among those who challenged Mrs Ormiston Chant, but she triumphed by having a screen of canvas and trellis erected between the promenade and the bars, and the prostitutes were discreetly concealed. The public won the day, however, because the following week, a crowd at the Empire tore down the barricade. It was never replaced.

Marie Lloyd was not immune from this moral onslaught. The story goes that Mrs Ormiston Chant interrupted Marie Lloyd's act at the Empire and began a famous confrontation between Marie Lloyd and the Licensing Authorities. One of their objections was to a line in a song about a girl who 'sits among the cabbages and peas'. Marie Lloyd agreed to change it – and did – to 'sits among the cabbages and leeks'. She was eventually called to sing the offending song to a Committee of the LCC. She did so, without any double entendre. The committee could see nothing offensive in the song and dismissed her. Before leaving the court Marie Lloyd burst into *Come into the garden, Maud*, a perfectly innocent song, which she laced with every conceivable double entendre, before sweeping out of the room.

Although the media are very different, the respectable face of music hall can be equated with television today, and just as Ellie Laine can't perform on television as she does in the clubs, so Marie Lloyd was excluded from the higher echelons of music hall. When the seal of approval was finally set on the music hall by the Royal Command Performance in 1912 Marie Lloyd was not invited to perform. She staged an alternative show down the road at the London Pavilion and the posters outside the theatre were pasted with special strips proclaiming:

EVERY PERFORMANCE BY MARIE LLOYD IS A COMMAND
PERFORMANCE BY ORDER OF THE BRITISH PUBLIC

Stand-up, however well or little known the performer, however great or small the audience, can be a breath-taking form of entertainment. At worst it can be deeply embarrassing. It is exciting when there's the surprise of discovering common experience. Pauline Melville:

> I did a whole lot of working men's clubs during the miners' strike and that was very odd. Before I went on in Armthorpe in Yorkshire, the chairman of the club came up and said: 'You'll never make 'em laugh here – we had Bernard Manning sweating . . .'

But she won the audience over:

> It was magic. I did some material that made the connection between black people being beaten up and the miners being beaten up. I heard a gasp of recognition – although it was a joke – that at last they'd realised what had been happening. It was hilarious and everybody fell about, but you knew that your humour was binding a community together.

To the mining community at that time, Pauline Melville, an alternative comedian from London, had more impact than Bernard Manning. The effectiveness of art in any political struggle is debatable, but there are times when it works. Pauline Melville:

> In certain countries . . . take Chile, for example – they had a tremendous left-wing arts movement that changed things, it made the conditions different. What's happened in Britain is that this political (alternative) comedy has altered nothing, it's just been a form of entertainment. This society hasn't altered one bit. So it's become completely safe, whatever you do.

Trevor Griffiths, talking about a very different environment from the left-wing arts movement in Chile, makes a very similar point about the radical potential of comedy. Eddie Waters:

> A joke releases the tension, says the unsayable, any joke pretty well. But a true joke, a comedian's joke, has to do more than release tension, it has to *liberate* the will and the desire, has to *change the situation.*

No one could claim that Britain is in the midst of popular revolution comparable to Chile's. There have, however, been strong political movements and events which have propagated political art. Some has been turgid and vanguardist but some of it has been genuinely popular. When art is part of real change in society, it's exciting.

Not all entertainment, and certainly not all stand-up, can hope to change society, but in popular political entertainment the exchange between audience and entertainer is, ideally, fresh, vital and surprising. Not every woman comedian wants to change society, or even change the position of women by doing her act, but if she is good, if she is a dynamic performer, she will not only delight audiences, she will inevitably, even if unconsciously, effect change. Every woman who can do stand-up is slowly breaking into what has traditionally been a male-dominated area. She is proving that she can survive and thrive in it: doing the job and doing it well.

MALE/FEMALE HUMOUR: IS THERE A DIFFERENCE?

When people say 'As a woman do you think such and such?' you
never know whether you think it as a woman or as yourself. People
don't expect that of men. The question doesn't exist.
(Lise Mayer, writer)

A woman going up on stage is somehow saying 'I'm available to you'.
But it doesn't work in exactly the same way for men: they're not
sexually available because they're always seen as the aggressor.
(Jenny Lecoat, stand-up comedian/actor/writer)

Men resented women in those days being in any way funny. I don't
know why. I still sometimes think they're not overkeen. But I mean,
that's something I think 'knickers' to.
(Beryl Reid, actor/writer)

I feel that humour transcends sex, by which I do not mean it's better
than sex, although let's face it, it often is. Traditionally, male humour
has been 'bluer' but that's on the way out. In fact if Mae West and
Marie Lloyd had their way – and history infers that they certainly did
– it would have gone out long ago. Women have been known to have
a secret humour amongst themselves for aeons – men resented it
and called it bitching. Bitchiness exists and men AND women love it.
Quoting George Eliot and Dorothy Parker is too easy – of course
there will always be exceptions to any rule. In general,
Victorianism has taken a good century to allow us to talk dirty, to tell
jokes and to score points off men. And in my experience, most men
love it. I've NEVER had a man turn nasty on me when I told jokes
and I've been telling them for hundreds of years. Humour either
works it or doesn't work – irrespective of race, colour or sex.
(Maureen Lipman, actor/writer)

Men and women laugh at each other. I feel that one of the reasons
for being here is to stop the stereotypes.
(Mandie Fletcher, TV director)

What men laugh at at the rugby club, what men laugh at on their
own, and what men laugh at when they're in the company of women,
are all very different things, in the same way as women all out on a
hen night as opposed to women in the company of royalty.
(Helen Atkinson Wood, actor)

Women aren't supposed to be dirty, but in fact are much coarser than men are a lot of the time.
(Jennie Campbell, radio producer)

There's some kind of subconscious link in people's heads that if you see a girl out there doing her stuff when it's dark – it's a little bit different – so we don't bother to do really late shows.
(Flamin' Hamsters, street performers/actors)

I'm very wary of saying that I think there's a difference in male and female humour, because I see people as individuals. But I do think that the 'tickle' mark is a lot higher in women than in men. They also tend not to laugh so much out loud. They smile more and they think. Even though we can be completely absurd and frivolous and laugh at very silly things, I think we are more demanding of what we want on television and of what we laugh about openly in public.
(Vicky Pile, writer)

Q: Do you think your kind of stand-up comedy is any different from male stand-up?
A: Well, I don't know many men who stand up and say 'I'm a lesbian.'
   (Claire Dowie, stand-up comedian)

Q: How do you feel about comedy as a woman?
A: I do find it an impossible question, 'how do you feel as a woman?', well, I've never been a man. And in terms of 'has it been harder?', well, I've got no terms of comparison. I've never lived twice. Or lived once as a man and once as a woman. I truly believe that there is no sex discrimination in comedy because I don't believe the audience is interested. I don't believe there's any prejudice from the audience, I think the prejudice is from the press. I know there are fewer women in comedy, or in stand-up, say. But I don't believe any audience has ever gone 'Oh God she's a woman, I'm not going to laugh.' I don't think there's a problem because I think personality transcends gender in comedy.
   (Victoria Wood, writer/performer)

No. Because we're all clinging to this planet as it hurls round spilling radioactivity all over.
(Denise Coffey, writer/performer/director)

Radio

On radio you don't have farce, soliloquies, or mention Jesus.
(Sue Limb)

For many years, radio was one of the most accessible media for
women to work in. Performers were cast for vocal ability rather
than appearance, and so radio provided opportunities for character
and voice work often denied women in live theatre and film. At first
women comedians were as frequently heard on radio as their male
counterparts. But eventually their contribution to radio became less
significant and they were employed as supports rather than central
figures. The reasons why women may have drifted away from
playing a major part in radio Light Entertainment are examined in
this chapter, as we look at some women who have made a major
contribution to the medium and at women in areas of writing,
performing and producing today.

As the music hall gradually died out, radio and film played an
increasing part in public consciousness. In 1901 Marconi sent the
first wireless message between Newfoundland and Cornwall. By
1905 music and speech were 'on air' for the first time. In 1922 the
British Broadcasting Company was formed, with J.C.W. Reith as its
general manager, and by 1923 it had gained its licence and
broadcasting began on a regular basis. By 1926 the British
Broadcasting Company became a Corporation, playing to over 2
million listeners.

Dance music was one of the most popular areas of entertainment
and a Revue and Vaudeville section of the radio was formed with
shows such as the intriguingly titled *Wireless Willie* and *Our Lizzie*
going out. However, the 1931 radio yearbook was not optimistic
for the future of radio light entertainment:

Few comedians are capable of writing their own material, and a
dearth of clever humorous writers is even greater.

The BBC took no risks with the performers it used, and the much-loved Beatrice Lillie was the first musical comedy 'star' to broadcast from the light entertainment section.

Amongst the pioneer comedy series were *Radio Radiance*, *Songs from the Show*, *The White Coons Concert Party*, and the popular *Music Hall*, compilations of already popular stage variety shows. Eventually the BBC produced its own musical comedies and in 1931 the first soap opera, *The English Family Robinson*, went out, featuring Mabel Constanduros (later to become quite a star on radio with her Grandma Buggins character in the radio soap opera of the same name). Throughout the 1930s radio was establishing itself as part of the way of life for many, and by 1937 the BBC had issued over 4 million licences.

Reith, however, held out against a separate light entertainment channel: the unsavoury music hall connotations of a single 'light' channel were anathema to him. When, in 1933, Eric Maschewitz was made head of the Variety department things began to change. Maschewitz (who was married to comedy performer Hermione Gingold) was keen on establishing a new look department and turned to American radio for ideas. He encouraged soap opera – a very popular form in the States – and imported *The Vagabond King*, a soap in which the leading role was taken by Bebe Daniels, later to work in British radio with Ben Lyons as part of the husband and wife team of *Hi Gang* and *Life with the Lyons*. By 1934 it was estimated that half of all radio listeners tuned into all of the variety programmes. Realising the potential of radio light entertainment, Maschewitz searched for new variety acts with whom to create a new type of show. He produced *Bandwagon* with Arthur Askey and Richard Murdoch, which paved the way for one of the greatest radio successes of all time: *It's That Man Again* or *ITMA* as it became known. Written by Ted Kavanagh, the first show went out on air in July 1939. Built around the fast-talking Tommy Handley, the show depended on pace and puns, introducing many comedians who later became household names. The female characters were an integral part of the show, and an impressive list of women took part: Hattie Jacques, as Ella Phant and later Sophie Tuckshop, Mollie Weir as Tattie Macintosh, Diana Morrison as Miss Hotchkiss, Joan Harben as Mona Lott, Jean Capra as Poppy Poopah and perhaps most memorably, Dorothy Summers as Mrs Mopp, with her catch-phrase 'Can I do you now, sir?'

For many reasons radio comedy has been an interesting and fruitful area for women. As mentioned, it is of no importance what an actor looks like in radio. It can eliminate the worries that many female comedy performers feel on stage about their appearance. A

Hattie Jacques in *Carry on Doctor*

voice can be convincing where an appearance may conflict with a character. However, Hattie Jacques, who was a large woman, was unimaginatively cast as the 'fat person' in *ITMA*. She appears to have had no qualms about her weight being an object of fun:

> It was planned that I should play a character 'Ella Phant'. Ted thought the laughs would come on the size gags but, being radio, and coupled with the fact that my voice didn't have the timbre of a 'heavy' person, that didn't really work out. It wasn't until one show when Tommy was supposed to be passing through a department store and knocked a speaking doll (me) that the audience reacted favourably. A large body with a very little voice seemed to hit the spot, so 'Sophie Tuckshop' was born – the terrible child who never stopped eating, with sickening results. (Hattie Jacques, from *The ITMA Years*, by Ted Kavanagh)

And so the inevitable jokes were made. It is notable that the radio audience would not at this time have been acquainted with Jacques' appearance and so they were simply laughing because the jokes were about someone fat. This tendency makes it difficult for such women to escape stereotyping.

> Handley: Why, Sophie Tuckshop. Fancy you're eating waxcakes now –
> Sophie (Hattie Jacques): Well, only one.
> Handley: Only one, eh? Well how did you keep it down?
> Sophie: I didn't – but I'm all right now. Would you like a roll:
> Handley: No thank you. I've just had lunch with a Scotty.
> Sophie: Ooh – did you have haggis?
> Handley: No, just a handful of biscuits and a rubber bone – but I'm all right now. I suppose you came here to study history. Who's your favourite character?
> Sophie: Henry VIII. He ate such a lot, and with his fingers.
> Handley: Aren't you thinking of Charles Laughton? I bet you'd have liked to have lived in those days.
> Sophie: Oh, yes – I'd have have stood behind him, and caught the bits he threw away.
> (*ITMA*)

During the years of World War II theatres and cinemas closed down, and radio was, for many, the main source of entertainment and information. The World Service was developed, and with the pressures of war, the BBC decided that although listening hours were to be cut, the evenings should be more or less devoted to comedy. Entertainments National Service Associates (ENSA) was set up to take entertainments to the troops and an ENSA half hour was on radio each week, much to the distaste of those who felt that some of the 'entertainment' on offer was substandard. Gracie Fields, on the other hand, was extremely popular at this time, with her wise-cracking humour and terrific singing voice. Known as 'Our Gracie', she was constantly on the radio and in film during the War years, and, like *ITMA*, was thought to be one of the reasons why the UK won the war.

Although many women moved into manual work during the War, housewives were still a target for propaganda, and Mr Harry Pepper broadcast *Up Housewives and At 'Em*. There was a demand for greater information broadcasts. Women comprised much of the listening population during the war, and so naturally no schedule was complete without a cookery programme. The radio stars Gert and Daisy (Doris and Elsie Waters) broadcast cookery sessions with recipes encouraging thrift and suggesting lovely things to do with reconstituted food. *Workers' Playtime* was a successful programme where comedians performed to men and women in factories and places of work, which then went out on network radio. Throughout the bombings and air-raids, radio was a vital part of British morale, and true to the idea that humour thrives in adversity, comedy flourished. Suzette Tarri was a comedian with a unique style of topical humour, who apparently managed to tell riotous jokes about the war in her own show *Tarri A While*. But the best-loved female double act of the war years and beyond was Doris and Elsie Waters alias 'Gert and Daisy'.

Through the 1940s and 1950s radio had the capacity that television now has to make 'stars', two of which were the Waters sisters. Born in Bow to keenly musical parents (their father set up a little family orchestra in which the large family played), they started their careers performing genteel 'after dinner entertainment' in respectable London hotels and dining places. Their 'set' consisted of Doris on the piano and Elsie on the piano or violin. Doris, the younger of the two, would tell some stories and in between Elsie would play a violin solo and they'd finish up with a duet, all of which took about 20 minutes. Like present-day cabaret acts, they might play two or three different venues in one evening. Whilst doing this they were invited to make a record for Parlophone. This proved successful, and they did three or four more until they ran out of material. The night before their next recording they were desperate for ideas. When we visited Elsie Waters in her elegant house near Brighton, she recalled over tea and home-made cake how the immortal characters of Gert and Daisy were born. In the face of having no musical material to perform, they simply decided to talk to each other on record.

Their choice of subject was weddings, and, that settled, they set about deciding what they should be called. Elsie Waters:

> What shall we call them, these two people? So Doris said 'Well,
> I'll call you Gert, 'cos I like saying it' and I said 'I'll call you
> Daisy because there's always a Daisy amongst them.' And so we
> called them Gert and Daisy.

They cut the record, making up the conversation as they went along. The record was a hit, unbeknownst to the sisters until about ten days later when they arrived at the Savoy to give one of their concerts. It was their third show that evening and they couldn't understand why they had been inundated with requests for their wedding record:

> When we got to the Savoy, this chap said 'Will you do your
> record? We said we don't know what you're talking about. He

Gert and Daisy

said, 'the wedding bells song'. 'Oh dear,' we said, 'we don't know if we can remember it. Will you put on a very long speech and we'll try and remember what we've done.' Then I took the handkerchief out of my violin case and put it round my neck, and borrowed an old hat and put it on back to front, and Doris put on a very old shawl (she used to do a song I wrote for her called 'Gone are the days' as an old Coster flower woman) and we went on and did Gert and Daisy for the first time. And we said to this chap 'Why do people keep asking for it?' He said, 'Well, Christopher Stone played your record on the wireless at lunchtime today.' And that's how you get known you see. After that it was the tail wagging the dog.

Miss Waters' recollection of how one of the most famous female double-acts came about also illustrates the growing power of radio. Despite the lamentations of the 1931 Yearbook, the Waters sisters were quite capable of writing their own material. Their ability to improvise their text was astonishing, as was their facility for topicality. If they heard an interesting news item in the morning it would be in their act by the evening. However, when they worked for the BBC they had to write down their material and submit it to be vetted. Any thing too risqué was taken out: 'And if you put it back in again, you were out' (Elsie Waters).

Their performance was relaxed, as if they had just sat down for a cup of tea and a chat. Their style is more realistic than say the Mrs Mopp character of the *ITMA* shows and has its modern counterpart in the comedy duo, French and Saunders.

Daisy: Married? Oh, not again. D'you know that girl gets married so often it makes the wedding bells sound like an alarm-clock.
Gert: 'Ere Daisy, I came round to see you last night and there was no answer.
Daisy: Last night? Oh no, we wasn't there. We'd gone up to Ted and Ada's – had a bit of a do on up there. Oh it was lovely, Gert. We danced to the wireless . . . Oh, there was a lovely man there, Gert. Oh, I fell for him. I looked at him and I thought 'Oh you gorgeous beast.' He took me dancing, and we was going round the floor together and all of a sudden I said 'Oh dear' I said. 'I do feel dizzy,' I said. 'Let's sit down somewhere.' So he said 'I know a nice dark corner.' I said 'I'm not so dizzy as that.' And then he told me his age, and I told him part of mine, and then somebody said supper was poured out. 'Ere, and after supper we had a bit of a sing-song. Ada's mother sang.
Gert: Did she?

Daisy: Yes, I'nt she a dear old girl?
Gert: Yes.
Daisy: She's a sweet old lady isn't she?
Gert: She's a sweet old lady.
Daisy: I like Ada's mother.
Gert: I like Ada's mother.
Daisy: She wasn't feeling too good though. Been in a draught and got
a stiff neck. Had to drink her Guinness sitting in a rocking chair.
(*Gert and Daisy, a Piano and How*)

Elsie Waters talked about their material and the problems of being well-known:

When it came to the patter we used to do it together . . .
Sometimes people would say they'd got some stuff, and they'd send us a script of the most ghastly muck you've ever read and you couldn't possibly use it, so you'd send them a cheque and forget the patter!

We asked Miss Waters what she felt was Gert and Daisy's appeal:

Well, we were lucky because they felt they knew us . . . I think it was that we didn't talk rubbish, we talked sense, and we made them laugh.

As Gert and Daisy they were known world-wide. They toured during World War II, taking their duologues to troops all over the world. Part of their appeal must have been that they represented people who lived much as the majority did, talking about problems with husbands or family life, mulling over incidentals with an unexpected quirkiness and wit. Although Elsie Waters is the only remaining sister, 'Gert and Daisy' were awarded the Burma Star last year for services to the country, and Elsie accepted on behalf of them both.

Doris and Elsie Waters were famous with the consistent characters of Gert and Daisy, part of their appeal being in their familiarity to their listeners. However, versatility has always been a major asset for women in Light Entertainment radio and many women on radio in the 1930s and 1940s were also involved in the popular Intimate Revue. Joyce Grenfell, who started her career in the revues of Herbert Farjeon, was supremely accomplished as a revue and radio performer. She worked extensively with radio producer Stephen Potter on his series of *How* programmes from 1943 onwards, although throughout the war she was a familiar voice guesting on such shows as *Monday Night at Eight, Henry Hall's Guest Night, Variety Bandbox* and *Workers' Playtime*. The *How* programmes were originally conceived as factual documentaries written by Potter. Joyce Grenfell was later brought in to provide a satirical touch to the series, performing pieces on 'How not' to do things. This was a fruitful time for Grenfell's gentle but achingly funny humour, and some of her best-known characters were created for the shows, including Fern Brixton, the hopelessly 'arty' and earthy vegetarian, and also the famous nursery school teacher. Grenfell's voice translated well to radio and created the world of her characters whilst maintaining her distinctive timbre which made her work so instantly recognisable.

The Waters sisters and Joyce Grenfell are good advertisements for the power of the writer/performer. Aware of their strengths, they insisted on using their own material whenever possible, and this is reflected in the quality of their performance. Obviously many writers have no desire to perform and vice versa, but those women who have combined writing with performing have usually been the stronger for it. With a few notable exceptions, such as Jean de Cassalis creator of the character 'Mrs Feather' who embarked on long eccentric one-sided telephone conversations, or Mabel Constanduros who also wrote for herself, writing has not been a particularly female domain in the world of Light Entertainment radio. Joyce Grenfell's long years on radio (she was 19 years with the *How* programmes) are witness to her creativity.

The best comic writing in whatever medium is often the most truthful to the author's individual sense of humour. This may seem startlingly obvious, but radio comedy can sometimes be written to order without any real imaginative input. It undoubtedly has the potential to be original and inventive, inviting the listeners to imagine the absurd and fantastical. Stephen Potter experimented with radio's unique scope in the Features department, but it seems that the first writers to do this in Light Entertainment radio were Frank Muir and Denis Norden in *Take it from Here* (1948). Each show started with some chatty conversation between the cast, moved into a satirical or topical sketch and ended with an increasingly absurd parody, usually of a film. The cast (as themselves, but scripted) commented on the actions of their radio characters, utilising the actors' personalities in an original way. According to Barry Took in his book *Laughter in the Air, Take it from Here* was a show that 'called upon the listeners' intelligence without losing its mass appeal.' Joy Nicholls was the original female star of the show, but she eventually returned to Australia, and was replaced by the popular singer Alma Cogan, and the actor June

Whitfield. The show became *The Glums* (1950), of which the characters and catchphrases such as June Whitfield's 'Oh Ron' became nationally known.

> Dunhill: This week we find Ron and Eth in a bedroom. Ron is lying on his back on top of the bedspread, hands behind his head, gazing up at the ceiling. Eth is sitting guiltily on the edge of the bed. So let us go, straight away over to the Glums.
> Orchestra: The Glums
> Whitfield: Oh Ron . . . I don't think we should be doing this.
> Bentley: I don't care. I like it Eth.
> Whitfield: But Ron, this is the Ideal Home Exhibition. People keep filing through and staring at us. Beloved you're just supposed to walk through and admire this Regency bedroom, not lie down on the bed and take your boots off.
> Bentley: My feet hurt Eth. (blows three times)
> Whitfield: Now what are you doing, sweetheart?
> Bentley: Blowing on me big toe.
> Whitfield: Oh, take it away from your mouth, Ron, do. You're not the only one whose feet hurt remember. I've walked miles and miles. That's the worst part of these exhibitions, they –
> Bentley: (tragedy) Oh! Oh, Eth! Oh!
> Whitfield: What is it, Ron?
> Bentley: I've sat on me free samples.
> (*Laughter in the Air*)

June Whitfield, who received her formal theatrical training at the Royal Academy of Dramatic Arts, and her comedy training working with Wilfrid Pickles, was in the show *Love From Judy* when she received a telephone call from Frank Muir and Denis Norden asking her to audition for *Take it from Here*. She got the part and that was her introduction to radio Light Entertainment. Despite her success in *The Glums* she has never had her own radio series and for many years she has played the feed to the men she has worked with. However there is always a strong sense of dignity in her performance which often means that she ultimately achieves the upper hand in a comic situation. This is also borne out in her television work with comedians such as Tony Hancock and Terry Scott. When asked what originally made her want to play funny characters, she said:

I think it comes from lack of confidence and embarrassment, because you think, 'well, if I'm going to get up there and make an

June Whitfield
© BBC Enterprises 1983

idiot of myself, and if they're going to laugh anyway, they might as well be meant to.'

At RADA she ended up playing the male parts in the productions, something that was common to many of the women to whom we spoke. If they were at an all-girls school either they were too tall, or too fat or too funny to play the traditional romantic female lead. Once the boy's kit was on, it was licence for the girls to be funny on stage. June Whitfield spoke about audience reaction to the funny woman:

When I started, women were not supposed to be particularly funny. Women were supposed just to be the foil. The kind of stuff that Victoria Wood and Julie Walters and everybody does now was not really quite done. And I think audiences had a slight built-in resentment of women being funny. Women were losing their dignity by being in comedy things. Beryl Reid was a great champion of that when she did all her musical stuff, I mean, marvellous . . . I was always delighted because not many women wanted to do it . . . they were rushing off wanting to be Juliet and I was quite delighted to hang about and pick up the comedy that was going. Suits me fine. I would still much rather be associated with something that makes people laugh than makes them think or cry.

A major point here is the reluctance of many people (even other women) to view women as innately funny. June Whitfield was slow to admit that her popularity was connected to her ability to interpret and perform comic scripts:

> It's nothing to do with me. I think again it's that thing of familiarity, I really do. I suppose it wasn't to start with, I like to think I have a sense of comedy, and I see the humour in things, but I couldn't possibly spend hours talking about my approach to comedy. My approach to comedy is pick up the script and read it and hope that something comes of it.

Familiarity is undoubtedly an important element in many areas of comedy. That June Whitfield is now a household name means that the audience feel safe with her, they know her style and respond to it, whether it is in *Terry and June* or an old *Carry On* film or at a recording of a radio show. We witnessed this audience relaxation when watching her record a *News Huddlines* show for BBC Radio. It was as if the audience felt that whatever else might happen, June Whitfield would remain calm and professional. This air of familiarity has always been a successful ingredient of radio comedy. The interminable catchphrases of the early broadcasts (and many of the later ones) bear witness to the fact that the listeners like to know or guess what is going to happen next, and that nothing will go horribly wrong.

In 1950 came the popular *Ray's a Laugh* with Ted Ray, Fred Yule, Kenneth Connors, Peter Sellers, Kitty Bluett and Patricia Hayes. Patricia Hayes was a favourite on radio and is well-known for her television appearances including *Hancock's Half Hour, The Lady is a Tramp*, and for her award-winning performance as *Edna, the Inebriate Woman*. She started her acting career playing a wealth of servants and maids (like so many character actors of quality) but she always welcomed her radio work because of its adaptability.

> At the time my marriage had broken down and I had three children to bring up. During the five years I worked with Ted I was never out of the house for more than half a day a week. (*Laughter in the Air*)

The familial responsibilities that women traditionally bear often conflict with their performing work. But radio is quick work, and comedy especially is done with a minimum of rehearsal. An ability

Patricia Hayes

to get things right first time is an advantage, often to the overall effect of the piece.

However, being a radio star is still demanding and so even though many women found radio a practical medium in which to work, their emphasis seems to have been on speed and ease rather than innovation. Those women who did achieve fame on radio seem, interestingly, to have had fewer family ties. The Waters sisters were unmarried and childless, Joyce Grenfell had no children, and Bebe Daniels brought her family into the studio along with her in *Life with the Lyons*. The familial demands on many women's lives meant that they were well-advised to corner the market in a particular voice or range of voices, to carve out a niche for themselves that could not easily be filled by anyone else. Beryl Reid was very successful at this, and the characters she created for the radio in the 1950s have remained with her. Like Joyce Grenfell, she was a popular guest on such shows as *Variety Bandbox*, *Workers' Playtime* and *Henry Hall's Guest Night*. Her early work on radio was apparently restricted by the fact that she had married a BBC radio producer, Bill Worsley, and consequently was only allowed to do six broadcasts a year for the BBC (although as this rule was not affirmed to us by the BBC it may have been an unofficial departmental arrangement). It was on Henry Hall's show that she first did the schoolgirl that was to become so popular as Monica on *Educating Archie*. She dressed up in full schoolgirl outfit for the recording of the show, and was a roaring success. Apparently the Head of radio Light Entertainment happened to be listening in to the show, and said 'Whoever that is, we've got to use her all the time' (Beryl Reid: *So Much Love*).

And it seems they did just that. Although they didn't give her her own show, she took the part of Monica in a new series *Starlight Hour* where she started a successful partnership with writer Ronnie Wolf. As a radio performer her dyslexia must have been a tremendous handicap: she had to learn all her radio scripts in advance (not at all common in radio). However, it did mean that she embellished her radio parts, and made the utmost of a script. *Educating Archie* (1953) was based around the ventriloquist Peter Brough's dummie, Archie Andrews. As Monica, Beryl Reid provided an impish St Triniansesque element to a cast which included Max Bygraves, Tony Hancock, Alfred Marks, Harry Secombe and Hattie Jacques. Eric Sykes was writing for the show at the time, and in her autobiography Beryl Reid recalls that he found it easier to write for Hattie Jacques than for her and consequently her part in the show suffered. This illustrates how dependent a performer is on a good writer to interpret style and provide material. As a result, a few writers are in constant demand, and they are bound to find people for whom they prefer to write. Luckily Ronnie Wolf stepped in at this point as Beryl Reid's full-time writer, and, with the help of additional material from Warren Mitchell, Monica continued to be a success.

> (*Door opens in distance*)
> Beryl: Hello – where's the grapes?
> Archie: Gone.
> Beryl: Goodbye!
> Archie: Monica, come back!
> (*Applause*)
> Peter: Now Monica, how are you?
> Beryl: Cheesed! You see when I'm at home, they all say I should be in school – and when I'm at school they all say I should be in a home.
> Archie: And how do you feel about that:
> Beryl: Frankly I'm frustrated!
> Peter: I'm not too good either.
> Beryl: Poor Mr Brough, you do look feek and weeble. Never mind, there's lots of illness around – our form mistress is away sick.
> Achie: What's the complaint?
> Beryl: None – we're all delighted!
> Peter: (*coughs*) Monica, do you know what's good for a sore throat?
> Beryl: Well, when Stephanie had a sore throat, I was told to get some hot salt, put it in one of her stockings, then wind it round her neck. I did, and she screamed like billyo! I didn't know I was supposed to take the stocking off her leg first. Still, she's all right – her leg comes out of plaster soon.
> (From Peter Brough's *Educating Archie*)

In the early 1950s, radio was still the quickest way to national fame and Beryl Reid benefited from her radio exposure:

> Peter Brough had this extraordinary gift for getting people just on the crest of a wave. He and his assistant Wally Ridley gave us all that push that we needed to become well known. I think, perhaps that I was the very last person to make a name through radio.
> (*So Much Love*)

Then came a new era. As television took over, the radio-listening population rapidly declined. Ironically radio comedy took on a new lease of life with such popular domestic comedies as *Life with the*

Beryl Reid as Monica in *A Little Bit on the Side*

Lyons (1954) with Bebe Daniels masterminding and co-writing the shows. They were based on the life of the Lyons family and they used a slick, gaggy style:

> Daniels: (coming on) Richard, why did you drag those old boots into the living-room?
> Richard: Because I want to polish them. Barbara and I are going riding with Mary and Derek.
> Daniels: Well, that's nice.
> Robin (Richard Bellaers): Who's lending you the horses?
> Richard: Violet Hemmingway's going to let me have hers.
> Daniels: You mean the four of you are going to ride one horse?
> Barbara: Of course not silly. Derek's getting the other three from the Marble Arch stables.
> Lyons: Well, be careful. Some of those animals can be pretty wild.
> Daniels: Your father's right. When I was a little girl I was thrown off a horse and knocked senseless.

Bebe Daniels
© BBC Enterprises 1970

Lyons: (chuckles) And you can see how long it's lasted.
Daniels: Well it's only been – Ben!
Robin: Mommie, I didn't know you could ride.
Daniels: Oh yes, I used to own my own horse, and what wonderful
    times I had galloping across the prairie.
Robin: Did you ever take a five foot jump?
Daniels: No dear, my legs were too short.
(*Laughter in the Air*)

Life with the Lyons matches the wise-cracking style of many American films and television shows of this era. At the same time there were many British variety style shows going out including *Variety Bandbox*, produced by one of the few women producers in radio Light Entertainment history, Joy Russell-Smith. It was a Sunday night variety show consisting of a series of acts linked by a compère. It was designed to 'present the public with the more avant-garde and "with it" comedians and singers of the day' (*Laughter in the Air*).

Among its artists were up-and-coming young comics Peter Sellers and Miriam Karlin (later to feature in the hit television show *The Rag Trade*). *Music Hall*, by contrast, was broadcast on Saturdays and was more traditional, featuring Doris and Elsie Waters, Vic Oliver, Rob Wilton and others. In 1959 came *Just Fancy* and *The Clitheroe Kid* which included in its strong support cast Diana Day, Carol Gardner and Patricia Burke. There is no denying that there have been a lot of women involved in radio comedy, but apart from the few such as Grenfell, Tarri, the Waters, Bebe Daniels and some others, they have rarely been innovators. In 1951 a startlingly original show, *The Goons*, abandoned any pretence to verisimilitude and blasted its way through Broadcasting House. With Peter Sellers, Michael Bentine, Harry Secombe and Spike Milligan, it showed that there was potential for change within the department. So if there is potential for change within radio structure, why has it not been generated by women? Is it lack of confidence in a male-dominated area, or lack of interest in the medium? The style of *The Goons* was manic and uncompromising, and it seems to have been generated through the desire to disrupt current modes of comic expression. Women in radio on the other hand have tended to fit in where they can.

Tony Hancock also hit the jackpot with his distinctive comedy at this time, supported by the scripts of Galton and Simpson and casts which included Sid James, Bill Kerr, Kenneth Williams, Moira Lister, Andrée Melly and Hattie Jacques. Hancock's humour was less anarchic, more traditional than *The Goons* and was based on the misfortunes of the Hancock character. He travelled through his misadventures like a forlorn reject from a Henry Fielding novel, snubbed and thwarted by those around him. His virtuoso style was impressive but tended to reduce the supporting characters on the radio, and later on television, to ciphers or stereotypes. The women naturally came in for this treatment. This excerpt, in which Hancock is telling Ted Ray about his new 'fiancée,' Joan Heal, who is about to appear on the programme, illustrates this point:

Ray: . . . By the way, where is Joan?

Hancock: Well I haven't read on, but I believe she's on the next page. You see she's with us on the programme tonight.

Ray: (*excited*) Joan Heal – here on the programme? Oh that's wonderful, wonderful! Quick where's the mirror? Just see if I've got my eyelashes on straight. Oh Ray, you brute you . . . (growls) How is it you've got so much?

Hancock: Nobody else wanted it. Anyway Ray, it's no use sprucing

up. It won't do you any good. This bint is Hancock crazy. She
hasn't got eyes for anybody else. She's completely under
Hancock's old spell. See how her minces light up soon as she sees
me. Oh – she loves me!
(*Door opens*)
Heal: (*delightedly*) Why, Teddy – darling.
Ray: Joan Heal.
(*Applause*)
(*Ted and Joan start necking, ecstatic moans, sighs, kisses, etc.*)
Hancock: (*Pause, embarrassed laugh*) Oh – er – Ted, I'd like you to
  meet my girlfriend, Joan Heal.
(*Laughter in the Air*)

Dennis Main Wilson who produced the early Hancock shows
remembers that Galton and Simpson didn't write particularly well
for women: 'It was always a man's idea of a woman.' This refers to
a major tendency in comedy: men write best for men, women write
best for women, but very many more men than women actually
write at all. This is a suitable point to study some female radio
writers and also some women working in other areas of radio
production.

There seems to be no lack of encouragement for the few women
who write for the BBC radio Light Entertainment department.
Andrea Solomons, (*Weekending, Lenny Henry Show, Spitting
Image, Carrott's Lib, Now Something Else*, etc.) who started
writing for radio but who now works more for television:

I got into comedy really by sending some stuff in to John Lloyd.
He was script editor at Light Entertainment Radio, and he invited
me up and suggested I start writing for *Weekending*. Then Paul
Mayhew Archer who later produced *Weekending* gave me every
encouragement to come back again.

Alison Renshaw (*Weekending, Now Something Else, Unnatural
Acts*) is one of the only women currently writing regularly for radio
Light Entertainment. She felt very unsure of herself when she first
started writing and says that she thinks that this is deep-rooted in
women: 'I think it's confidence. Women are not brought up to
believe that they can crack jokes, make people laugh.'

Alison Renshaw was at first encouraged by producer Jamie Rix
(now working in television), and subsequently by Paul Mayhew
Archer. So the support is there, but it's actually the fear of rejection
prior to sending in material that is the hardest to overcome. We
asked Sue Limb, who writes extensively for radio and who has won

a Sony Award for her work in children's radio, why she thought so few women ventured to write for the medium:

> For the same reason why women have taken a while to move into a lot of activities. I don't see why radio comedy should traditionally be male. Women have always been comic novelists, and there is no reason why a woman shouldn't write for radio. It's just as easy as writing a novel. I think it's all to do with the 'old boys' club' atmosphere that surrounds it, and in which, really, radio comedy has its origins.

By referring to the 'old boys' club' Sue Limb means the past tendency of radio Light Entertainment to employ Oxbridge graduates. It is not an image of which the department is fond, as it rightly recognises that it is intimidating and classbound. It has recently taken steps in its selection process to cast its nets wider, but radio is an area which does seem to attract Oxbridge graduates with a penchant for comedy. Limb wishes that more women would become involved in radio Light Entertainment:

> I love radio. I think it's a shame it hasn't got more prestige . . . when it comes to women, and the way women are presented, I'm quite sure that radio has more room than TV to escape stereotypes.

However, it is an inescapable fact that the BBC is still a particularly male-dominated area, and traditional hierarchies of all descriptions still exist.

Despite the ever-decreasing listenership in the 1960s and 1970s good new shows were being produced, such as *We're in Business* (by Barry Took and Marty Feldman) with Irene Handl, and *Round the Horne* whose cast included Hugh Paddick, Kenneth Williams, Kenneth Horne and Betty Marsden:

> Grams: *Isn't it Romantic?*
> Marsden: Oh Charles, are you still experimenting?
> Paddick: Yes, Fiona, I think I've stumbled on something big – very big indeed.
> Marsden: You must rest, Charles. You can't keep driving yourself like this.
> Paddick: I can't give up now. It's all I live for. I think I've hit upon something. Look through this microscope.
> Marsden: In here, Charles?
> Paddick: Yes, at these slides.
> Marsden: Good heavens, Charles. It's me on a donkey at Margate.

Paddick: And here, look – see hundreds of them.

Marsden: They're terribly small, Charles.

Paddick: You can't see them with the naked eye – but for years I've known they were there.

Marsden: Bacteria, Charles?

Paddick: No thanks, not while I'm working. There, see – just an ordinary piece of Gruyère cheese.

Marsden: But I don't understand. What are you doing with it?

Paddick: It's an experiment, Fiona. Watch   I do this   and this and that.

Marsden: Don't do that, Charles.

Paddick: Oh I'm sorry. Not that. I'll do this then.

Marsden: That's better.

Paddick: Then I take it so and hold it over the Bunsen burner. Now do you see what I've been up to all these years?

Marsden: Oh Charles, you've done it at last. One day millions of people will recognise your achievement.

Paddick: Yes, Fiona. I shall be known as the man who discovered – Welsh Rarebit.

(Fiona and Charles discover Welsh Rarebit – from *Round the Horne*, written by Barry Took and Marty Feldman)

Sexual innuendo seems to play a large part in radio comedy, sometimes to the extent that it makes a mockery of radio censorship. Some scripts have reached peaks of sordidity in an endeavour to conjure visual explicitness out of verbal innocence. These double standards can make radio comedy occasionally risible. Even a show like *News Huddlines* contains an alarming degree of double entendre. Some of the newer shows have tried to explode the titillation of the double entendre by undercutting it and exposing its implied meaning (cf. *Radio Active* and *In One Ear*), but the subtlety is not always appreciated.

By the mid to late 60s BBC radio had had its day as a popular medium. Pirate Radio Caroline was set up in the early 60s, Radio Luxembourg was well established, and the growing interest in the 'pop' culture market meant that BBC Radios Two and Four lost their listeners to other frequencies. Radio One emerged in '67, but as an exclusively music station; its listeners did not necessarily tune into Radios Two, Three or Four. The Radio Four show *I'm Sorry I'll Read That Again* (1965) appealed to a youthful market. It was innovative, very funny and was performed by an excellent cast who were soon to realise their full potential in television as members of the *Monty Python's Flying Circus* team. Unfortunately there was only one woman in the cast – Jo Kendall. In the 70s, Douglas Adams' cult programme *Hitch-Hiker's Guide to the Galaxy* (1978) wooed a considerable audience, but was not enough to revive a flagging medium. Like many areas of the arts, radio is financially impoverished, hence the popularity of game shows on radio: they are cheap to produce and take little time to rehearse. Such conditions are not expedient to women. The smaller the cast, the cheaper the show, which often means that the status quo of one woman in a sketch-show will remain. If one woman is versatile, why have two? However, for many women, who often have little material to play with, the idea of being the only woman in a show means greater possibilities.

Alison Steadman:

> Actually, in a funny sort of way, I quite like it, being the only woman, because you get all the parts. There's more variety.

Two familiar performers on contemporary radio are Denise Coffey and Miriam Margolyes. As Denise Coffey put it:

> It's either me or Miriam dragged out to do the pilot for something or other.

Both women have a terrific ability to vary the tone and range of their speaking voices, and to switch characters with lightning speed. But for both, radio is an unlucrative sideline, and they are more involved in instigating interesting theatrical projects elsewhere. Miriam Margolyes, who successfully backed and toured the play *Gertrude Stein and a Companion*, also works in TV, film and voice-overs. Margolyes was the more disenchanted with women's parts on radio, feeling them to be:

> Absolutely fucking appalling. I really don't think that there's much good stuff written for women. Only Victoria's (Wood) stuff approaches the range and power we deserve. We're just foils, and I'm tired of that.

Miriam Margolyes was however highly complimentary about the work of Sue Limb, in whose radio comedy *The Wordsmiths of Gorsemere* she and Denise Coffey performed. *The Wordsmiths* is the story of a family not dissimilar to the poet Wordsworth:

The Wordsmiths of Gorsemere

F/X: (Fade in) kitchen sounds
Iris: So 'tis five for dinner tonight, then, missus? Shall I set about it?

Miriam Margolyes

Dorothy: Oh, please, dear Iris – do. But what can we provide?
Iris: The garden be full o' greens, missus.
F/X: Door to garden opens. Moorland sounds
Dorothy: Are the beans ready yet?

Iris: (*Outside*) Nay, but I got a few handfuls o' Pellitory-by-the-Wall,
missus. (*Coming indoors*) That'll make a bonny salad for they
gentlefolks, wi' a morsel o' groundsel tops an' all.
Dorothy: – Oh dear –
William: (*Entering*) Dorothy?
Dorothy: Yes, William?
William: I wish to speak frankly with you on a subject close to my
heart.
Iris: Don't ye take no heed o' me maister. Remember I be stone deaf.

During the mid to late 1970s and early 1980s there was a spate
of sketch-shows which were indebted to university revue for their
style and content. *Injury Time* featured ex-Footlights member
Emma Thompson, who has subsequently worked in other radio
shows as well as West End theatre and television. The transition
from radio to television is a common one for both performers and
producers. The Light Entertainment department is thus a curious
mixture of producers who have been there for a great number of
years, and who will stay there, and the newer producers, many of
whom see radio as a springboard to greater things. Writers too
move to television at the first available opportunity: it is better paid
and less restrictive.

Radio Four's *Radio Active*, however, is intrinsically suited to
radio. First produced by Jimmy Mulville in 1981, it has completed
its sixth series and is one of the success stories of recent years. The
show centres around the idea of the Radio Active independent radio
station complete with its own DJ, features and news items, and
parodies of contemporary pop songs. The show is largely written by
Angus Deayton and Geoffrey Perkins (also cast members), and
Michael Fenton Stevens, Philip Pope and Helen Atkinson Wood
play numerous characters, from chatshow hosts to people ringing in
with their problems. Helen Atkinson Wood is an especially versatile
performer, and two of the main characters she plays are presenter
Anna Dapter, and Agony Aunt Anna Rabies (who started life as
Joanna Jaundice). This extract is from a radio phone-in sketch in
which Joanna Jaundice and the radio Doctor are answering callers'
problems:

Caller: Well, I've been married and living in Croydon for three years
now and for the past few months I've been having an affair with
another woman.

Doctor: Yes, well three years is a particularly critical period.

Joanna: Oh, do shut up for goodness' sake. Now first things first. Have you told your wife?

Caller: No, you see . . .

Joanna: Look, the only way you're gonna solve this problem, luvvie, is to be completely honest with yourself *and* her. And that means telling her the whole story.

Caller: But she'd kill me if I did . . .

Doctor: Caller, could I ask you one question . .?

Joanna: Oh, just shut it, can't you? What's your name luvvie?

Caller: Well, I'd rather not disclose my . . . .

Joanna: What's your name? You gave it to the receptionist?

Caller: Well, I did, but I'd rather you . . . .

Joanna: 'Peter Bainbridge' I hear over my headphones. Is that right.

Caller: Oh, no. You've gone and blown it . . . .

Joanna: Mrs Bainbridge, if you're listening or if anyone's listening who knows her, perhaps they'd let her know that her husband is having an affair with another woman. It was just one, was it?

Caller: Oh, God. She's just come in . . . . .

(Sound of fighting, yelling, breaking glass, etc.)

Joanna: Hello, Peter? Well, we seem to have lost him there for a minute, but I think we can safely say that Peter, that's Peter Bainbridge of Croydon, has been having an affair with at least one other woman. Of course it could so easily be more. Doctor?

Doctor: Yes?

Joanna: Piss off. Hello? Next caller.

Helen Atkinson Wood, who trained in Fine Art, also works extensively in theatre and television (*The Young Ones, Kelly's Eye, The Comic Strip Presents*). She joined *Radio Active* rather than heading into 'straight' theatre because:

I always wanted to be funny. Once you've dared yourself to be funny, it becomes so interesting and exciting.

She finds radio very liberating:

The thing that I like about radio is that I get to play a leggy brunette if I want to, and interesting and exciting people, as opposed to chubby, spotty blondes.

Self-deprecation aside, the parts she plays with *Radio Active* are well-observed parodies of the smug presenter-reporter type and characters of her own devising. She has a distinctive but adaptable voice and because of her comic ability and sense of timing she plays a major part in each radio show.

76

Helen Atkinson Wood (picture by Daily Mail photographer Jim Hutchinson)

Radio

The only Light Entertainment radio show which has had more women than men in the cast was the notorious *Three Plus One on Four* which featured three women – Alison Steadman, Denise Coffey and Emma Thompson (who was later replaced by Susan Deneker as she was unable to complete the series) – and one token man, David Jackson Young. The show was produced by one of the only two women producers of recent years – Jan Ravens. Jan Ravens (also the first woman President of Footlights) became a radio producer in 1981 after directing the Perrier Award-winning Footlights show *Cellar Tapes*. She recognised the importance of her position as the only woman producer, but she didn't want the material in *Three plus One* to be overtly feminist. Her main criterion was that it should be funny. She felt that feminist elements would be more powerful if they subtly infiltrated:

> I wanted it to seep insidiously into people's brains that women could be as funny.
> (Jan Ravens)

Although:

> It's very difficult to know where you're doing women down, or where you're parodying something in women you don't think is necessarily very good.

Jan does not feel that the series was a wild success, and a particular sketch about orgasms (which went out one Saturday tea-time just before *Desert Island Discs*) caused much disruption amongst the department and public, contributing to, according to David Jackson Young, one of the authors of said sketch, some 'severe tickings off' and *Three Plus One* only lasting for one series. This is the offending sketch:

Metro Magazine

(Door opens)
Deirdre: Ah, come in Irma, Tom, Anna. Take a seat.
All: Deirdre.
(Door closes. Scraping of seats.)
Deirdre: Right – so what have we got for the November issue of metro mag? Irma?
Irma: Well, Deirdre, I thought I'd write a piece on the female orgasm.
Deirdre: Good, good.
Irma: Entitled 'The Female Orgasm: does it exist? *Metropolitan* goes on the hunt.'

Deirdre: Fine. What sort of area will you be uncovering?

(*Laughter*)

Deirdre: No, seriously Irma.

Irma: Well, I thought I'd answer those questions that most non-orgasmic women want answered abut the female orgasm.

Deirdre: Such as?

Irma: Well – where can you get one for instance? How much will it cost? Does it hurt? Can you take it back if it doesn't work? That sort of thing.

Deirdre: Sounds like just the sort of thing we're looking for.

Irma: It should be – I read it in *last* month's *Metro*.

(*Laughter*)

Deirdre: Tom?

Tom: Well, I thought I'd write a really sexist, but humorous, tongue-in-cheek article on the problems of being a working mother.

Deirdre: Title?

Tom: 'Working mother – Tom Crabapple tells you how you can have an orgasm a day.'

Deirdre: Hahaha. Love it Tom. How long?

Tom: Sorry?

Deirdre: Your column – how long?

Tom: Wha–

Deirdre: How many inches? Your article?

(*Sound of Tom flashing*)

Tom: Oh. Sorry. Ha haha. I thought you were talking about my . . . ha ha.

(*Laughter*)

Anna: Lips.

Deirdre: Can't wait to see it Tom.

(Sound of zipper undoing)

Deirdre: No Tom – put it away – your article.

(*Laughter*)

Deirdre: OK Anna – so what's new for November?

Anna: Right. OK. Look.

Deirdre: What?

Anna: Look Deirdre – today's woman is a complex, sensitive creature, full of unexplored potential, and capable of achieving so much more than our sexist, male-orientated society allows. I mean, we've got a woman Prime Minister, for Christ's sake!

Irma: Right, right . . .

Deirdre: What's your point Anna?

Anna: I think *Metropolitan* has a right – no, a *duty* – to say that there can be more in a woman's life than simply 'an orgasm a day'.

Anna: A multiple orgasm a day.

> Deirdre: Good point. So your piece will be . . .?
> Anna: 'Margaret Thatcher and the multiple orgasm.'
> Deirdre: Brilliant. Science Fiction – we haven't had one of them!

Despite complaints the programme was well received:

> Billed as a knock about feminist comedy. While some of the
> feminism seems a little uncertain (some of the jokes had a
> distinctly self-mocking character) this show does have moments
> of extreme hilarity. Last week's show contained a very funny
> sketch on the way Pamela Stephenson promotes herself together
> with a comic but damning send up of the way female
> employment agencies of the 'Kelly Girl type' provide services of
> dubious usefulness. All in all this was the funniest twenty-five
> minutes I've heard on radio for years. Let's hope the team can
> keep it up – would it not be possible to encourage more women
> to write for it. It seems a shame that a feminist comedy show has
> to depend on a stock of material written by men.
> (*City Limits*)

Jan Ravens left the BBC in order to follow a career as a
performer and director, areas in which she has subsequently had
much success. Her place at the BBC was taken by another woman,
Jennie Campbell. When she applied for the job, Jennie Campbell
felt that the BBC was more concerned to break the Oxbridge
tradition of young producers than they were with the unequal ratio
of men to women in the department. Like Sue Limb, she feels that
radio Light Entertainment's image is disconcerting:

> It's very much a male stronghold. And for that reason I think
> people are put off from applying.

Moreover, once on the inside:

> When you're there, it doesn't make any difference at all. It's very
> much a profession where you all work in your own way, and
> people respect that. And the fact that you're a woman doesn't
> make any difference at all.

Although:

> At the very beginning there was a tendency to suggest that I do an
> all-woman programme with female performers and writers which
> I did resent.

However, Jennie Campbell dispelled any notions that she might be suited to a specifically woman-orientated area by proving herself first and foremost to be a good producer. Once she'd done that, the pressure decreased. Whilst generally dismissing any claims about sex discrimination in radio she did mention one particularly male-dominated area – panel games:

> In a panel game there are usually three men and a token woman, and that does make me very cross . . . But at times it is easier to find witty men than it is women who are prepared to be funny. It's a horrifying thing if you're sitting on a panel and you tell a joke and it doesn't go well, and the three men beside you tell jokes that go uproariously. It would put anybody off.

As the only woman producer, she felt that her position as a critic of other women was difficult:

> To criticise a woman, her performance or her writing, is scary. There is always the let-out, from a lot of women, that the criticism is not aimed at the performance, or the material, it is aimed at them because they are women. That's a shame because I feel that women should be criticised and take criticism. There's a tendency at the moment, because they are women, and because the profession has been against women, to think that they have a God-given right to succeed.

Jennie Campbell felt that to make allowances for woman would lead to their being judged by a different set of standards. She argued that radio afforded unique opportunities for women:

> People who work for radio have a voice that can bring people in. A lot of women have that timbre to their voice. I think people should be trying to use radio more, because it provides fantastic opportunities. It's not even necessary for a woman to have a voice that is tremendously versatile. Radio Light Entertainment has been looking for a new Kenneth Horne for about twenty five years, and if that turned out to be a lady, it wouldn't matter at all.

Although less optimistically:

> Within television and radio I think there is definitely less prejudice against women performers. Although I do think that the radio audience is perhaps slower to change than any other, and perhaps for that reason women are going to find it quite difficult.

Jennie Campbell has left the Light Entertainment department to move to Edinburgh. So, unless the BBC elects another woman in her place, the light entertainment corridor will remain an all-male bastion.

Most producers are aware of the sexual imbalance and strive to find and encourage female writers and performers. Helen Lederer writes for and performs in the award-winning live show *In One Ear* produced by Jamie Rix. Helen Lederer has worked as a stand-up comedian and latterly in television (*Happy Families, Girls on Top, Naked Video*). *In One Ear* was based on the interaction of the cast (Nick Wilton, Clive Mantle, Steve Brown and Helen Lederer) and the success of the series depended upon the appeal of these four personalities.

Often Helen Lederer's character draws attention to her minority position and, by pinpointing the pitfalls into which the only woman in a sketch-show might fall, she eliminates these dangers. The men in the show, who are constantly trying to be 'right on', cover their tracks in case they have inadvertantly made a sexist or racist comment. The show satirises the current attention to 'ideologically sound' comedy, and much of the humour comes from their attempts 'not to notice' that Helen Lederer is the only woman in the show:

> Clive: I don't know how to make a pancake. Ask Helen.
> Nick: Helen?
> Helen: Yes Nick?
> Nick: Do you know how to make a pancake – eh, not that I expect you to, I mean, I hope you didn't think that I was being sexist – assuming that you knew how to make a pancake – no reason you should. Why didn't I ask Steve? Why not indeed? Bloody good point. Look, it wasn't sexist of me asking you if I was being sexist, was it? Why should I expect you to be the judge of what's sexist, just because you're a girl – I'm not using girl in any derogatory sense, please don't think that, I was using it descriptively, purely descriptively. I wasn't trying to imply, girl – i.e. a person less able than a man, or, 'Get back in the kitchen, girl' I didn't say that, OK? (etcetera . . .)
> Helen: Calm down Nick. You're not being sexist, I don't mind you asking me if I know how to make pancakes.
> Nick: Well do you?
> Helen: Yes.
> Nick: Well go and bloody make some then.

The performance and concept of the show are strong and imaginative and make lively listening. *In One Ear* also illustrates the potential for good radio shows.

Radio Light Entertainment now has many other independent stations with which to compete. The listenership of Capital Radio (which now includes comedy in its repertoire) is in the region of 4 million, whereas Radio Four at peak listening time only attracts hundreds of thousands. The medium cannot work when it is out of step with other areas of entertainment. It is difficult to imagine BBC Radio Light Entertainment regaining its former popularity, (although in some young professional circles, Radio Four is becoming 'chic'). At present (1986) there is no female Light Entertainment Producer in BBC radio, whereas there are sixteen men. Even in comparison with the BBC Drama Department which has thirteen women and thirty-four men, the statistics are unbalanced. It would be interesting to see more women performers with their own half-hour shows, but sadly there is no reason why new talents should choose to work in radio over and above the more remunerative field of television. As former Chief Producer of BBC Radio Four Light Entertainment Alan Nixon pointed out in an article in *Broadcast* (February 1984):

> Why should the Comic Strip team try out a pilot sit-com for radio, when there's enough money for half-a-dozen small film budgets on Channel 4? The impact, money and success are instant and perhaps temporary. It is sad, however, that writers and performers of talent have not been made aware of radio's unique qualities. We may not have the money but we have the power to stimulate the imagination in a way second only to the written word.
>
> 'Alternative' comedy could be as transient as punk rock. Yet the size of its audience reflects the need for the new. By not tuning into that audience in radio are we guilty of losing another generation of listeners? The modern 'alternative' comedy style is as popular at Leeds Polytechnic as down South; eight and nine year olds quickly spot the new and exciting. BBC2's *The Young Ones* has had an avid following among 14-year-olds. These are the middle-aged listeners of the future and we will keep them by ensuring that there is room for new comedy. We must ensure a variety of styles, listen to the grass roots response and educate the new writers and performers in the art of radio. That way we will build a positive and exciting future even if it upsets some of the loyal and faithful traditionalists on the way.

Alan Nixon brought the *Cabaret Upstairs* series to Radio Four. The series aimed to take the best of the live acts on the London cabaret circuit and bring them to radio. However, it took him four years to get this kind of show on air. In 1981 Alan Nixon made a recording of a group of the best-known alternative comedians at the Comedy Store, London. Amongst those recorded were *20th Century Coyote* (Rick Mayall and Adrian Edmonson), *The Outer Limits* (Nigel Planer and Keith Allen), and French and Saunders, and the evening was compered by Alexei Sayle. The recording was taken to the then Head of Radio Two and it was deemed unsuitable to go out on air, or if it did, it would have to go out at one o'clock in the morning, and even then severely edited. When a few months later, Alexei Sayle won a Pye Award for his Capital Radio show *Alexei Sayle and the Fish People* and was profiled in *The Times*, Nixon was asked why the Light Entertainment Department had not picked up on Sayle. Alan Nixon has now left radio and works as a television producer.

Although radio can be a tremendously liberating medium, it also has limitations. Radio Four especially maintains a rather genteel image and the disproportionate attention given to the few letters of complaint it receives rather than to the many thousands that it does not is alarming. This obsession with the minority, perhaps a hangover from the notorious *Green Book* – the first published form of BBC censorship, printed in 1949 (which banned the use of certain phrases such as 'winter draws on' because of its lewd connotaions) – proves restrictive and discouraging to writers. Radio may be more permissive than it was but it still lags behind television in interpreting current trends in comedy. By refusing to acknowledge the humour of a whole generation of comedians for whom explicit language and unorthodox images are the norm, BBC Radio has lost listeners through its pursuit of the permissible. But then, mass appeal may not be its criterion.

It must not be forgotten, however, that many women enjoy performing for radio and are always keen to work in it. It would perhaps be wise to see radio as a valid training ground, before the increasingly inevitable move to television; a training ground where women can perfect their abilities and develop ideas. In doing so they can acquaint radio listeners with new movements, such as the new wave of female comics, before translating them elsewhere.

ON LOOKS, GLAMOUR AND IMAGE

If you look like me, short fat and Jewish, people really don't know what to do with you. Instead of using your peculiarities like they do in America, they don't know what to do with you here. They're frightened. There's too much of a cult of perfection.
(Miriam Margolyes, actor)

I think you have the advantage if you look peculiar, because then that's the first joke.
(Helen Atkinson Wood, actor)

Society has conditioned us to think that an attractive woman cannot be funny – it's just the law – she can't because she's too good-looking to have any problems. 'Course she's got problems.
(Kit Hollerbach, stand-up comedian)

I think it's interesting on the circuit how many women stand-ups dress to look like men. Kit Hollerbach's an exception, but most of us all wear trousers, or suits. I don't think there's anything wrong in it, but it's quite interesting that that's the one compromise that a lot of women make.
(Jo Unwin, performer/writer, The Millies)

I find dressing up and putting make-up on puts you in the right frame of mind, it gives you a certain confidence of coping, it makes you stand in a certain way.
(Jenny Lecoat, stand-up comedian/actor/writer)

I will know that I'm truly liberated when I can bear to go on stage without an inch of make-up, nothing, not even look in the mirror before I go on. I would love to be able to do that, but I can't and I don't know any other female comics who can.
(Rebecca Stevens, actor/writer/stand-up comedian)

What I like about Victoria Wood is that she is so ordinary, you could actually imagine living next door to her.
(Adele Anderson, performer/writer, Fascinating Aïda)

Women in television have an obligation to look pretty; and it really irritates me that the few women who are in television who aren't pretty have the piss taken out of them mercilessly, like Esther Rantzen and Janet Street Porter – she's all right, but she gets ripped

to shreds because she doesn't sound middle-class and doesn't look smug. I want to see women equivalents on television of Patrick Moore, Robin Day, Magnus Pyke, David Bellamy . . .
(Abi Grant, writer)

If someone's stunningly good-looking it's very difficult for them to get the audience's sympathy.
(Rebecca Stevens)

They used to say to me 'You've got to wear a dress.' And I said 'but I hate wearing dresses. Please don't make me wear a dress.' And they said, 'No, you've got to.' And so I did, 'cos I thought I had to do what they wanted me to do. And in the end I got so upset about it, being dragged round these awful dress shops and being put into eiderdowns, I made an appointment with the producer . . . and I said 'Excuse me, please can I wear trousers?' and he said 'Yes don't bother me now.' So it was all right after that.
(Victoria Wood, writer/performer)

Victoria Wood was always an inspiration, not because I wanted to copy her, but because she was not preoccupied with her sex, her looks, or what she was saying about men, but was getting on with a whole range of humour and being really funny.
(Helen Lederer, stand-up comedian/actor)

An audience doesn't want a woman to look stupid. They want her to look glamorous or vulnerable.
(Jan Ravens, actor/director/producer)

Someone said to me, 'Eve, when you first came on stage you reminded me of Bette Midler. But when I looked again you reminded me of Ronnie Barker.'
(Eve Ferret, actor)

I don't try to have an image. I just try to be myself.
(Victoria Wood)

Victoria Wood – I think she's easily one of the most attractive female comedians without doubt.
(Helen Atkinson Wood)

Character actors, monologuists and women's theatre

> You should be prepared to go to extraordinary lengths. I don't care
> what I look like, whether I play the part of a tree or anything. If it's
> funny and you can make it funny, you shouldn't have conditions.
> (Su Pollard)

Character acting is a female forte. It is argued that while women
can't or won't tell jokes, they excel at portraying a wide variety of
ridiculous and eccentric women. Edith Evans's Lady Bracknell,
Margaret Rutherford's Miss Prism, Hylda Baker's 'She knows, ya
know!' and Joyce Grenfell's 'George, don't do that!' have all
become common currency. This chapter celebrates the quantity and
diversity of women's character work and looks at the qualities and
technique which make a good character actor as well as the
limitations and psychological hurdles which women have experienced in this area of work. Are women's roles as character actors
inevitable, or are they mutable? Have changes in women's roles in
society been matched – for better or worse – by changes in the
nature and technique of women's character acting?

It is in the area of character actors that 'women in comedy' are
perhaps hardest to define. There are and have been many fine
British actors who have interpreted comic roles in theatre, both in
classical texts – including Shakespearean and Restoration comedies
– and modern plays. Contemporary supremos in this area include
Judi Dench, Julia McKenzie and Maureen Lipman and, although we
admire their skill, we have not discussed their theatre work at
length. We have chosen to talk to women working in clowning,
women's theatre and their own shows, as well as women in
conventional comedy. Thus we have attempted to comment on the
nature of comic performances and women's perception of their
comic potential rather than the interpretation of theatrical texts.

A key quality of the British character actor is eccentricity. While
the lead actor is often young, attractive and lucky or lost in love,

the character actor tends to be older, quirkier, unpredictable, offbeat – and funny.

Nellie Wallace (1870-1948) made an art of her oddity and was eventually billed as 'The Essence of Eccentricity'. Although she began her career in music hall, she had none of the inviting sexuality of music hall singers such as Marie Lloyd or Vesta Victoria. She was a thoroughbred clown who started as a clog dancer, was hopeless as a serious actor but excelled in music hall and pantomime. She cultivated an outrageous and outraged stage character – a scrawny hen of a woman who never got her man but never ceased to be infuriated by rejection. Because her work carried over into the twentieth century, there are more accounts of Nellie Wallace's act than there are of most music hall women. These include Alec Guinness's description of his early infatuation with Nellie Wallace after he was taken to see her at the Coliseum. He was 7 years old (it was 1921) and was highly impressed:

> I don't believe I laughed at Miss Wallace on her first appearance. Truth to tell, I was a little scared, she looked so witch-like with her parrot-beak nose and shiny black hair screwed tightly into a little hard bun. She wore a loud tweed jacket and skirt, an Alpine hat with an enormous, bent pheasant's feather, and dark wollen stockings which ended in neat, absurd, twinkling button boots. Her voice was hoarse and scratchy, her walk swift and aggressive; she appeared to be always bent forward from the waist, as if looking for someone to punch. She was very small. Having reached centre stage she plunged into a stream of patter, not one word of which did I understand, but I am sure it was full of outrageous innuendoes. The audience fell about laughing but no laughter came from me. I was in love with her.
> (*Blessings in Disguise*)

John Fisher describes Nellie Wallace as 'The Queen of Low Comedy' (*Funny Way to Be a Hero*). She excelled in the art of coarse clowning, which Alec Guinness describes:

> She turned up in a bright green, shiny and much too tight evening gown. She kept dropping things – bag, fan, handkerchief, a hairbrush – and every time she bent to retrieve them the orchestra made rude sounds on their wind instruments, as if she had ripped her dress or farted. Her look of frozen indignation at this pleased me enormously . . . I laughed a lot but didn't fall out of my seat until Nellie's next act, in which she appeared in a nurse's uniform ready to assist a surgeon at an operation. The patient, covered with a sheet, was wheeled on stage and the surgeon immediately

Nellie Wallace (1870-1948)

Mother would never let us wear high-heeled shoes as she said it made one's ankles swell, but one day Doris went up West and bought a pair of high-heeled shoes and said to us all 'I've been to the Holborn Empire and saw such a funny lady called Nellie Wallace, and she sang "My mother always said look under the bed" . . . Oh she was good.'
(Elsie Waters)

> Man: I wonder why a woman as intelligent as you troubles to run a
>   club like this.
> Nellie: I'm doing this to forget a man.
> Man: Crossed in love?
> Nellie: No worse – I've been run over.
> (from *Queen of Clubs* by Weston and Lee, as performed at the
>   Holborn Empire in 1932. (*Funny Way to Be a Hero*))

set about him with a huge carving-knife. Nellie stood by looking very prim, but every now and then would dive under the sheet and extract with glee and a shout of triumph quite impossible articles – a hotwater bottle, a live chicken, a flat-iron, and so on. Finally, she inserted, with many wicked looks, a long rubber tube which she blew down. The body inflated rapidly to huge proportions and then, covered in its sheet, slowly took to the air. Nellie made desperate attempts to catch it, twinkling her boots as she hopped surprisingly high, but all in vain. The orchestra gave a tremendous blast as she made her last leap; and that is when I fell off my plush seat and felt faintly sick.

Nellie Wallace's work has resonances in present-day comedy. Influenced by the French mime teacher Jacques Lecoq, Philippe Gaulier has developed a distinct theatrical style.

In 1986, his company (Compagnie Philippe Gaulier) presented an all-women piece: *No Son of Mine*, at the Institute of Contemporary Arts. It featured a triumvirate of buffoons – three decaying, desexed creatures who formed a bizarre iconoclastic Trinity. This potentially disturbing piece, played to a London fringe audience, must sound like a far cry from Nellie Wallace's revue sketches, but the pessimistic side of *No Son of Mine* was offset by outrageous and irreverent buffoonery, not dissimilar to Nellie Wallace's style. The actors in *No Son of Mine* had the same sense of the grotesque, a complete disregard for conventional female appearance and a delight in playful clowning.

Fine character actors and clowns have emerged in British theatre despite the potential constrictions of fashion or form. In the stylish ambience of inter-war revue, Beatrice Lillie stands out as an anarchic original.

Born in Canada, she made her London debut in 1914 and soon became a star of revue and cabaret where she sang grotesque songs and played in 'strange, often slightly surrealistic sketches many devised by herself' (*A Dictionary of the Theatre*). Kenneth Tynan, in his essay on Beatrice Lillie in *A View of the English Stage*, called her 'the most achingly funny woman on earth'; her style defied categorisation:

She is *sui generis*. She resembles nothing that ever was, and to see her is to experience, every time, the simple joy of discovery that might come to an astronomer who observed, one maddened night, a new and disorderly comet shooting backwards across the firmament.
(Tynan)

91

No Son of Mine

Beatrice Lillie revelled in her own anarchy:

> She will do anything to avoid making sense – lapse into a clog
> dance, trap her foot under an armchair, or wordlessly sink
> beneath the weight of a mink coat . . . What she has been doing
> for the last 40 years is conducting guerrilla warfare against words
> as a means of communication . . . Nobody is a more devout
> anthologist of the whimpers, sighs and twitters that the human
> race emits in its historic struggle against intelligibility.
> (Tynan)

While many comedians depend and thrive on direct contact and
communication with the audience, Tynan deduced that part of
Beatrice Lillie's art was to ignore the audience entirely:

> Her gift is to reproduce on stage the grievous idiocy with which
> most people behave when they are on their own: humming and
> mumbling, grimacing at the looking glass, perhaps even singing
> into it, hopping, skipping, fiddling with their dress, starting and
> stopping a hundred trivial tasks – looking in fact, definably batty.

The contemporary work of Rose English – though totally
different in form from Beatrice Lillie's – nevertheless has resonances
of the revue star's unpredictability and comic originality. Having
trained at art school, worked as a designer, performed with various
theatre companies, including Lumière and Son, and collaborated on
Sally Potter's film, *The Gold Diggers*, Rose English now writes and
presents highly original, mainly solo shows. Although she hates the
terms 'visual theatre' and 'performance theatre' because they imply
that theatre normally has no performance and is not visual, her
shows undoubtedly highlight these qualities.

The starting point of her most recent show, *Thee Thy Thou
Thine*, was the desire to remember the moment of conception and
the action initially focussed on trying to recall the child's first

---

No Son of Mine

Celia Gore Booth (centre) is Wilfrid Brambell as God – a monstrous
tyrant dispelling bubonic plague at whim; Linda Scott (right) is an
impish Holy Spirit with a dreadful line in jokes; and Annabel Arden
(left) is the Son, a holy soppy nurd dispatched to earth to remove him
from God's presence.
(*Time Out*)

Beatrice Lillie

For my money, the funniest woman there has ever been.
(Joyce Grenfell in *Joyce Grenfell requests the Pleasure*)

Gertrude Lawrence (1898-1952)

Sometimes, in *Private* Lives, I would look at her across the stage and she would simply take my breath away; I can think of nobody living or dead who ever gave to my work as much as she did. (Noel Coward in *Gertrude Lawrence*)

Gertrude Lawrence was enormously popular in Britain and America from the 1920s through to her early death. She exemplified the droll witty women of Noel Coward's plays. She appeared in many of his works and they often performed together.

Rose English in *Thee Thy Thou Thine*

The spirit of a gazelle, the body of a pelican, the mind of Edward
Lear, the costumes of a bag lady.
(*City Limits*)

> 'Are there enough hats in this show?'
> 'No!'
> 'What sort of hats should there be in this show? Bonnets?'
> 'Do you know what a bonnet is?'
> 'Yes.'
> 'Am I wearing a bonnet?'
> 'Yes.'
> 'Oh yes I am!'
> 'Oh yes you are.'
> 'Yes I am.'
> 'Yes you are!'
> 'Yes.'
> 'Yes.'
> 'Yes.'
> 'Yes.'
> 'Get it?'
> (from *Thee Thy Thou Thine*)

contact with formal art. In Rose English's case this was the film *Oklahoma*, and she spent part of the show trying to create her own dusty revival. The ostensible theme of the piece is not crucial to its effect, because, as Rose English admits, anything can happen in her shows and it is impossible to predict what the audience will draw from the experience. Whereas Beatrice Lillie largely ignored her audience and was like 'a child dressing up in front of the mirror, amusing herself while the grownups are out' (Tynan), Rose English can also be a child, but one who's just discovered a theatreful of new friends. She revels in contact with the audience, continually departing from the script to 'play' with them, inviting comment and discussion, often taking assorted objects from her big wicker box of props. On the night we saw the show she repeatedly offered an apple to a man in the audience and asked questions such as: 'Are there enough hats in this show?' at intervals during the evening. Though her shows have a script, Rose English ad libs extensively and the impact of the show lies not in its subject but in its performance.

Rose English is another original among comic character actors who are all highly individual but who together can be seen to form a comic tradition. Hermione Gingold and Hermione Baddeley are two important eccentrics in this gallery of unconventional women. Sheridan Morley paid tribute to this quality in an article he wrote on Miss Gingold in *The Times*:

> Miss Hermione Gingold is an original: a 100 per cent eccentric. She's also her own invention and contribution to the twentieth century. The proud possessor of a face that has clearly launched 1,000 jokes and a voice that makes Lady Bracknell sound positively suburban . . .

She was on stage by the age of 10 and was all set for a legitimate career in theatre, but instead became a star of inter-war revue. In his essay 'Four Eccentrics' in *A View of the English Stage*, Kenneth Tynan points out that:

> . . . she is not a diseuse, she does not sing, and she is not properly a satirist. She does not parody anything or anyone especially well, except herself: and if we must define what she does, we can only call it self-mockery . . . Your true original makes no attempt to satirize people who already exist: he is himself the germ of a new sort of human being.

Hermione Baddeley was also a child performer who started working in a double act with her sister Angela (now the famous Mrs Bridges in TV's *Upstairs Downstairs*) at the age of 10. They worked on tours and in musicals and by the 1920s Hermione Baddeley was starring in Cochran and Coward revues and musicals. During the war she teamed up with Hermione Gingold and they appeared together in revues, although they eventually split up and became arch rivals. Hermione Baddeley describes, in characteristic style, what happened, in an interview with Sheridan Morley in *The Times*:

> Bea Lillie told me there was a lady at a little club up the Charing Cross Road who was doing imitations of us both, and hadn't we better go and see what she was like? So off we went and there was Gingold and she was really hilarious, so I got her into a revue with me called *Rise Above It* and that was where we started being the two Hermiones.
>
> Mind you, it wasn't easy; she's never been as nice as me, and far more trouble to work with. Also she never cares for being reminded that I gave her a start in the business, and so she's always jolly catty about me but I rise above it because I'm like that.
>
> After the war, you know, when I came back from 2 years of troup concerts in my natty little uniform, Bernard Delfont asked Gingold and me to be the ugly sisters in *Cinderella* and Gingold refused because she said she wasn't ugly enough. Gingold! Can you believe it? So after that I went off on my own and we took to doing rival revues and we haven't spoken much since; not since she was doing one called *Slings and Arrows* and I went to a matinée dressed in full armour with a helmet. She didn't laugh once, silly lady. Mother Gingold, I always called her. We seem both to have ended up in America surrounded by lot of very small dogs, but we never meet. She's in New York, I'm in California; I think it's better like that.

This catalogue of women who have excelled at eccentric comedy suggests that successful character acting is simply a case of natural talent finding appropriate performing opportunities. This is not necessarily the case. It's true that some performers have never had any qualms about appearing ridiculous, but a significant number are aware that for a woman to be comical is not always sociably acceptable. Dillie Keane, one of the highly successful all-female musical and comedy trio, Fascinating Aïda, comments:

> Traditionally, women are decorative. Ideal women do certain things, but one thing they always do is look nice. And for women to make fools of themselves goes against the grain of years and years of conditioning.

Hermione Gingold and Hermione Baddeley

If being comic means departing from acceptable female behaviour then it is no wonder that there are a limited number of comic parts for women and that only a relatively small group have felt totally uninhibited about going to grotesque extremes. Annabel Arden, who played the Son of God in *No Son of Mine*, is sensitive to women's inhibitions but positive about overcoming them:

> I'd love to see women creating characters who are as known and loved as the Goons, Monty Python, that sort of stuff . . . that's what makes people laugh the most, it's total looniness . . . you look at them and you think: 'how can they be so stupid?' and I think that what's so difficult for women is to let go of all kinds of saving graces, in the broadest sense, to be one thing and one thing to the hilt.

Peta Lily trained as a dancer and mime artist, was a member of Three Women (one of the first and few all-women, feminist mime companies) and now works as a solo mime artist in Peta Lily Mime Theatre. Her experience of teaching mime has revealed that women can be afraid of the grotesque extremes of clowning but, ironically, they can also be frightened of femininity and the sexuality they may discover in their own clown personality:

> Clowning brings out something inside you and I think that the problem with some of the women I've taught is that they've resisted the silliness in themselves because they've not wanted to be a girly clown. They've anticipated what they might be like but they fear it and so they block, and the minute they block, they can't play the clown. The clown is open and vulnerable and in the shit. We love the clown when it's in the shit. The clown is funny when it's in the shit, but I think this is a problem a lot of woman may be encountering. I think it's a form of censorship.

Su Pollard (perhaps best known as Peggy in the TV show *Hi-de-Hi*) feels that there is no point in hitting out at the obstacles. Whatever the pressures, it is up to women to push themselves to extremes:

> It's up to women, whatever part they've got, to bring something of their own into it, so you can't always blame the writer for putting a woman in that situation. I tend to get fed up of women bemoaning their lot in the entertainment world. There aren't enough women prepared to look a prat.

A performer will never create a successful character if she censors herself, but neither should she force herself to be grotesque if this

Peta Lily in *Whole Parts*

makes her feel uncomfortable. There can be no rules about comic personae and each performer has to find the milieu in which she can discover her comic character. Dillie Keane appreciates that the security of a small and independent company such as Fascinating Aïda has been a fertile base from which to explore comic styles, but she first discovered her clown when she was in a production of *Pirates of Penzance* in Dublin:

> I was in the chorus and we were all encouraged to have a
> separate character, and they gave me a book as a prop, so I said:
> 'right, well I shall have glasses' and then they gave me a wig and I
> plaited it and had freckles, and then the make-up became more
> and more extraordinary and I suddenly realised, about 2 months
> into the run, that I'd discovered my clown . . . we used to have
> these clown classes at drama school – you know – 'everybody
> has a clown inside them' and all that – and I was looking for my
> clown and I couldn't find anything and I was really terrible at
> clown classes, but this discovery was a revelation and it was the
> most wonderful thing.

This discovery is crucial. Whether by intuition, experiment or training, women have to find the type of clown they want to be. You cannot judge or censor the role your clown may adopt. It just has to feel comfortable and appropriate.

While clowning characters are expansive and can give the impression, by their lunatic behaviour, of not simply playing the fool but *being* the fool, the monologuist's art is more measured and passive. The monologue focusses on the linguistic aspects of character, and because the monologuist dips in and out of character and often appears on stage, initially and intermittently, as herself, there is a greater distance between actor and character, a greater opportunity for satire.

Women have excelled as monologuists. The form grew in popularity and early exponents included Dora Bryan and Beryl Reid. Reid's characters, Monica, the schoolgirl, and Marlene, the streetwise Birmingham dance-hall girl, were extremely popular.

The monologue combines well with other elements in the one-woman show. As well as creating excellent television series, Victoria Wood has become a supremo of the genre. She is totally at ease with a form which was once a mystery to her:

> When I first heard this expression 'one-woman show' I didn't
> know what it was (I knew that Libby Morris had done one) and I
> had this idea that I wanted to do something – I'd seen Joyce
> Grenfell and I liked that a lot, I was about 6 when I saw her, and

Victoria Wood

Leila Webster

I met her too. My sisters wanted to meet her, and they went backstage. My sisters were about 9 and 12, and they thought I was too young to go, so they went. They told Joyce Grenfell about me and she came out and said hello which I thought was highly charming – so *anyway* I had this idea buried so low I couldn't even have dug it up – an idea to do something on my own on stage that was to do with comedy. But not knowing anything to do with the business, I didn't know what you had to do to do that . . . I'd no idea how you became a comedian. I knew I wanted to pull faces as well. I thought, how do you pull faces for a living? I know now, I didn't know then.

Eleanor Bron is another talented monologuist. Her work in Footlights and the Establishment Club is discussed in the chapter on writers but she has also presented a one-woman show (*Eleanor Bron – on her own*). Sheila Steafel's solo shows, performed mainly in the 1980s, have been largely based on the monologue. Sheila Steafel has used the simple device of a pair of shoes, plucked from the shoe tree, to indicate character.

Our trip to Belfast introduced us to Leila Webster, who is something of a Belfast heroine. She informed us of this: 'I'm not a big headed person by any means . . . but . . . I'm really a legend here.' As well as starring in plays she has put on her one-woman show in which her monologues, such as *The Belfast Home Help*, satirize local types and accents, as well as undermining pretension, as she does in *WI Meeting*. The style combines Beryl Reid's cheekiness with the type of gentle parody which was the speciality of the best-known monologuist of the century: Joyce Grenfell.

Joyce Grenfell had always displayed a talent for accents and mimickry, and an impromptu performance at a dinner party (in 1939) which radio producer Stephen Potter attended led to an audition with Herbert Farjeon who immediately put her into the *Little Review* at the Little Theatre, London. She performed in three editions of the *Little Review* and then in *Dimensions* and *Dimensions 2* at the Wyndhams, London. During World War II she toured military hospitals in the Mediterranean, Middle East and India and afterwards returned to London revues, performing in *Light and Shade* at the Ambassadors, Coward's *Sigh No More*, *Tuppence Coloured* and *Penny Plain*. She first performed her solo show *Joyce Grenfell Requests the Pleasure* in 1952 which toured with great success.

Described in the obituary in *The Times* (1.12.79) as a 'gently mocking, affectionately amused commentator on English manners and social customs,' Joyce Grenfell, influenced by the monologuist

Character actors, monologuists and women's theatre

Ruth Draper who was a close family friend, created a wide variety of comic characters, but her approach was constant: however unworldly, misguided or downright ghastly the characters, Joyce Grenfell's portrayal was never malicious nor deeply satirical:

> When I began I was amused by silliness, snobbery, lack of humour, pomposity and heartlessness; now I am more interested in people as individuals than in their follies. Perhaps I have grown more tolerant; or it could be that I became bored more quickly.
>
> With one exception I don't believe I ever sat down to write a monologue. I always knew the character I was after; the way into it came through the voice and accent. It was the voice that

---

Joyce Grenfell's *Flowers*

Children – we're going to do our nice 'Moving to Music' this morning, so let's make a lovely fairy ring, shall we? And then we'll all be flowers growing in the grass.

Let's make a big circle – spread out – wider – wider – just finger-tips touching – that's it. Sue, let go of Neville –

Because flowers don't hold hands, they just touch finger-tips.

SUE. Let go of Neville.

And Sue, we don't want GRUMBLERS in our fairy ring, do we? We only want *smilers*.

Yes David, you're a smiler – so is Lavinia – and Peggy and Geoffrey.

Yes, you're all smilers.

QUIET PLEASE.

Don't get so excited.

And Sue is going to be a smiler too, aren't you Sue? That's better.

George – don't do that . . .

Now then, let's all put on our Thinking Caps, shall we, and think about what flowers we are going to choose to be.

Lavinia? – what flower are you?

A bluebell. Good.

Peggy? A red rose. That's nice.

Neville?

A *wild* rose. Well done, Neville!

Sidney? – Sidney, pay attention, dear, and don't pommel Rosemary – what flower are you doing to choose to be?

A *horse* isn't a flower, Sidney.

(*George – don't do that . . .*)

106

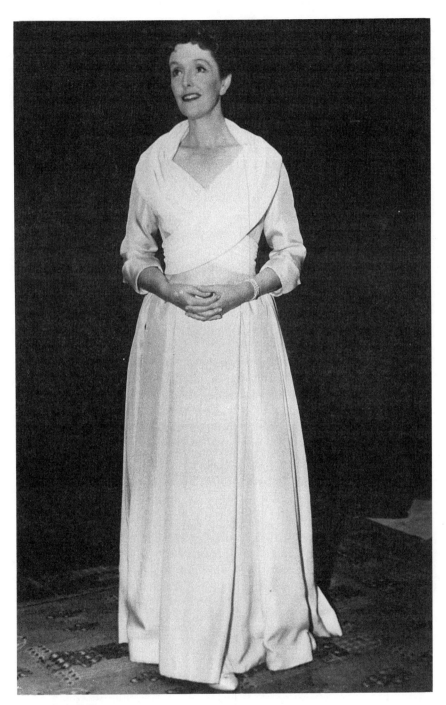

Joyce Grenfell

brought the character into focus and with it instinctively came mannerisms and movements. I talked out loud to myself as I moved about the flat, thinking in the manner of the creature I was trying to bring to life. Sometimes I visualised backgrounds – bedroom, clothes, tastes (if any). The story-line was the last thing to be thought about. Throughout the building-up process – anything from two days to a month – I made notes of key-words and phrases, and so the piece took shape. Only then did I write it out in full.
(Joyce Grenfell *Joyce Grenfell Requests the Pleasure*)

With faith and optimism, Joyce Grenfell believed in the positive potential of humour:

In her we recognized someone who made fun without malice, depicted absurdity with love.
(Bernard Levin in *Joyce Grenfell – by herself and her friends*)

The nature of Joyce Grenfell's humour prompts questions on the general nature and function of comedy. Athene Seyler, in one of the few good theoretical books on comedy, *The Craft of Comedy*, writes:

. . . to me comedy is inexplicably bound up with kindliness. As soon as a comment on character is inspired by contempt or anger it becomes tragic and loses the light of laughter. Irony, satire even, must all be charitable and compassionate at heart or they stray into the realm of serious comment . . .

How does this instinct of 'kindliness' show itself in practice? Patricia Routledge, a most distinguished and accomplished character actor, has, with characteristic thoughtfulness and perspicacity, come up with some telling comments on why and how we laugh:

I suppose the first time I ever realised that humour could save a situation was when I was very small. If I had fallen over and was crying. My mother had a simple cure. She would say 'Have a toffee.' 'I don't want a toffee.' 'Have a toffee.' 'I don't want a toffee. I want a jube-jube.' '*Have a toffee.*' It always worked. I would stop crying. Years later I asked her, 'Why a *toffee*?' and she said 'Well you can't cry and chew a toffee at the same time,' which is true. The business of crying and trying to chew a toffee resulted (of course) in laughter and the growing exchange of laughter between oneself and another person – that person enjoying the situation (who happened to be my mother) and me knowing that I was looking quite funny not being able to get on with my grief. It was a salvation. That was my first awareness that hurt could be eased, even eradicated, by something ridiculous. And this comes back to me often when my heart is breaking.

This sense of salvation created a bond between individuals. As Patricia Routledge realised from her reaction on her first trip to the pantomime at the Empire in Liverpool, this bond was a crucial element in theatrical comedy:

You felt you knew them. They had something magical about them, and it opened up the world for you; just as when somebody laughed at your joke, at school, or at home, it opened up the world for you. It made a contact for you, it took your isolation away.

Comic performance does not always engender this generosity and the comic instinct is not always kind. The most fundamental of gags – slipping on a banana skin – makes us laugh because the victim has been made to look ridiculous, their status has been reduced. We laugh at the mighty falling, at pretension being exploded; we laugh because the crisis is not happening to us. This is 'the exquisite terror that isn't yours' as Patricia Routledge describes our laughter at Harold Lloyd hanging from the New York skyscraper. We find the same humour in the excruciating social embarrassment of Alan Ayckbourn's comedies. We recognise the situation from having ourselves suffered nightmares and we laugh partly from relief, because this isn't happening to us. There's a similar chilling social acuity in Mike Leigh's plays which have included *Abigail's Party* and *Nuts in May*.

Laughter at ghastly characters and unenviable situations implies recognition of life's more desperate sides. It would be unrealistic to claim that laughter always results from a sense of sharing human follies. The comic, by nature of her grotesque appearance, dislocated intellect or foolish actions, not only allows us to laugh at the uncomfortable experiences we fear and avoid but to which we sometimes fall victim, but, she also allows us to believe that she is always immersed in this comic pit, that she is genuinely inferior because the disasters that create comedy are all she ever experiences. This is the emotional make-up of the clown who is morose and depressed, who sees her role as a constant reminder of life's ennui. Denise Coffey described this kind of comedian:

The whole point about comics is that they're outside the vortex. They're the ones looking in saying: 'excuse me, have you noticed

Maureen Lipman in *Outside Edge*

how peculiar humanity is?' What's funny about comedians is the way they draw people's attention to the frailty of human life and existence. And they make you think about death. *But* they make you laugh about it, and that's why they are mainly extremely profound and melancholy, neurotic, difficult and upset, because they can't join in.

Although this approach is very different from Joyce Grenfell's, the two are not necessarily at odds. They are two parts of the same equation. Gentle satirists such as Joyce Grenfell never plummeted to the potential dissonance at the root of personality; but, conversely, the bleaker kind of comic who points to the desperate side of life is able to relieve her anxiety by creating humour. However tragic the human condition, the comic instinct has positive elements. Patricia Routledge:

> I want the theatre not to give me escape but to take me out on the uplands and make me realise that life in spite of set-backs and pain and evil, can go on, at its best and most enjoyable; and above all (and this embraces the tragi-comical condition of mankind) that the human spirit will triumph. I think the *proportion* that comedy gives to apparently ill-assorted circumstances is of the greatest possible importance.

There is no reason why women should not express the comical condition as often or as well as men, but because women have enjoyed less power in society than men, they have had less access to

---

Maureen Lipman's credits include the film *Educating Rita*, the sitcom *Agony* and, most recently, *Wonderful Town*. First comedy performance:

> As a 'layman' was at the Palace Theatre, Hull, aged eight. 'Are there any children in the audience who would like to come up on stage and sing–' VROOM! Lipman, hair tortured with Twinkie, knock of knee and horizontal of teeth, is first up on stage – gives out with Alma Cogan impersonation 'You dream boat – you lovable dree-eam boat', with the catch in the throaty voice, and the rolling eyes. The house was duly brought down, and so should I have been – a peg or twenty.

Heroes:

> Hylda Baker, Beryl Reid, Joyce Grenfell, Lucille Ball.

Ambitions:

> A one-woman show about Joyce Grenfell, a comedy series which doesn't need a word altering and a lot of cameos in movies.

artistic expression. It is essential that their status as equal performers be respected.

The functioning of the comedian's status in performance is complex, and obviously connected to the comparative status of genders in society. Because women have had very little real status in society, it has been difficult for them to adopt the mock inferiority of the clown. Thus, the pantomime dame is comic because the prospect of a man becoming a woman is laughable – he has lost his customary social status and appears ridiculous in the generic trappings of a woman. Traditionally, the process is not reversed when a woman cross-dresses, although, with the advent of feminism and the re-evaluation of gender roles, women (particularly in feminist theatre companies such as Spare Tyre) have dressed and performed as men to great comic effect.

For women to become clowns is a positive step because it indicates that they have enough self-worth to adopt a mock low status, to allow an audience to laugh at them. The dual action of performer and role is at work here, just as when the audience laughs at the clown it is deriding her foolish behaviour but also affirming the skill with which it is executed.

This dual reaction is facilitated in comedy performance by a greater distance between actor and role. Athene Seyler:

> . . . emotional acting of a serious part involves absorption in the character – identification with it, losing one's own self in another's . . . on the other hand, comedy seems to be the standing outside a character or situation and pointing out one's delight in certain aspects of it.
> (*The Craft of Comedy*)

Beryl Reid also cited this duality when she talked about comic technique and her memory of comedian Sid Field:

> You felt, in the audience, that you and he were in league against everybody else on stage, you had a secret, a little secret, you were sharing with him.

This response is based on a strong and affectionate response which the actor is able to inspire in the audience. Beryl Reid:

> I've got a theory that if people are going to laugh with you, at you, whatever, they've got to like you first, there's got to be a great bond of affection between you and the audience before they can really feel relaxed. Then they can sit back and think: 'Oh no, whatever's she . . . oh how daft! . . . oh look at . . .' But there's a feeling of great affection.

Patricia Routledge *in When we are Married*

Building on this affectionate response, the performer has the strength to 'play' at being the clown, someone who thinks she is greater than they are, but whose pretension is, finally, exploded. Patricia Routledge:

> I come from a part of the country (the North) where pretension is quite rife. I do find pretension undermined very funny indeed.

The comic device of pretension exploded is brilliantly explored in J.B. Priestley's *When we are Married*, playing at the time of writing at the Whitehall Theatre in London. The pretensions of three bourgeois couples from the north of England, celebrating their twenty-fifth wedding anniversary together are completely destroyed when they discover that because of a legal hitch they may not be married at all and have therefore been 'living in sin' for the last quarter of a century. The three wives are beautifully played by Patricia Routledge, Prunella Scales and Elizabeth Sprigges, with Patricia Hayes as the cantankerous housekeeper, Mrs Northrop.

Priestley was expert at exploring and observing local characteristics. Then acting skills of performers who originate from the north of England are equally astute. Some of our best character actors have northern roots: Patricia Routledge, Patricia Hayes, Maureen Lipman, Hylda Baker and Dora Bryan have already been mentioned; Thora Hird's gorgeously funny northern women, portrayed particularly well in the plays of Alan Bennett, should certainly not be forgotten. There is a tendency to undervalue actors whose skill is not mainstream and classical, as Alan Bennett pointed out in a South Bank show (London Weekend Television) interview with Melvyn Bragg:

> There are some actresses, Patricia Routledge is one and Thora Hird's another, for whom it's sheer pleasure to write. I always think Thora should be a Dame. I think she was made an MBE last year, and thought it was more than she deserved, probably. But if she'd been an opera singer or worked for the RSC or subsidised companies, she'd have been a Dame years ago, but because she works in popular theatre, the great and the good who decide these things presumably think that's not appropriate.

What, then, is the secret of the great character actor's performance? Is it a question of cultural background, good writing, training and experience or is it comic instinct? Athene Seyler writes of the comic point of view as 'a state of mind which cannot be induced . . . it is a quality of mind which is either born with one or not.' This premise was borne out in our interviews. Time and time

Hylda Baker © BBC 1957

was the chatty half of a pair of comic young women, tall and short; Cynthia, in fact a man in skirts, was silent:

> 'Where have ya been? We've been stood here waiting for you. I told you to be soon, didn't I? "Be soon," I said, "Be soooon." (And then confiding to the audience:) 'She just looks through ya! No, I wouldn't care, but she knows, y'know! She just won't let on, that's what!'
> (*Funny Way to Be a Hero*)

again performers talked of their involuntary ability to invite comic situations. Su Pollard:

> I pinched a pork chop in a café, once. I was only 18 and I was really hungry. I thought he'd left his dinner and gone out but he'd only gone to put some money in his meter and he came back and there was no food there. I'd ate it. 'Where's my dinner?' he said, and I thought 'Oh God!' I dashed out the back, went to the toilet, never came back. I couldn't face it. The manager was getting it in the neck something chronic, you know.

Even her audition for *Hi-de-Hi* was comical. The fact that Su Pollard looks somewhat unconventional confused matters:

> I went along to see the director, he lived in Westminster. It was a beautiful flat, 300 stairs, and he opened the door and said: 'We don't want any pegs' – he thought I was a gypsy.

Barbara Windsor remembered that even as a child she had a taste for the ridiculous:

> My cousin said, the other day: 'You was always very funny. You had us in stitches. Do you remember the time you had measles and you kept banging on the wall?' If I didn't have attention . . . the family, they were obviously my audience . . . and my mother said: 'Oh leave her.' I got to the point when I said: 'You'd better come up now 'cos you're going to get a big shock.' I'd cut all my hair off – I had these big spots – and all my hair off and was beginning to cut up everything else in the room. And she said: 'You looked so funny, with no hair, and this little round face and all these spots – everybody fell about.'

Denise Coffey felt that a comic understanding was such an intrinsic part of her life that she did not isolate it as a separate quality. She quoted George Bernard Shaw to illustrate this point:

> He was asked what he wanted to be, did he always want to be a great writer? and he said: 'Well, when I was a young man I wanted to be a pirate, and then I wanted to be a great composer, and a great painter, and a great opera singer, but I never thought of being a great writer because writing to me is like the taste of water in my mouth, I don't notice it because it's always there.' And the same goes for the kind of outlook you have on life, the world around you which is classed by others as comedy, but to you seems to be a perfectly ordinary viewpoint on life. So it's kind of a natural bent that I discovered you could actually make a living doing it.

116

Leila Webster recognised this innate comic ability in her performance:

I have this something which God gave me – whatever it is I have it and I don't know what it is.
　And when we asked her: 'What is it about a comic character that makes it funny?' she answered:
　This may sound really dreadful – me.

Patricia Routledge made a similar observation:

I think truly funny people have a secret which they can't keep secret. It's a congenital condition with a contagious influence in spite of any conscious intention otherwise. Lucky for us that it is so.

Natural comic talent is obviously essential but it is undeniable that years of performing experience enable the actor to learn her craft. Beryl Reid was convinced of this:

To be a comical person and to be liked, it's a long, long apprenticeship. It's the longest.

Vicky Pile, one of the comic writers we interviewed, believed, similarly, that:

Comedy isn't something you're born with. You might be born exceptionally good at performing, or making people laugh, but to be good at it as a career, you need to serve your apprenticeship. Ten years on the boards and you'll be good.

Beryl Reid's years of experience have enabled her to distil some of the essentials of her technique:

When I've found out what's good, I cut all the rubbish. Comedy is always enhanced by being brief. There's got to be heart in it, they've got to see that you're vulnerable . . . the audience has to know everything that you're thinking, what's happening to you. Never play for sympathy, 'cos you'll never get it if you play for it. Play it straight out and you'll break their hearts.

If the actor is as sure of comic motivation as Beryl Reid clearly is, she can build comic performance and business to a virtuoso pitch: Beryl Reid describes her performance as Lady Wishfort in *The Way of the World*:

There was a scene I had to do when I was practising what I was going to say to this man when he arrived, and I did it on a chaise longue, and I did about seven minutes business in it, which

117

Charabanc Theatre Company (l. to r. Sarah Jones, Maureen
MaCauley, Carol Scanlan, Brenda Winter and Eleanor Methuen in
Lay up Your Ends) was formed in 1983 by five Northern Irish actors
whose preoccupation was the lack of employment available to them
and the poor quality of work offered by established theatres. As
women, they were interested in history from a woman's point of
view. Their first show, *Lay up Your Ends*, was about the Belfast linen
industry, a largely female preserve. At the time of writing they are
touring America with their latest show, *Gold in the Streets*, about
Irish emigration. Charabanc, a majoritively female company, are
extremely popular with a wide and varied audience; their material
combines the humour and the agony of the Irish experience.

Congreve had obviously *meant* the person to do. I used to dangle my foot a little bit, and then of course she gets it in the hem of her long skirt, and I finished up forward with my bosom always hanging out and trying to get up and saying: 'There is nothing so alluring as a levee from a settee.' That was sort of invention.

Leila Webster acknowledges that she has refined her technique to such an extent that business is reduced to a minimum:

I have eyes that speak. I can be on the stage and talk to somebody and I could have a silence of a few seconds and I could look down at the audience and they'd be in fits. I wouldn't have to say anything.

Minimum action should not, however, be equated with minimum effort. Leila Webster:

I don't just like a few laughs. People have actually had to go out . . . tears and wetting the seats . . . there's got to be punchlines all the time. I'm not the sort of person who just goes out and hopes for the best.

It is undoubtedly admirable that a significant number of women are acclaimed character actors, but focussing on successful women does not give the whole picture. Female actors are, in general, poorly served in terms of the number and nature of the parts they play. The Equity Women's Committee (founded 1978) collects and discusses information on the current work situation and problems of women members of the Union, and CREE – Campaign for Real Equality in Equity – campaigns for equal opportunities for women as well as for ethnic minorities and those with disabilities.

The lack of opportunities for women in theatre, together with the increased feminist awareness of the 1970s, gave birth to a vibrant women's theatre movement in Britain. Companies included Monstrous Regiment, Women's Theatre Group, Spare Tyre, Sensible Footwear, Siren, Hard Corps, Burnt Bridges, Sadista Sisters, Beryl and the Perils, Little Women, Scarlet Harlets, and Mrs Worthington's Daughters. Some, with the support of Arts Council funding, have survived into their second decade, others, because of the limitations of project funding, the demise of the Greater London Council and the accumulated political pressure years of Thatcherism have achieved, have disappeared or been put on ice.

One of the major contributions of women's theatre was to depict women, not as men see them, which most plays, because they are written by men, inevitably do, but how women choose to depict themselves. Women's theatre has also increased the scope of women's humour. By creating and presenting their own material, women's theatre companies have discovered ways in which women enjoy laughing at themselves.

New departures in performance have also brought new audiences. Since 1979 Spare Tyre have toured with a series of shows, initially based on Susie Orbach's *Fat is a Feminist Issue*, but later on self-image, health, motherhood and, in 1986, on women in their mid-30s. The work has had practical applications: Spare Tyre have had discussions with the audience after the show, set up self-help groups, returned to groups to do follow-up shows and talks and developed a strong working relationship with the Women's Therapy Centre in London. They tour all over the country, playing in community centres, fringe theatres, at benefits, to women's groups, mother and toddler groups and self-help groups. They are committed both to women's issues and to reaching more than the tiny elite that normally go to the theatre. Katina Noble of Spare Tyre:

> It was very important to feel that I wasn't just performing to a
> very small elitist group of feminists. From my experience, the
> majority of feminist theatre is still playing to that kind of
> audience – which is lovely for them and very supportive and
> encouraging and affirming of one's feminism, but it seemed to me
> that there were very few women's groups that were actually
> working with a broader audience in mind.

Spare Tyre have always offset the seriousness of their subject with humour: 'There was so much pain, you had to make it funny' Katina Noble.

Sensible Footwear have toured a wide variety of community venues, presenting cabarets and theatre shows on women's social and political confinement (*Out of Control*), violence against women (*Ladies First*) and self-image (*In Whose Image*). Like Spare Tyre, they incorporate humour into their shows, particularly for youth audiences:

> We think it's important to use humour because you can get away
> with things using humour that you couldn't get away with
> playing straight, especially with kids.
> (Sensible Footwear)

Those who oppose the notion of feminist theatre sometimes accuse it of always being simplistic and humourless. This is simply not true. In some early feminist theatre work, agitprop was appropriate and well received, but women's theatre groups are increasingly exploring more complex issues. Siren are a lesbian

Spare Tyre – l. to r. Harriet Towell, Katina Noble, Clair Chapman

socialist theatre company, cabaret troupe and rock band founded in 1979. Hilary Ramsden, one of the all-women collective, talked to us about the aims of her work and the place of humour within it:

> There'd be no interest for me to just give a long spiel about society's wrongs and how we're going to better them. There have to be contradictions in there, the insecurities of how I feel about doing it. The undercutting that all the time brings humour.

Underfunding and minority appeal can restrict the market of women's theatre. Many groups do not, however, wish to reach a mass audience if the price they have to pay is a loss of control:

> I think what's of paramount importance to us is that we have total control over what we do. We find it totally unacceptable to perform something we're not 100% happy with.
> (Sensible Footwear)

The Women's Playhouse Trust aims to capitalise on the pioneering work of women's theatre and to increase opportunities for women in mainstream theatre while maintaining the artistic control that fringe groups have enjoyed.

It was founded in 1980 by a group of women who were concerned about 'the lack of opportunities existing for women in the conventional structures and organisation of traditional theatre' (Women's Playhouse Trust brochure). The Trust, whose steering group includes established actors such as Diana Quick, Jane Lapotaire, Miriam Karlin, Glenda Jackson and Pamela Stephenson, aims to buy and run a West End theatre which will provide a mainstream venue and a home for major women writers, directors, actors, designers, musicians and technicians.

Greater performance opportunities and perhaps a greater understanding of women's comic potential will be achieved when more women are in decision-making positions, but, sadly, women theatre directors are still relatively thin on the ground in British theatre. In 1982 the Standing Committee of Women Theatre Directors and Administrators conducted a survey of all branches of theatre including National Theatre, repertory, fringe, alternative and community; the statistics revealed that in the 119 theatres surveyed, only 12% had female artistic directors and the statistics for associate directors (17%), assistant directors (41%) and freelance directors (24%) were hardly higher. Sheila Hancock is one of the very few women to have directed at the National or the RSC and the only one who has directed at both. She describes the pressures that women directors face:

> It was tricky trying to work with that male mafia at the RSC, it's very difficult for women. I started doing the jokey bit, trying not

---

Krissie Illing

is one of the few women who work largely in street theatre. Having trained in dance and mime, she formed a male/female double act with Mark Britton. The duo, Nickelodeon, were the Time Out Street Entertainers of the year in 1985 and have now performed street theatre all over the world. One of the aspects of her work that particularly pleases Krissie Illing is the fact that she makes a living from an apparently precarious occupation.

> It's taken me 29 years to prove to my father that I can work and earn a living like this. He used to say, 'why don't you take an office job and keep your dancing as a hobby?'

Krissie Illing

to frighten them, because they're very frightened of somebody invading their club. I did get very stroppy sometimes.

Though she knows she can survive in this atmosphere, she describes clearly how women are at odds with the male hierarchy at the RSC:

I try to operate in a way that I think women will always do in an organisation, in a way that doesn't happen in a male hierarchy. The difficulty is that these companies are run as male hierarchies: for example, they have meetings going on until one o'clock in the morning, which for women with children is very difficult. So until these systems change, it's bloody difficult for a woman. In these establishments, and certainly at the RSC, it is their life, they are absolutely obsessed with the RSC – 'the greatest company in the world' – and I don't think that a lot of women are prepared to be so obsessed. I mean I do totally immerse myself in my work, but I have another life. I have other responsibilities – it's very difficult to operate in this building if you have.

She disputes the claim that her work at the RSC – directing the regional tour – was in any way inferior to a main house production:

. . . It always annoys me that whenever feminists write about the lack of women directors at the RSC and the National, which they're quite right about, they always dismiss the fact that I've *only* been given the tour, which makes me bloody angry because I actually think that the tour is possibly one of the most important branches of the RSC.

Whatever women may feel about the relative merits of their directing work, there's nevertheless a general reluctance to credit women with positions of responsibility. Denise Coffey, who has directed extensively in Canada, has found the British theatre narrow-minded about its women directors:

In this country, not only if you're a soppy girl but if you've also done funny shows, they assume, ergo, you are a nit-witted, pea-brained rat-bag. In Canada, where there's no evidence for this except the strangeness of my productions, they don't mind if you're little or fat or thin or tall, if you can do your work, you're in. That's it, no questions.

If women with artistic energy, innovation and dedication can find a platform for their work, there's no limit to what they can achieve. Joan Littlewood's theatre workshop at Stratford East radically changed British theatre. She reintroduced popular theatre, breaking away from the elitist world of the West End to produce naturalistic plays which used a different kind of actor:

> Gone were the hallmarks of mainstream English acting – the dignified poise, well-cut profiles, modulated tones. They didn't look like actors, they looked like people.
> (*Working with Joan*, by Clive Goodwin and Tom Milae)

The revolution was particularly liberating for unconventional actors. Sheila Hancock:

> When I was young it was *so* difficult for women – I mean Claire Bloom was the archetypal actress, that was what you had to be, so if you were like me you just *weren't* . . . I mean I was in weekly rep for 8 years and nobody would look at me, and then Joan Littlewood came along. My audition for her was St Joan because that was what you did. She just roared with laughter, she was hysterical, and said: 'But you're a clown my darling, you're a wonderful clown,' and then she got me to do an impro [improvisation] which I'd never done in my life, she said, 'wonderful' and she just liberated me because she allowed me to go back to my roots and bring out something different, instead of going around in flat shoes to appear smaller and wearing amazing concealing make-up. With Joanie you didn't have to be like that and it was wonderful.

Barbara Windsor's roots were geographically close to the Theatre Royal at Stratford but she, initially, had no truck with the naturalism of the Littlewood approach. She was working in a night club, and caught up in the glamour of West End night life, when she was called to an audition with Joan Littlewood at the Wyndhams Theatre. She told the lady at the door ('a little fat lady with funny clothes and a funny woollen hat' – Barbara Windsor) that she didn't want the job because she was involved in her West End show. Barbara Windsor thought the lady was a char: she turned out to be Joan Littlewood. She got the part, and was a great success in Frank Norman's *Fings Ain't What They Used t'Be*, which transferred to the West End. She admits that Joan Littlewood 'changed my life, because that made me a star.'

Joan Littlewood proved that what makes a good actor and good theatre are not universal qualities but ones which can change with the kind of political commitment which can liberate women from character stereotypes. Women's theatre companies have achieved similar ends. At the same time, it's undeniable that individual women working outside a political context have created original

Joan Littlewood at a news conference in Edinburgh, 1964

and unconventional comic styles. While it's worth celebrating those who have triumphed in their originality, it should also be borne in mind that some women have been hampered by sexism and limitations. For those who sometimes feel lost and doubtful, it's worth bearing in mind that some of the most successful actors have serious self-doubts – Beryl Reid:

> I always think 'I can't do that', and I've said this to directors: 'I don't think I can do that – I quite honestly don't think I'll manage' and people who know me say: 'Well, give it a try . . .'

Happily, those misgivings are balanced by a strong sense of self-worth. The two characteristics are not at odds, they are part of the character actor's emotional make-up: contradictory but complementary. Beryl Reid again:

126

You've got to know what you're up to, to learn, and to know exactly what you want to do and go out and jolly well do it . . . I've had terrible disappointments and setbacks but it's never made me unhappy because I've always known what I wanted to do, and if you know that, you're 3/4 there.

SHOULD THERE BE MORE WOMEN IN COMEDY?

My idea of hell is ten young women my age who are just absolutely brilliant.
(Jenny Eclair, performer)

Women need to get in everywhere.
(Jill Tweedie, writer)

I think that this is the most exciting and interesting time to be a woman, in all areas of work.
(Helen Atkinson Wood, actor)

I think that women in comedy have had to fight just as they have everywhere else. There's no reason why women aren't as funny, or why they don't have as many shows written about them as men.
(Miriam Margolyes, actor)

There should be more women.
(Faith Brown, impressionist)

If somebody said to me 'There are 50% more women comics on the circuit than there were this time last year' I'd say 'Oh good.' but if I hear there's another female stand-up comic on the same bill then I do feel more threatened because because she's in my category; people are going to judge us one against the other.
(Sheila Hyde, stand-up comedian)

Q. – Didn't it scare you when you looked around (the alternative cabaret circuit) and saw that there weren't any other women?
A. – No. I was delighted. It was my market wasn't it?
(Jenny Lecoat, stand-up comedian/actor/writer)

I'm awfully glad that Victoria wood is around because she is unashamedly female, she's very funny. Mind you, she's very funny about other women, which probably means that feminists get uptight about her portrayals of female vanity and stupidity and emptiness. I love the way she sends up sex. It's very subtle and terribly funny. (Germaine Greer, writer)

Q. – Should there be more women in comedy?
A. – No thank you.
(Marti Caine, stand-up comedian/actor)

Film

I think that the *Carry On* films should go down in history. Although they drive me mental.
(Barbara Windsor)

For many years America has dominated the film world, mass-producing and marketing films of various types and qualities. American comedy has flooded the international film market and has produced a notable line of funny women, from Mabel Normand through to Mae West, Deanna Durbin, Judy Holliday, Katherine Hepburn, Doris Day, Lucille Ball, Goldie Hawn and Diane Keaton. All these women have had distinctive comic styles and a considerable effect on the perception of the 'funny woman' in American film. The British film industry has had a varied history which has resulted in a dependency on selling to the American market for its commercial existence. It has fluctuated according to financial stability, and has moved between innovation and imitation of American film, and consequently what should have been the steady development of British comic women in film has been interrupted. This chapter takes a look at the role of the female comedian within the comic film.

In 1906 Britain's first proper cinema was opened. The film-maker Léon Gaumont who had set up the Gaumont Film company in 1898, started the tradition of using music hall artists in film. Two British film-makers, James Williamson and George Smith, working from their own studio in Hove, advanced film techniques and churned out hundreds of comedies up to the end of World War I. Story lines were basic, and, as film was silent, it was easily transferable from one country to another. This meant that more actors were becoming internationally known although, rather as with advertising today, the actors were anonymous.

World War I had a crucial effect on British film. America superseded Britain as the major film-producing country:

130

The British Cinema had never really succeeded in progressing from the artisan to the industrial stage of development; her film makers had lost the pioneering lead of 1900, and fallen into the habit of stagey literary adaptation which was to persist for many years.
(David Robinson, *World Cinema 1895-1980*)

American film, meanwhile, forged ahead, with the influential work of David Wark Griffith and director/producer Mack Sennett, who together contributed to changing the American film world and developed it into an industry. The post-war years brought dramatic economic change, as the 'consumer' took on a new identity. Basic aspects of British everyday life were vastly improved for a growing middle class, and communications such as radio, newspaper and cinema were now within common grasp. Smaller families were in vogue, suburbia expanded and more money was available for leisure activities. The demand for film increased, but it was not met by Britain. With such new comedy stars such as Mary Pickford, Buster Keaton and Charlie Chaplin, America established itself as the largest film-producing country in the world, with comedy as one of its main commodities, while British comedy, pandering to the new, upwardly mobile class, produced a spate of unremarkable comedy-romances. The film world lacked originality and lifted its ideas from the music hall and the West End stage or from American films.

By 1925, 95% of British screen-time was occupied by American films, and most of the studios that had grown up during wartime had disappeared. There seems to have been an inability to consider film on its own terms, independent of theatre, and consequently, many actors innately unsuited to film were transferred from theatre or music hall to celluloid. Vesta Tilley worked with cinema producer Walter Gibbons and later with G.B. Samuelson on a full-length feature *Jolly Good Luck to the Girl Who Loves a Soldier* in which she acted all the parts. Sara Maitland, in her book *Vesta Tilley* notes, however, that:

She loathed the experience of filming, particularly the business of repeating scenes endlessly and the long hours of work.

In 1924, Michael Balcon (later to become famous as the head of the Ealing studios) set up Gainsborough Pictures, and created some of the early stars indigenous to cinema. Ivor Novello and Betty Balfour were performers, and Anthony Asquith and Alfred Hitchcock directed. Betty Balfour was one of the first successful female comedians of the silent film era, but there is very little written about her. All we discovered is that she was a 5ft 2in blue-

131

eyed blonde who made her music hall debut at the Wood Green Empire at the age of 12. At 17 she made her screen debut in the film *Nothing Else Matters* and through the 1920s she was the most popular British female comedy star. It is difficult to discern her particular style of humour but the titles of some of her films may be self-explanatory: *Somebody's Darling*, *Squibbs*, *A Little Bit of Fluff*, *Bright Eyes* and *The Brat*. She also worked with Hitchcock on the film *Champagne* in 1928. She was one of the first internationally known stars, but one whose career declined with the advent of 'talkies'.

In America female stars such as the angelic-looking Mabel Normand (and a little later Bebe Daniels under the direction of Hal Roach at Pathé films) made the funny woman an accepted feature of the wacky Keystone comedies of Mack Sennett. The Americans seem to have arrived more quickly at an ease with film comedy, regarding it as a separate medium. Comedy, more than drama or tragedy, is an intrinsically live art, dependent on audible audience reaction for its success. At best the live comic relies on chance and welcomes an irregular response, using it as material. The live comic actor discovers different nuances and new laughs each night (this may be presenting a somewhat romanticised view of the live performer who is often tempted or bored into unimaginative repetition of material) but these techniques, and the audience, are denied the comic actor on film, (unless the film is a recording of a live performance e.g. *Richard Pryor live at Sunset Strip*). The film audience is required to employ new codes and methods of interpreting comedy on screen. In a cinema, the lights go down and it is generally understood that the audience are silent in order to absorb the film. They may of course laugh, but discussion or interaction amongst the audience during the film is discouraged, as it disturbs concentration and could drown out important lines. It is fascinating, then, that so many of the actors used in film comedy had come from the flexible noisy and responsive world of live comedy.

In film comedy, the camera acts as one of the code-interpreters, often as an interloper. In a way, it is the camera that has the sense of humour and decides which of the actions on set should be offered to the viewer as funny. This makes the camera (or director) the arbiter of taste or at least of sense of humour, and so it is endowed with intrinsic power. This power is constantly discussed in relation to the effect of violence on film. If we are to believe that such images can be deeply effective, then the same power should be attributed to the comic film, despite the reputation that comedy has, and which it is too often in danger of perpetrating, of being light and trivial. The manipulative power of the camera might therefore be regarded as a bonus in comedy. It can coax an audience towards a laugh, position them and then release the laugh. It can structure a comic situation with precision. Little is left to chance. As the camera leads the audience towards the things at which it wants them to laugh, the traditions of humour come into play. Because the camera is making decisions on behalf of the audience about what is funny, it must rely on history or tradition for some of its assumptions. So if women have played certain roles, or have been perceived in a particular way, then it is likely (though not always the case) that cinema will endorse and build on that.

Early film may have had its advantages for women in comedy. The undesirable connotations of appearing in music hall would have been eliminated, and a woman in film would potentially have had greater security and respectability. Given these factors it might be expected that more women would have been attracted to the medium, and in America a new kind of comedian, the wise-cracking quick-talking attractive young women who became known as the 'screwball' comedians, were born. Perhaps because America did not have the inflexible traditions regarding a 'woman's place' that Britain had, the screwball heroines possessed a streak of dizzy but witty and belligerent independence that women in British comedy didn't seem to find until the 1940s and 1950s.

The screwball comedies were largely based on the initial conflict and ultimate harmony of the sexes. Although they often ended in tears as the heroine acquiesced to male will and got her bottom spanked by her rugged male counterpart, elements of female rebelliousness were there. These comedies, largely the work of directors Frank Capra and Howard Hawks, were full of knock-about pseudo-sophisticated verbal sparring matches; women were companions rather than Theda Bara-style sirens. British cinema meanwhile took time to recover after the slump of the 1920s. Typical of the film comedies of this era was the husband-wife partnership of Jack Hulbert and Cicely Courtenidge. Together they performed in film versions of the type of Aldwych Farce then very popular in London. In 1931 Courtenidge made *The Ghost Train* followed by *Jack's the Boy* and *Aunt Sally*, all middle-class affable comedies. They, like so many of their British counterparts, went to Hollywood eventually, but they never achieved any great success there. However, their popularity in this country must not be underestimated, and eventually Cicely Courtenidge was made a Dame.

Perhaps the biggest female light comedy star of the 1930s was Jessie Matthews. Born in Soho in 1907 she started performing at

Cicely Courtenidge and Jack Hulbert in *Under Your Hat*

the age of 12 and by 1926 she was a West End star. She moved into films, but her early film career was dogged by a much-publicised affair with actor/director Sonnie Hale who left his wife for her. This was seen as such a scandal that when her first film success, *The Good Companions* (1932), became the first talkie to have a Royal Première she was barred from being presented to the King and Queen. It wasn't until her biggest screen success, *Evergreen* (1934), that she became socially acceptable. Offers from Hollywood poured in, but she turned them down, afraid for the stability of her marriage. (It's interesting to see how domesticity has often trumphed over stardom in the lives of many of the women we have looked at.) With her next films, *First a Girl* and *It's Love Again*, she was a top box-office star in Britain. By 1935 she decided to go to Hollywood, but sadly a deal with MGM fell through, as eventually

Jessie Matthews

did her marriage. She was charismatic, with a remarkable physique, and was an excellent dancer. However, despite her box-office success of the mid-1930s, by the end of the decade her heyday was over. She made films up to the end of her life, but died of cancer in 1981 aged 74.

In the late 1930s more studios were built and cinemas refurbished and the film production, distributing and exhibiting process made more efficient. Directors such as Michael Balcon, head of productions at Gaumont British and at Gainsborough Films, had, during the early 1930s, imported actors mainly from Hollywood in order to capture the American market ('alien' accents were still found disconcerting on both sides of the Atlantic). Balcon, however, later concentrated on cultivating British talents:

> British cinema, having failed to create a tradition of silent
> comedy, drew upon a rich music hall tradition at the very
> moment when it was already becoming extinct in the theatres.
> (David Thompson, *British Cinema*)

Far and away the biggest star on any terms in the 1930s was Gracie Fields. Born in Rochdale in 1898, she started her career performing in music halls and touring in musical productions. Her screen debut, *Sally In Our Alley* (1931) demonstrated the working

---

Sing as you go

Unemployed mill-girl Gracie has cycled to Liverpool to look for work. She meets a Policeman:

Grace: (*wearily*) Here, I say. Do you know where Lime Street is?
Policeman: Yes.
Grace: Well, where is it?
Policeman: In Liverpool. (*guffaws*)
Grace: Don't be funny. I want Lime Street, Blackpool.
Policeman: Never heard of it.
Grace: (*wearily*) All right, Sam. Pick up thi' musket.
Policeman: May I ask where you come from?
Grace: Yes.
Policeman: Well, where?
Grace: Lime Street, Liverpool – (*and pulls a face*)
Policeman: You be careful.
Grace: (*wearily mounting machine*) I shall have to be.
She rides off in *wobbly fashion*.
Policeman looks after her *threateningly*.

Gracie Fields

class, down-to-earth appeal for which she became famous. She acquainted middle-class cinema-goers with her deflating sense of humour. She represented hope to a country on the brink of war: the working girl who could triumph against all odds. Other of Gracie Field's films included *Shipyard Sally* (1939) and *Sing As We Go* (1945) written by J.B. Priestley and set in Blackpool's Golden Mile. Her style was a far cry from the elegant punning farces of the day. By the end of the decade, she was the highest-paid star in Britain, earning a phenomenal £40,000 per picture. She was renowned for her generosity, particularly to the people of her home town. Known to all as 'Our Gracie', her powerful singing voice and Piaf-like ability for pathos (the other side to her undercutting humour) made her songs signature tunes for the troops during World War II. In 1936 she made the film *Queen of Hearts*, directed by Italian Monty Banks, whom later she married. She had long been courted by Hollywood, but remained loyal to Britain. However, in 1938 when war broke out, her husband was in danger of being interned as an 'enemy alien,' so she made the unpopular decision to go to America for his sake. The British public were slow to forgive her for going, but eventually were won round and loved her American films just as much as the English ones. Like Jessie Matthews she was faced with a domestic dilemma which seriously affected her work and, like so many women, she chose the path most detrimental to her career. This is not a judgment, merely an observation. In the 1940s, Gracie Fields continued her film career in Hollywood and remained the top box-office success for the next eight years.

When Gracie Fields left the Ealing Studios they underwent a major box-office crisis. It is notable that a single performer could make or break the fortunes of a studio. She had, however, opened the market for other performers with her kind of broad humour, and had instigated a new interest in working-class life and in 'ordinary' people. When in 1939 Michael Balcon took over as head of Ealing Studios, it marked the advent of a prolific and interesting time in British movie comedy. *Cheer Boys Cheer* (1939) is seen to be the first of the famous Ealing Comedies, though not until after the war did they come into their own. During the war, the documentary film flourished and a film division of the Ministry of Information was set up. A new attention to social realism began to develop, giving rise to greater thought in the handling of feature film subjects. Britain emerged from the war optimistically, and with cinema attendance at an all-time high but still failed to break into the American film market; despite all odds, the Ealing Comedies estab-lished themselves representing a new movement in entertainment:

... they were written with intelligence and with the logic and seriousness due to comedy; and were played with all the extended skills of a generation of fine British character actors, led by the versatile Alec Guinness.
(David Robinson, *History of Film*)

The comedies were a creative breeding ground. In 1949, *Passport to Pimlico*, *Whisky Galore* and *Kind Hearts and Coronets* appeared. The appeal of the comedies is described by Janice Anderson in her book *The History of Movie Comedy*:

The Ealing Comedies reflect in their kindly and humorous, but often also sharply satiric way, all that is worst and best in the English character: its lunatic fringe and its rational core, its chauvinism and its tolerance, its pomposity and its self-depreciation and, above all, its ability to deflate the pretensions of others. These films also display a sophistication of attitude to morality, society and the world in general hardly seen before in British film comedy.

In Peter Noble's *Films of the Year 1955-6*, Michael Balcon wrote on the subject of film comedy:

Comedy-making is a good way of making comment on contemporary conditions and it is realism that we try and make the keynote of our films today – the superimposition of a curious or comic character (or characters) against real people and real backgrounds.

He goes on to comment that 'comedy as a film subject' almost disappeared during the war years because the film industry was over-attentive to the national effort rather than giving the public something to laugh at, and that the country might have benefited from more comedy. But:

In dealing, however with vital war-time subjects in the way we did, there is no doubt that the film industry discovered itself.

Balcon's comments on the 1950s define the context within which the films were made. The Ealing Studios themselves were:

... basically a middle-class institution of a mildly radical disposition, as well as a determinedly small-scale enterprise.
(George Perry, *Forever Ealing*)

The comedies introduced a plethora of female comedians to the screen. Many of them were an interesting brand of funny woman who looked more as if they had come from a church fête than a film

Joan Greewood in *Whisky Galore*

company. They were actors who had come from the theatre and were well known to the London theatre-going audiences: women such as Irene Handl, Hermione Baddeley, Hermione Gingold, Margaret Rutherford, and Katie Johnson. They were maiden aunts with too much to say, but who were always right in the end. The humour came most often out of the accuracy of the character acting, involving the audience, convincing them entirely of the type, and then elaborating on individual eccentricities. A good example of this kind of character is Katie Johnson in *The Ladykillers* (1955). She plays old Mrs Wilberforce, the landlady who takes on a new tenant (Alec Guinness). He pretends to have a chamber ensemble whose members regularly come round to practise, but in fact it is a gang planning a robbery. They perpetrate the crime, but Mrs Wilberforce discovers the money. The gang plot to kill her, but in trying to decide who should do the dirty work they actually kill each other. The police refuse to believe Mrs Wilberforce's pleas for help, so at the end of the film she ends up alone with £60,000 in cash. For her role as the adorable Mrs Wilberforce, Katie Johnson, then in her seventies, won an Oscar. In a review of the film in the *Daily Telegraph* Campbell Dixon wrote:

> The real hit of the film, however, is not one of the stars, but a little old lady of 77. Miss Katie Johnson has appeared in hundreds of plays and films – always so far as I can recall, in small parts.
>
> After 60 years she retired to Warwick, to spend the rest of her life with her family. Sir Michael Balcon, the producer, and Alexander Mackendrick, the director, persuaded her to come back for this one film, and the result is an autumn triumph.
>
> Miss Johnson is so sweet and gentle that she wins your love, so simple that when she recalls the husband that 'went down with his ship, standing at the salute,' she touches your heart, so unaffectedly absent-looking, that she makes the whole (and in particular the end) seem credible.
>
> 60 years – it has been a long climb. Everyone who sees this film will agree that if we must lose her – she has retired at the top.

The Ladykillers. Mrs Wilberforce interrupts the gang's robbery plans:

> MUM comes up the stairs. She reaches the landing almost exactly at the moment when the music finishes. She knocks at the door.

Film

C.9   *Int. Bedroom. Professor's rooms*
       The MAJOR, LOUIS, HARRY and ONE-ROUND are poring
       over the map which is laid on the bed, arguing in heated
       whispers which cease at once as they hear the knock.
       Moving in unison the four men rise, file into the outer room.

C.10   *Int. Outer room. Professor's rooms*
       They take up their stations, assume their instruments. The
       MAJOR plays the Professor's part, closing the gramophone
       case and unlocking the door.
            LOUIS (in a whisper, mimicking Mum)
            Excuse me, Mr. Courtney, I wondered if perhaps you'd
               like some tea . . .?

       The MAJOR opens the door. MUM speaks at once.
            MUM (sweetly)
            I wondered if perhaps you'd like some tea, Mr. –

C.10ᵃ *Outside Professor's rooms. Day* (Studio)
       SHOOTING across MUM on to the MAJOR, LOUIS, HARRY
       and ONE-ROUND beyond.
            MAJOR
            No, thank you, Mrs Wilberforce. Please don't bother.

       The door is shut before she could reply. She turns away.
       She goes two steps down the stairs, pauses and comes
       back, knocks. The door is opened again.
            MUM
            I could make some coffee, if you prefer.

            MAJOR
            No, thank you. You're very kind. Thank you. Thank you.

       The door is closed again.

C.11   *Int. Outer room. Professor's room. Day* (Studio)
       They wait a moment before they move. Nothing happens. So
       they put down the instruments, turn towards the bedroom.
       As they do so, the knock sounds again. The MAJOR reopens
       the door.
            MAJOR (with saintly patience)
            Yes, Mrs. Wilberforce?

            MUM
            I'm so sorry to bother you, Mr. Courtney, but before you
               start again, could one of you hold General Gordon for
               me? I have to give him his medicine, you see, and I
               can't quite manage by myself.

Katie Johnson in *The Ladykillers*

C.13   *Int. Bedroom. Professor's Rooms. Day* (Studio)
REVERSE ANGLE. MAJOR turns in desperation to HARRY,
who is nearest.
MAJOR
Of course, Mrs. Wilberforce. (to Harry) Mr . . . Mr . . . Mr.
  Robinson, would you mind lending Mrs. Wilberforce a
  hand?

HARRY (with false gallantry)
Mind? Of course not! I'd be delighted, Mrs. Wilberforce.
  You will excuse me, gentlemen . . .?

MUM (as Harry goes out to her on the landing)
It's extremely kind of you, Mr. Robinson. He does dislike
  taking it, you know, but if someone holds him . . .

The MAJOR shuts the door.
LOUIS
Tea! Coffee! Mend the plumbing! Give the parrot his
  medicine! (incredulous) *Give the parrot his medicine?*

143

C.14 M.S. Major
      The MAJOR opens the suitcase, removes the quartet. LOUIS
      enters shot, glances at the small pile of records, finds one
      that is clearly a trio and hands it, poker-faced to the MAJOR.
      As the MAJOR puts it on, LOUIS goes into the bedroom.

C.15 *Int. Bedroom. Professor's Rooms. Day* (Studio)
      As the trio starts, LOUIS resumes his position before the
      map. ONE-ROUND and the MAJOR join him. From below
      comes a distant cry.

C.16 *Int. Sitting-room. Mum's House. Day* (Studio)
      HARRY is nursing an injured finger.
          MUM (distressed)
          I'm *terribly* sorry, Mr. Robinson. I do apologise. He's
          never bitten anyone before.

Margaret Rutherford, who, like Irene Handl, didn't start acting until quite late in life, has become the archetypal British eccentric. She became famous on stage for her performance as Madame Arcati in Noel Coward's *Blithe Spirit*, made into a film, and later in the Ealing Comedies and as Miss Marple in the Agatha Christie murder mysteries (*Murder Ahoy, Murder She Said, Murder at the Gallop* and *Murder Most Foul*). She represented the fading days of the Raj and the British Empire, the acceptable face of the intelligent upper-class, fiercely independent. For her performance as Madame Arcati she received numerous excellent notices, among them this one from Simon Harcourt Smith in the *Daily Mail*:

> The Madame Arcati of Margaret Rutherford achieves the hardest of all feats in acting – she portrays a character absurd without being ridiculous, a woman who beneath her Girl Guide jargon hides both sense and heart. In certain respects indeed, she steals the picture.

As with Katie Johnson, much humour came with the absolute conviction of the character in whatever she was doing. Admittedly the women in Ealing comedies rarely take the leading roles, but they are always conspicuous and, because the films are well written, never superfluous. However, this area of precise eccentric character comedy is one that became less apparent after the early 1950s. Today, women such as Beryl Reid and Irene Handl carry on the tradition, as do Thora Hird, Patricia Hayes and Dora Bryan. Some of these women started their film careers during the Ealing days. Many of them appeared in the St Trinians films, the first of which

Irene Handl in *Morgan – a suitable case for treatment*

was made in 1954 and was based on the sketches (drawings) by Ronald Searle, of horrific-looking schoolgirls. The St Trinians films looked at women in a different way. The school, run by headmistress Miss Fritton (ironically played by Alistair Sim in drag) was a menagerie of girls whose conduct was ten times worse than that of any boys. Operating as a ghetto for monster children, the St Trinians films showed that girls could be just as disruptive, dirty, noisy, unappealing and clever as their male counterparts. In the first film, *The Belles of St Trinians*, Clarence, the headmistress's brother (also played by Sim), who is a bookie, puts his daughter into the sixth form to pick up racing tips from the daughter of a race-horse owner. The horse, Arab Boy, is being backed by the fourth form, Miss Fritton and the school fund to win a fortune. The sixth form kidnap the horse, but it gets rescued, naturally wins the race, and St Trinians is saved from bankruptcy. The film was a massive

Margaret Rutherford as Madame Arcati in *Blithe Spirit*

Belles of St Trinians with (r. to l.) Alistair Sim, Beryl Reid and Joyce Grenfell

box-office hit, and boasts a catalogue of comic performers including Beryl Reid as the bizarre maths and french mistress Miss Wilson, Renée Houston, Hermione Baddeley, Irene Handl, Joyce Grenfell, Betty Ann Davies, Joan Simms, Shirley Eaton and Barbara Windsor. All gave memorable performances, particularly Joyce Grenfell as the love-lorn gawky policewoman, Ruby Gates.

In a different vein, 1954 featured the first of the 'Doctor' series of films, *Doctor in the House*, based on the novels of Richard Gordon. This film was the top money-spinner of the year, and starred Dirk Bogarde as the aspiring young doctor Sparrow. These films were largely representative of the young middle-class male experience of the 1950s and, as with the later *Carry On* films, women were

147

generally introduced as battle-axes or as 'sexy pieces.' The latter were usually in the shape of demure nurses or the chief surgeon's daughter, variously played by Joan Simms, Shirley Eaton, Joan Hickson, Brigitte Bardot and Kay Kendall.

Kay Kendall was a very popular light comedy actor of the 1950s. She is best known for the 1953 comedy *Genevieve* (in which Joyce Grenfell also appeared) as Kenneth More's sophisticated, bored, trumpet-playing girlfriend. The film celebrates eccentricity, and Kendall's trumpet-playing, the battle of the sexes and the British competitive spirit are sources of humour. Kendall bore similarities to the American stars of the Screwball comedies, a 'British Katharine Hepburn' (David Thomson: *A Bibliographical Dictionary of the Cinema*). She was beautiful, witty, exciting and odd, and, like Hepburn, she was attractive to both men and women. Sadly her career was cut tragically short as she died of leukemia at the age of 32.

Kay Kendall has been likened to Joan Greenwood, now familiar to television viewers as Lady Carlton in the *Girls on Top* series with Dawn French, Jennifer Saunders and Ruby Wax. She made her film debut in the 1940s and reached her peak of popularity from about 1948 to 1955. She was a regular in the Ealing Comedies, including *Whisky Galore*, *Kind Hearts and Coronets*, and *The Man in the White Suit*. She possessed:

> . . . the unerring capacity for exaggeration and restraint, drawing forth in unison. What seemed at first like a mannerism proved within minutes entirely genuine: a rather dotty, genteel sexpot.
> (*A Bibliographical Dictionary of the Cinema*)

Joan Greenwood has come to exemplify the rather odd but quirkily funny young women of the Ealing films. She and Kay Kendall struck a delightful balance between glamour and wit in their work, and Joan Greenwood has endured as a comic performer of distinction.

The seaside postcard blonde was an image perpetrated nowhere more successfully than in the *Carry On* films, the first of which was made in 1958. Despite the growing competition from television, the early films achieved surprising box-office success. With the *Carry Ons* British comedy was seen to forsake the subtle intricacies of the Ealing era and was:

> . . . reduced to endless gags and grimaces and trousers falling down or being torn off.
> (Janice Anderson, *History of Movie Comedy*)

However, it seems that the British public was ready for a bit of slap and tickle and lots of shots of Barbara Windsor's bra pinging

Kay Kendall in *Genevieve*

off into Bernard Bresslaw's face, and the *Carry On* films ran for twenty-two years. The plots were simple and usually revolved around the exploits of a group of people thrown together under the control of some establishment (*Carry On Nurse*, *Carry On Admiral*, *Carry On Teacher*, etc.) The first of the long line was *Carry On Sergeant* (1958), closely followed by *Carry On Teacher* (1959) and *Carry On Nurse* (1959). *Carry on Nurse* has the archetypal plot line, it is set in the men's surgical ward at Haven Hospital, the patients misbehave, to the increasing wrath of Matron (Hattie Jacques), and the action culminates in an unofficial operation on a patient who wants to get away for the weekend. The operation fails (surprise, surprise) after everyone falls under the influence of laughing gas. The sexes are always polarised in these films, with the men being afraid of the female authority character whilst pursuing the shapely harmless nurses.

Although Barbara Windsor is almost entirely associated with the cheeky chirpy blondes of these films, she has had a varied and interesting career. Born in Shoreditch, she went to stage school: 'A camp place called "Madame Behenna's Juvenile Jollities"' (Barbara Windsor), and then on to the Aida Foster stage school, where she was told by Aida Foster: 'I think you'd make a fine comedian, though you're not the kind of girl we have at this school.' She describes herself at this stage as 'short, fat and very loud,' a far cry from the sort of girl that they did have at the Aida Foster school who was usually in the Jean Simmonds mould. Barbara Windsor soon went into pantomime and at the age of 14 took the part of Sadie Kate in the award-winning show *Love From Judy*. She came out of the show wanting to be a 'white Lena Horne' and so she developed a cabaret act, but when she attempted pathos in the act, the audience seemed to find it funny. She stayed in cabaret for a while and in 1959 was asked to join Joan Littlewood's 'Theatre Workshop' at Stratford East.

At their first meeting, Littlewood had remarked that Barbara Windsor was 'a pretty little thing' and Windsor remembers this being the first time anybody had ever said that to her. It seems remarkable to a generation who see her as a 1960s sex-symbol that she should not have thought of herself as attractive, but it makes her laugh to think of herself as such.

She was in the film *Sparrers Can't Sing* (1962/3) which was about East End housing deprivation, and was in the vein of the 'kitchen sink' dramas then pervading the London stage and the film world. She went to Broadway with Theatre Workshop's production of *Oh What a Lovely War* and it was while she was in America that she received an offer to do the next *Carry On* film:

My agent said 'It'll go one way or another with you. It's a wonderful way to learn your art in *Carry On* films' (they'd been going twelve years before I came in). But it took me away from my *Sparrers* direction. I was known as the *Carry On* lady after that, and I've only done nine out of thirty-three. *Sparrers* and my *Beggar's Opera* kind of got lost along the way. People still say 'I wonder how your career would have gone if you'd not done the *Carry Ons*' and I think, 'Well, that's life. I might be in oblivion.' You don't know.

Her appeal was huge, considering how few of the *Carry On* films she actually made. She is inextricably linked with the regular *Carry On* team, and also with her indissoluble image as the archetypal 'bubbly blonde'. She attributes the success of the *Carry Ons* to their 'McGill postcard' appeal, saying that people liked to identify with them despite their 'over-the-top' quality. She also thought that their accumulative effect – 'they crept up on people' – and the fact that they were released during school holidays had something to do with their success. They had family appeal: they were just rude enough to titillate but not dirty enough to offend. Barbara Windsor often played the subversive minor authority figure who fraternised with 'the lads', and who was generally revealed in a state of semi-nudity at a crucial moment. The constant re-runs of the *Carry Ons* have kept this image intact, and to the British public she will always be a 'cute sexy little lady', as she puts it. During the 1960s she resisted offers of work from America because:

I'm very London orientated and I'd just got married. A year later I was appearing on Broadway in *Oh What a Lovely War*. When the show finished I was asked to audition for *Laugh In* and the Broadway show *On a Clear Day*, but I said no. I wanted to be a star in Britain. I wanted my friends to say, 'Oh, Barb's done everso well' and I thought 'they won't know if I'm over there.'

She remains philosophical about her career and about the difficulties of her specific image in comedy.

In the *Carry On* films, there was always a Barbara Windsor character (before her it was Liz Fraser) who was the comic sex object, but there was also an Anita Harris or Shirley Eaton figure, an altogether more demure 'brainy' type who managed to ward off the men by being cleverer, and who usually ended up with the young doctor or the young teacher (often played by Jim Dale). Another feature was the Hattie Jacques or Joan Simms character. Joan Simms incidentally, started off playing the sexy glamour parts and ended up playing frumps who nobody fancied because they

Barbara Windsor in *Carry on Camping*

were big and fearsome, but who turned out to have a heart of gold, or to have a crush on the wimpy male authority figure (often Kenneth Williams). There were also 'char lady' characters played by the likes of Esma Cannon and Irene Handl, or the angry wives and mothers-in-law played by Thora Hird and Dandy Nicholls. Stereotypes were endorsed time and again, although in the beginning they contained a Ben Jonson grotestequerie which worked as a comic formula. Eventually, the later *Carry Ons* became, as Barbara Windsor put it, 'more like *Confessions* films' the stereotypes were cruder, and the films lost their charm. Whatever they may have become, the *Carry On* films hold a place in British cinema history, along with the Ealing Comedies, as representative of the popular taste of the time, and they are interesting documents of a particular era in the presentation of women in film comedy. They gave rise to the *Confessions* films of the 1970s in which the plot generally consisted of the unappealing Robin Asquith 'getting off with' a lot of women. Other films from this camp were the *Please Sir* and *On The Buses* films which had come from successful television series. In the *Please Sir* films, actor

Carry on Girls

Hope Springs (Barbara Windsor), in crash helmet and leather
jacket, meets beauty contestant promoter Sidney Fiddler (Sid
James):

> HOPE TO SID: Excuse me.
> SID TO HOPE: Not now sonny, I'm busy.
> HOPE TO SID: Sonny? You want your eyes tested!
> (*She unzips her jacket to show her ample bust. SID reacts*)
> SID TO HOPE: Excuse me, I always thought they built the shock
>   absorbers into the bikes!
> HOPE TO SID: Saucy!
> HOPE TO SID: Here, you the bloke in charge?
> SID TO HOPE: That's right, Fiddler's the name.
> HOPE TO SID: Oh, nice to meet you.
> SID TO HOPE: How do you do.
> (*They shake hands*)
> HOPE TO SID: I'm Hope Springs.
> SID TO HOPE: Hope Springs? I don't believe it.
> HOPE TO SID: True. Well . . . actually me real name's Muriel
>   Bloggs, but it was hardly right for this game, was it?
> SID TO HOPE: What game?
> HOPE TO SID: Beauty contests, of course.
> SID TO HOPE: Hang up, wait a minute. Don't tell me you're a
>   competitor?
> HOPE TO SID: Course I am.
> (*She turns round to reveal the 'Miss Easy Rider' written on the back
> of her jacket.*)
> HOPE TO SID: See!
> SID: Miss Easy Rider.

Carol Hawkins played Sharon, the sex object, and in the *On The
Buses* films Anna Karen played 'Olive' the stereotypical frump
desperate for sex but unlikely to get it. Barbara Windsor felt that
the young female comedians of the 1980s have rightly rejected the
style of humour for which she was so well known:

> They stopped all that because they didn't want to be like that.
> Mind you, having said that, funnily enough, they said 'we don't
> want to be like the *Carry On* type ladies' but I've noticed their
> work has become more like it. But I like the way comedy's gone

Fenella Fielding in *Carry on Screaming*

for ladies. They're not just the girl who walks in and says 'Oooh, 'ello!' which is all it was, unless you had that Irene Handl-Thora Hird look.

Barbara Windsor's perceptions of the current vein of women in film and television comedy are interesting, as they show how the feminist awareness of the 1970s has enabled the comedians of the 1980s to indulge in comic stereotypes, but ironically.

Fenella Fielding became the archetypal mysterious siren in the films of this era. She represented the frightening side of sex, and although presented as a dominant woman, her sexual voraciousness set her aside as a comic siren and therefore limited her comic interaction with other characters. Different again was Dora Bryan, who often appeared in films of this era as the rather vague dizzy woman, the sort whose children got their heads stuck in chamber pots, or to whom some minor disaster was bound to happen. She, along with others of the *Carry On* regulars, also worked extensively in the new style of tragi-comedy 'slice of life' film and television drama of the time. These films documented the struggles of the working-class, and of youth trapped within the confines of an unstimulating social background, economically destined to stay there, but emotionally disposed to escape. Examples of the genre are *Look Back in Anger, Saturday Night and Sunday Morning* and *This Sporting Life*. Many of the older generation of comic women were used to play aunts, mothers and neighbours, and many showed themselves to be excellent actors, displaying a kind of raw regional humour. Hylda Baker in *Saturday Night and Sunday Morning*, playing Albert Finney's aunt who performs the abortion on his lover, gave an excellent portrayal of wit and wisdom against the odds, skilfully revealing the more sinister side of bad social conditions. Dora Bryan in *A Taste of Honey* gave an Oscar-winning performance as Jo's (Rita Tushingham's) mother. She plays a vacuous and selfish woman, whose only aim in life seems to be to get a man. She is a fading goodtime girl, whose treatment of her daughter is unforgivable, and yet she is also funny and appealing. She represents a specific view of the single mother, financially and emotionally dependent on men, at once fearless but philosophical:

Dora Bryan as the flightly mother, is given her first chance in films to be more than a music hall turn and she takes it. Without sacrificing the bawdy comedy of the part, she succeds in slipping us the serious emotions under the counter.
(Thomas Wiseman, *Sunday Express*)

Dora Bryan in *A Taste of Honey*

Towards the end of the 1960s, films became preoccupied with swinging London and youth. The Beatles had made their first film *A Hard Day's Night* in 1964 and followed it in 1966 with *Help!* in which the ex-Cambridge Footlights member and star of *The Establishment* comedy club, Eleanor Bron, appeared. She was also in *Alfie* (1966), playing the doctor. Lynn Redgrave was delightfully artless as Georgy in the film *Georgy Girl* (1966) and later teamed up with Rita Tushingham for *Smashing Time* (1967). Tushingham and Redgrave personified the rather ignorant girl to whom things 'happened' rather than the 'with it chick' that women such as Susannah York, Julie Christie and Susan George tended to play on film. Sex was another essential ingredient of these films, either discussing it, having it or trying to get it (cf. *The Knack*, 1965, and Tony Richardson's epic *Tom Jones*, 1963). Women's Liberation had raised skirts and sexual expectations, and everyone had to be swinging (whatever that meant) in order to have a good time. Seduced by the abundance of young British talent, American backers began to pump money into British films, but with largely unsuccessful results. Towards the end of the decade, the enthusiasm faded as did the quality of film. Surprisingly (and a little depressingly) the surviving formula among 1960s subject matter has been the James Bond films.

The Bond films – based largely on the novels of Ian Fleming – started off as glossy but classy big-budget feature films. In recent years the budget has grown, but the classiness has not. The first James Bond, played by Sean Connery, was macho, but also tongue-in-cheek, and the women in the early films were clever and glamorous, usually rival double-agents who (lucky for Bond) would always try to seduce him in order to get the information they wanted. Alternatively they were the athletic assistant ready for whatever adventure might come their way. One of the most memorable of the Bond Girls was Diana Rigg, in *On Her Majesty's Secret Service* in 1969. She played opposite George Lazenby, who took over Bond for one film. Rigg, who had made her television debut with Harry Corbett in the ITV comedy *The Hothouse* in 1964 and was well known as Emma Peel in the television series *The Avengers* (1965-69), had the ability to play superwoman parts whilst retaining a sense of self-irony. Her comic ability has never been fully recognised in this country. She made an American sitcom *Diana* in 1973 which ran for only a season. She is of course an established 'straight' actor, and comedy may not be her main concern, but it would be interesting to see her do more. She manages to retain credibility and style in her work and her familiar

Glenda Jackson in *A Touch of Class*

half-smile suggests a complicity with the viewer and a facility for not taking things too seriously.

The 1970s witnessed a falling-off in cinema attendance, with cinemas closing down and backers hard to find. Television superseded cinema, and was plundered for film ideas. Much of the writing for commercial cinema was poor, and appealed to the lowest common denominator. What had once been amusing in the *Carry Ons* was now crude and tedious, and the final *Carry On* film, *Carry On Emmanuelle* (1980), was a mere shadow of its forerunners. However, the decade did give rise to a completely new comedy movement which transferred its style to film with great success: the Monty Python team.

Their major films include *And Now For Something Completely Different* (1971), *Monty Python and the Holy Grail* (1975), *The Life of Brian* (1979), and *The Meaning of Life* (1983). Despite the innovation of their work on every other front, the Python team have never provided many good opportunities for women. Many women have shown exceptional comic ability elsewhere during this period, but none have really had the benefit of participating on equal terms in this wonderfully surreal area of film comedy. It was not really until the films of the Comic Strip group that women

A Touch of Class

> *Vicky (Glenda Jackson) and Steve (George Segal) are alone at last. However, disaster strikes at the crucial moment in the form of a disagreement over who should sleep on which side of the bed:*

STEVE: Would you do me a very big favour?

VICKY: I thought that's what I was doing.

STEVE: Would you mind getting on the other side?

VICKY: What's wrong with this side?

STEVE: Nothing. It's just that it's more natural for me being on that side.

VICKY: Well, I don't want to make an international incident out of this, but it's more natural for me on this side. We always started this way.

STEVE: We?

VICKY: Me and my Italian. You see, he had tennis elbow and a bad shoulder, and well anyway, I just got used to this side.

STEVE: It doesn't work for me.

VICKY: Why not?

STEVE: I'm deaf in my left ear.

VICKY: What's that got to do with it?

STEVE: I won't be able to hear you.

VICKY: I'm not going to say very much.

STEVE: You're going to breathe aren't you? Sometimes that sounds pretty good. Who knows, a word of encouragement may slip out at the right moment, could do wonders.

VICKY: Shall I walk round?

STEVE: What?

VICKY: Shall I walk round?

STEVE: Oh no, why don't you slip over and I'll slide under.

VICKY: Oh no, I think it's better if I slip under and you slide over.

STEVE: I tell you what, why don't we just kind of roll towards each other.

VICKY: Look, it's getting awfully late. Why don't you just get on top and hope for the best.

---

achieved equal writing and performing status within a major comic film movement.

As well as the James Bond extravaganzas of the 1970s, there were a spate of comic one-off films, featuring actors well known for their stage work. Rachel Roberts, who had appeared as Albert Finney's down-to-earth, married lover in *Saturday Night, Sunday*

Morning, was later superb in the roles of Gloria, Mint Paillard and Mrs Richards in Lindsay Anderson's *O Lucky Man* (1973). In a wonderful coffee-tasting scene with Malcolm McDowell, Rachel Roberts is positively demonic. She had the ability to be both threatening and sympathetic, hard but funny. An actor with similar qualities is Glenda Jackson. Best known on film for her portrayals of passionate intellectuals and doomed royals (*Mary Queen of Scots*, 1971, *Elizabeth R*, 1972, and *Women in Love*, 1970, she broke the mould in 1972 with her Oscar-winning performance as fashion designer Vicky Alessio in *A Touch of Class*.

In her film affair with George Segal, Jackson displays vulnerability which gives rise to comedy. In forsaking her familiar intransigence, her character, Vicky, is left open to misadventure. Jackson is adept at both the slapstick elements of the film (when, for example, Segal ricks his back during a love-making session) and the verbal slanging matches that frequently occur between the couple, who have gone abroad on an illicit 'dirty' holiday. Her assumed poise and superiority make the deflations even funnier. In this role she displayed an impressive knowledge of comic technique which surprised audiences and critics alike, and defied the stereotyped role of 'serious actor' that had, until then, been her public image. She possessed a superb sense of self-irony, yet her skill as a tragedian enhances much of the film, most memorably in the scene where she has prepared a romantic lunch at which Segal fails to appear.

Although the film occasionally veers towards the sentimental, it is rescued by the central performances. No sooner had Jackson displayed her considerable comic talents than she was seized by the comedy film world; once a comedian, it is hard to be taken seriously again. Jackson, however, has proved that this does not have to be the case and, like the actor Maggie Smith, she has the stature to keep a balance.

Maggie Smith is one of Britain's most accomplished stage comedians: her timing is impecabble and she conveys to the audience the slightest nuance. On film however, instead of powerful direct contact wth the audience, she uses minute characterisations to create a comic structure for the parts she plays. She creates characters that seem always to contain something of the 'essential Maggie Smith'. This is arguably an important aspect of film acting – that the viewers are encouraged to identify certain (however minute) characteristics of the actor as 'person'. This is, in fact, closely connected to the construction of the film star system: the projection of the actor's personality on to the role that he or she is playing, and vice versa. Maggie Smith won an Oscar for her part as Miss Brodie in *The Prime Of Miss Jean Brodie* (1968). She played the part as heroic, tragic, neurotic and ridiculous, and her perception of 'type' was reinforced by undercutting the characteristics before they became predictable. Perhaps her most memorable film performance was as the actor awaiting the results of the Oscar Awards in Herbert Ross's *California Suite* (1978), written by Neil Simon. Maggie Smith's performance was a tour de force of theatrical camp, her nasal voice churning out witticism after neurotic witticism as she frets and drinks the hours away before, through and after the Oscar ceremony. She forms a filmic double act with her bisexual screen husband played by Michael Caine. Together they pick at each other's insecurities like monkeys searching for fleas; once the fleas are caught the duo masticate maliciously. But beneath their derisive and divisive behaviour a touching warmth and affection is revealed. Maggie Smith obsessively adores her husband, and he, in turn, is devoted to her. Maggie Smith has the ability to veer convincingly between tragedy and comedy, and her perception of the part in *California Suite* equals her performances on stage. The Oscar she won for this part was well deserved.

In *A Private Function* (1985) written by Alan Bennett, Maggie Smith plays Michael Palin's socially climbing wife with a pinched reserve and characteristic archness. Her mother, played by Liz Smith, provides a further subtle comic element, as she approaches senility and incontinence still protesting that she is perfectly capable of looking after herself. Bennett's script slices through pretensions like a hot knife through butter. Alison Steadman plays the pampered wife of a local dignitary, displaying a great facility for character acting (familiar in her television work with Mike Leigh) and for the smallest looks and gestures which are detected by, rather than designed for, the camera. She appeared also in the film *Clockwise* as Mrs Stimpsom, wife of Mr Stimpson, played by John Cleese. She single-mindedly pursues her husband through a series of bizarre disasters all sparked off by his getting the wrong train out of Liverpool St Station. She retains an air of mad calm as the plot escalates to ever more bizarre degrees of confusion. Her outward control points up the absurdity of the situation.

The mainstream films of the 1970s were preoccupied with campness, sex, showbusiness (*The Stud, Shampoo, Emmanuelle*, the *Bond* and *Confessions* films) and flared trousers, which, happily, had disappeared by the turn of the decade. The early 1980s have seen a more positive aspect of the British film industry. A wave of optimism was heralded by the emergence of several new film-makers, one of the most notable being Bill Forsyth. His film, *That*

Maggie Smith as Diana Barrie in *California Suite*

Sinking Feeling (1979), paved the way for the critical and commercial success of *Gregory's Girl* (1980). The film is a simple love story. It starts between a schoolboy (Gordon John Sinclair) with a crush on Dorothy, 'the prettiest girl in the school' (Dee Hepburn). Gregory tries to woo Dorothy – who, incidentally, is an ace footballer – by coaching her, but she ends up taking his place in the school team. Gregory never gets his girl but, through a series of brilliant female machinations, he ends up with Susan, (played by

A Private Function.

> *Chilner's Garage. Day. Joyce (Maggie Smith) and Mother (Liz Smith) are sitting in the back seat of the pre-war Vauxhall Big Six. We do not see Gilbert (Michael Palin):*

Joyce: Where shall it be today, Mother? Any preference?
Mother: Where what?
Joyce: Our destination. I thought we might have a little run to Harrogate.
  (*The car is gently rocked.*)
Mother: Joyce.
Joyce: What, Mother?
Mother: We're in the garage.
Joyce: I have to breathe, Mother. I have to breathe.
  (*We see* Gilbert *cleaning the car.*)
Mother: Why doesn't he put the wheels on, Joyce?
Joyce: (*Winding down the window*) Because we've got no coupons, Mother. Gilbert can't get the juice. I've got a husband who can't get the juice. What are you eating, Mother?
Mother: A cream cracker.
Joyce: Where did you find it?
Mother: In my cardigan.
Joyce: Well, get out of the car and eat it. You know the rules. No crumbs in the car.
  (Mother *gets out.*)
Mother: He's missed a bit here, Joyce.
  (Joyce, *still in the car, looks out of the open window at the bit* Mother *is pointing at.*)
Joyce: You've missed a bit here, Gilbert.
  (*As* Gilbert *comes from the back of the car, with his polishing rag,* Joyce *gets out and we see it's on blocks.*)
Gilbert: I never have. I can see my face in that.
Joyce: (*Sadly*) So can I.

Claire Grogan), who had a crush on him all along. In Forsyth's films, the women are the generating force. They are the ones who are ultimately in charge and who subversively dominate the action. Forsyth's films are well cast and although they are commercially successful in America, and have become large scale (*Local Hero*, 1983, starred Burt Lancaster), they manage to retain a certain charm, without becoming twee. He usually avoids stereotype. However, Claire Grogan, who showed potential as a comedy actor, in *Gregory's Girl*, was merely decorative in *Comfort and Joy*. It is to be hoped that Forsyth's subsequent work will show the imaginative use of women of his early work.

A major movement in 1980s comedy has been the Comic Strip. Masterminded by Peter Richardson, the group have managed to capture the Punk and post-Punk teenage and student market. Their work particularly appeals to youth, and they reflect the humour of a generation. They work as a flexible co-operative company, writing and producing their own work. The double act of Dawn French and Jennifer Saunders is an integral part of this group (which also includes Adrian Edmonson, Rick Mayall, Nigel Planer, Keith Allen and sometimes Alexei Sayle). Together the Comic Strip have made a series of half-hour films for television, all written by different combinations of the team. The first of the Comic Strip films, *The Comic Strip*, was directed by Julien Temple (of *Great Rock and Roll Swindle* and *Absolute Beginners* fame) but their first real success was with *Five Go Mad in Dorset* (1982), a parody of the Enid Blyton Famous Five books, which was followed by *Five Go Mad on Mescalin* (1983). They found financial support for the early projects by approaching Channel Four television just as it was starting up. The production manager on the first four *The Comic Strip Presents* films was Sarah Radclyffe, who in 1983 took over as Producer. She subsequently set up Working Title and Aldabra Ltd, production companies which she co-directs with Tim Bevan. Her work with *The Comic Strip Presents* was an interesting forerunner to her current ventures. In writing for each other, the Comic Strip write to their strengths, and have always been critical of each other's work. They have never been forced into the position of doing projects that they didn't want to do. Their films have variously been directed by Sandy Johnson, Bob Spiers, Adrian Edmonson, Peter Richardson and Stephen Frears. Frears (director of *The Hit*), directed the film that French and Saunders co-wrote, *Consuela*. Dawn French:

> They were just great adventures. We used to have such a good time. Working with all your best chums, doing what you like best of all.

And Jennifer Saunders:

> It was so free because you learnt almost everything about the direction: you could even help direct certain scenes, learn how film works, how to work with the film crew; and everything you had a suggestion for was taken, and you could go and look at the

editing, and help the editor; so you had control all the way along the line, which in a lot of companies you don't get.

Most of the crews who worked with them on *The Comic Strip Presents* were there because they wanted to be, and this contributed to a good working atmosphere. They preferred the set-up in film to that in television:

> Most of the [Comic Strip] producers are women, most of the production managers, everything. It's a very female atmosphere in a way. So all the crews are used to working with women and under women, whereas in television companies it's fairly macho. (Jennifer Saunders)

Because the Comic Strip budget their own productions, they are able to allocate money to the areas they consider most important to the film rather than to personal comfort. In 1985 they completed their first full-length feature film, *Supergrass*, written and directed by Peter Richardson. It was a small-scale but ambitious project. They used 16 millimetre film rather than 35 millimetre, and had a production crew of about fifteen people. Although they found the concept of sustaining characters over a long period more taxing than with the half-hour films, overall they didn't find the experience more difficult. Their working situation is enviable, and contradicts the notion of fixed hierarchies that the film world perpetuates. It is encouraging to see women such as Dawn French and Jennifer Saunders participating in every aspect of production. The consistently high standards of their television films, and the potential shown by *Supergrass*, reflect the efficacy of gaining as much control as possible. In some ways their work is a cross between the Ealing Comedies and the *Carry Ons*, more anarchic and more bizarre than both. In *Supergrass* Jennifer Saunders as WPC Reynolds, the heroine, was cool and aloof, bringing comedy to the part by parodying the tough 'woman in a man's world' cop. She was believable, but ultimately risible. Dawn French, playing Andrea, the punk girlfriend of Adrian Edmonson (on whose behalf the whole thriller starts) was at her most brilliantly dismissive and bossy; it was a shame that she did not appear more often. In their half-hour films, and to a certain extent in *Supergrass*, the Comic Strip have concentrated mainly on parodies of other genres, and if they work together more in the future, it will be exciting to see what developments they make in style.

As a group the Comic Strip are rare. Whilst they must be lauded for their enterprise, their success also emphasises the dearth of other groups in the same position. This in part is due to the difficulties of finding funding for new projects. The Comic Strip have been lucky in having Peter Richardson to act as entrepreneur. In their self-sufficiency they stand apart from the rest of the 1980s film industry.

Thanks to video, more people are watching films in this country, which means that less are going to the cinema and so there are smaller box-office returns. The money known as 'Eady' money (a proportion of box-office money from cinema receipts which was channelled back into the British Film Foundation funds) was abolished under the Conservative Government's film act of 1984 and not replaced, and the NFFC (National Film Finance Corporation) was privatised under joint Rank/Thorn-EMI and Channel Four, thus creating a void in government film funding. This means that the only areas of public funding are the BFI (British Film Institute) and Regional Arts Associations. Various bodies have campaigned, so far unsuccessfully, for a levy on blank video-tapes to make up for the Eady money, but support for this has been unforthcoming. It is now near impossible for a commercial film to survive without an American backer or buyer – a pre-sale is essential. This has a serious effect on the types of film that are made; 'minority' interests tend not to be catered for and films by or about women are often seen as such. The recent success in America of British films such as *Chariots of Fire*, *The Killing Fields* and *Gandhi* has encouraged merchant banks to invest money in some films, but this is only a temporary solution which maintains a capitalist status quo, and discourages government funding.

The 1980s have indicated a potential audience for more experimental low-budget moves in Britain. Small alternative distributor circuits for low-budget films have been going for years, and pockets of activity have developed in London and the provinces, where they are funded by the BFI's regional film theatres. 'The Other Cinema' which distributes to political groups, film societies and regional cinemas, was the main alternative distributor of the 1970s. Films such as *My Beautiful Laundrette* directed by Stephen Frears and written by Hanif Kureishi, which was originally made for television on a low budget of £600,000, was one of the great box-office and critical successes of 1986.

The 1980s look more optimistic for women in film: they are breaking new ground on a production level and creating better situations for themselves. The feminist distribution group Cinema Of Women (COW), was set up in 1980, and has built up an excellent repertoire of material which is distributed to women's groups. 'Circles' is another feminist distributor which supports individual films and works in conjunction with the Four Corners Workshop in East London. COW attempts to make the public more aware of feminist cinema and they are responsible for the launch of *A Question of Silence* (1982) and *Born in Flames* (1983). They are the major feminist distributors in Britain, but they cannot go on for ever without outside financial support.

As Jennifer Saunders says, film is an area in which more women than usual have made headway on a production level. Women such as Verity Lambert (Director of Production at Thorn-Emi Screen Entertainment), Linda Agran (Deputy Controller of Drama at London Weekend Television and formerly Director of Scripts and Production at Euston Films, where she was responsible for *Widows* and *Minder*) and Sarah Radclyffe (Director Aldabra and Working Title Ltd) have reached the top of the film profession. But there is still a long way to go. The Women's Film and Television Network (WFTVN) was set up in 1981 to 'develop an information and advice and campaigning network for both women working in film, television and video, and those wanting to. The ultimate aim of WFTVN is the positive realistic and representative portrayal of women in this media.' They campaign for the 'serious employment of women at all levels of production.' Listed in their directory are 27 women directors in film in this country, 35 producers, and 28 'film-makers'. Although most of them are not as high-profile as Agran or Lambert, the statistics are encouraging, but disproportionate. In the BFI Film and Television Yearbook for 1985, there were only 14 women producers and 4 women directors who made or were working on a feature film in 1984, as opposed to 73 male producers and 63 male directors (statistics given are for British-made and financed features, US productions based in the UK and television films running over 73 minutes which began production during 1984. Statistics for 1985-6 were not available at the time of this book going to press.) However, recent successes include Sally Potter's *The Gold Diggers* and Bette Gordon's *Variety* both made with independent companies, *The Gold Diggers* with an all-women crew. In *British Cinema Now* these two films are cited as:

> . . . perhaps the only examples of film-makers from the independent movement who have been able to combine critical and reflexive concerns with the construction of pleasurable narrative.

A recent comedy, which did not receive much critical success was *Loose Connections* (1984), directed by Richard Eyre and written by Maggie Brookes. It is an interesting film which perhaps falls between two stools of trying to make a constructive point about feminism and trying to make it accessible to a large audience. Film writing is still a male-dominated area and unless women contribute

Film

Margi Clarke as Teresa in *Letter to Brezhnev*

more to the input of film subject matter, they are not going to be fairly represented on screen. French and Saunders write parts that they are going to enjoy playing: other women should write with this in mind, or at least with a view to what they would like to see other women playing.

With his film *Letter to Brezhnev* (1986), Frank Clarke disproved the argument that men cannot write for women. *Letter to Brezhnev* is cited as the first box-office success to be made by a collective of working-class people on the dole, about working-class life. Margi Clarke, sister of Frank Clarke, plays the character of Teresa, and Alexandra Pigg plays her friend Elaine. They go for a night on the town in nearby Liverpool (the film is set in Kirkby) after stealing a wallet. They meet two Russian sailors at a night-club, and decide to go all-out for a night of passion, booking into a hotel with the sailors. Although for Teresa the evening is pure lust, for Elaine it's true love. The Russians have to go back to their ship the next day, and from then on Elaine plans to go to Russia to marry her sailor.

Letter to Brezhnev

> *Teresa* (Margi Clarke) *and Elaine* (Alex Pigg) *have just picked up two Russian sailors in a night-club. They go to the toilet and, sharing a cubicle, discuss their options for the evening:*

Elaine: So what d'you reckon then?

Teresa: My one's friggin' gorgeous. He reminds me of that fellow in Dr Zhivago.

Elaine: He's nothing like Omar Sharif.

Teresa: He's got the same accent. You can imagine, can't you? You should see the lovely big thick arms on him. I love men with thick arms. What's your one like?

Elaine: Oh, he's gorgeous. He's got lovely eyes.

Teresa: So, em, what do you fancy doing with them eyes, later?

Elaine: Oh I don't know, Teresa. They're both dead nice and everything, but they might be a bit . . . strange.

Teresa: What's wrong with a bit of strange? You've been warring and moaning all night for a bit of romance, adventure, and here's your chance, looking at you straight in the face. Anyway, my one's just kissed the gob off me, and I don't know about you, but I'm getting in there for another slice of the cake. They're gorgeous, Elaine. Well better than anything we're going to find round here. So get your laughing gear round them.

Elaine: Yeah, you're right, come on.

(They flush the toilet and go)

This culminates in her writing a letter to President Brezhnev and eventually, against her family's wishes, going off to Russia. The relationship of the two women is the film's theme. They are at once wise, daring and funny, and the combination of Liverpool and female humour is riotous. Margi Clarke has talked about the particular style and origins of Liverpool humour:

> Liverpool comes under the sign of Scorpio and it's got those attributes – it understands Life and Death. It's not frightened of Poverty or Pain. Our sense of humour has replaced fear. If you're in a frightening situation, the easiest thing to do is laugh – it's a way of self-protection. The way you produce humour here is to insult one another. When you go to polite society you know that attack's gonna be the best form of defence – you knock 'em out with your humour.
> (Margi Clarke, *Spare Rib*)

The women support each other, but without sentimentality. Teresa and Elaine are the filmic counterpart of the male double act. We've had Butch Cassidy and the Sundance Kid, Bob Hope and Bing Crosby, Starsky and Hutch, Alias Smith and Jones, endless lists of golden-hearted bad boys who always come out on top thanks to male camaraderie and well-disguised sensitivity. Clarke and Pigg are out for a good time, they know exactly what they want and how to get it, and they do so with style and humour. However, we must beware of setting them up as icons. Clarke and Pigg are both socially and politically committed to their work:

> We've got to use images of Peace and Beauty. Beauty can be so shocking; and keep pushing Love and Hope. There's no shame in that . . . This'll lead to Socialism and in the end true socialism is a Matriarchal Society.
> (Margi Clarke, *Spare Rib*)

Letter to Brezhnev defies the economics of the film world, as did *My Beautiful Laundrette*. It is hoped that its success does not do it a disservice in allowing funding bodies to believe that all films can be made on a minute budget.

Liverpool humour was an integral part of one of the biggest film successes of the early 1980s – *Educating Rita* (1984). Written by Willy Russell, the film is a latter day *Pygmalion* with Julie Walters as Rita (a modern Liza Doolittle). The educating of Rita, a hairdresser from a small local salon, is the subject of the film and her relationship with her tutor (Michael Caine) and her family is the central theme as she becomes more self-aware and better informed.

As Rita, Julie Walters coaxes the viewers through the stages in her metamorphosis, from the cocky but intellectually insecure hairdresser, telling gags and attempting to shock her tutor, to the more reserved but enlightened student. Walters was excellent in the role and was offered several film parts as a result:

> The first thing I was offered was a Burt Reynolds film to play the part of a classy American stock-market whizz-kid who was involved with criminals. Well, I mean, sorry but why me? Old Burt just said I was so wrong for it and could play it so different from what it should be. I thought why bother? Then I was offered a lot of things like the Glenda Jackson and George Segal romantic comedies of the '70's and old dusty scripts were brought down off the shelf, you know what I mean, 'she's worth a bit of money now, let's ask her to do this'.
> (Julie Walters, *LAM*)

Unfortunately, she eventually plumped for a couple of fairly duff scripts, and her films *She'll Be Wearing Pink Pyjamas* and *Car Trouble* have not been well received. Hopefully her considerable resources will be tapped in her forthcoming film about Cynthia Payne, *Personal Services* and that in future she will be offered more scripts that allow her to explore her unique facility for comedy displayed in *Educating Rita* and her television performances with Victoria Wood.

Pace is an essential ingredient of any comedy, and film is no exception. The actors have to encourage the viewers to understand the internal humour of the film. A film such as *Letter to Brezhnev* acquaints the viewer with its particular language and rhythm so that moments of pathos can be juxtaposed with pure visual humour. A good comic film defines its criteria and helps the audience to understand them. A film such as Julien Temple's *Absolute Beginners* (1986), perhaps the most hyped film of the 1980s), generally ignored its own potential for humour. It never quite found the right balance between high camp, comic cameos and social documentation. The cameo roles were the most impressive and in the case of Eve Ferret who played Big Jill, the most amusing. We spoke to Eve Ferret, something of a latter-day Diana Dors, about her work in comedy. She started performing in the 1970s at the Blitz Club in Soho, a forerunner of the Comedy Store, as part of a male-female double act. She has done a variety of television work ranging from *Bottle Boys* to *Game for a Laugh* and most recently has been working on a film with Gene Wilder. She celebrates her individuality rather than her versatility:

> I don't fit into an ideal, but then, I look at myself and I think 'I
> feel quite normal.'
> (Eve Ferret)

As Big Jill she was outrageous, and although she only had a small part in the film she pumped it full of character. Inevitably cast as Big Jill because of her size, she realises that this is part of her appeal and that it is a positive step in the perception of the female image that directors are actually changing parts to suit her. Eve Ferret recognises her own potential and refuses to change herself for any market, in the same way that Pamela Stephenson also kept her characteristic flamboyance while breaking from television into mainstream feature films such as *Superman III*.

Women in 1980s films are attempting to break stereotypes. It is still an uphill struggle where the traditional film star image persists and pouting ingénues such as Patsy Kensit and Samantha Fox occupy so much of media space, but there is a new comic woman in film: independent, quirky, with humour that doesn't depend on bitchiness, dumbness or shape. At the beginning of this chapter we stated that America has generally been ahead of Britain in its representation of comic women. It has become obvious that this has been as much to do with the greater availability of funds for the production of films in the US as with the ability of women on either side of the Atlantic. Women in this country have not had the consistent opportunities to experiment with comedy on film; there have been imaginative contributions during times of healthier funding and inventive production, for example under the direction of Michael Balcon at Ealing, and the Free Cinema of the 1960s, but it has not been an area of security in which women could develop. If funds are low, then it is easier not to take risks, and if male comedians have worked well on film in the past, then it's safer to use them again. This seems to be the way the thinking has gone. However, this chapter has taken a look at women who have made a very definite contribution to British film.

If women are to progress in film they must move further into areas of writing and production, and funds must be found to keep the British film industry alive. Films provide a public service, that of entertainment, and many of the films discussed in this chapter show that entertainment need not be geared to the lowest common denominator. Most essentially, film is a potent form of communication and must be used as such. Good comedy films have appeared in the 1980s with women in the vanguard. Hopefully they will not disappear as the Ealing Comedies and the 1960s comedies did.

Eve Ferret as Big Jill in *Absolute Beginners*

Film

Video sales have the potential to destroy or revive the film industry and practical steps must be taken to fund and support this area of artistic and social importance. It is also important that women have the space to experiment and display their comic ideas. We've seen women in film being tragic, we've seen them be repressed, we've seen them in charge. We've seen them be funny before; now let's see them be funny again.

HOW WOULD YOU LIKE TO CHANGE THINGS FOR WOMEN IN COMEDY?

I don't think the situation is going to change until you get like-minded women going in at the top levels. You can do so much fighting from the grass-roots level – as performers, cabaret performers, actors and actresses. Ultimately, it's the people running venues, writing reviews, and more importantly, working in television, the people who actually commission the programmes, who'll give things a chance, let things grow and encourage them, who have the real power to change things. There's loads of people with talent and material to do great things, I think the problem is that the people at the other end are simply not imaginative enough.
(Jenny Lecoat, stand-up comedian/actor/writer)

Getting the fun back into it, and not having to fight women.
(Helen Lederer, stand-up comedian/actor)

I have no illusions about anything changing in the next five, ten years. I don't see anything changing for my generation (which is now twenty), but I hope that we'll plod foward and maybe in ten, fifteen, even thirty years time, it'll be better. Lenny Henry is doing an awful lot to break down racial barriers, but Lenny Henry on his own isn't enough. We don't have a black problem, we have a white problem, we don't have a women problem, we have a male problem. The more women you get in there, the more the attitudes of producers will change.
(Abi Grant, writer)

I'd change people's expectations. About what women should be about, and about what comedy should be about.
(Rona Munro, writer)

I'm just trying to have a good time, and to get everyone else to have a good time.
(Emma Thompson, writer/performer)

Good performers will survive because they're good performers. I hope that women become producers, especially in Light Entertainment. It's such a male-dominated area, but I think it's got to happen through natural selection rather than positive discrimination.
(Lise Mayer, writer)

176

I think it's essential that women make their voices heard as women – to counterpoint the men, there's been no counterpoint, no questions asked . . . I think women have got to fight to get into positions of authority, and they've got to fight to get other women in and prove that it works . . . I think we've got to the change the systems, the way they're run . . . I think it's very important for the future of the world.
(Sheila Hancock, actor/director)

We have to take the initiative. We have to push and we have to make the spaces.
(Miriam Margolyes, actor)

Women have to get more organised and be more ruthless with each other so that together we have more sense of our own critical ability.
(Annabel Arden, performer/manager/director)

More women . . . it's not just comedy, it's a whole attitude that women don't share with men. There is a way of dealing with people, a confrontational style that men have and women don't. It's very deep, and until you tip the scale you won't get anywhere.
(Jill Tweedie, writer)

I'm sure that the more women penetrate comedy, the more it will be subtle and deepened and humanly substantial.
(Sue Limb, writer)

Until you have a club where the women are paying for the men, you will never get the change that you really want. Most of the women who go to the working men's clubs have been taken out by their husbands who haven't taken them out for 6 months. That's another reason they're prepared to laugh. An insult every 40 seconds is a small price to pay for being outside the kitchen, I suppose.
(Germaine Greer, writer)

I don't really think that the creative arts change the world except in about one case in a million.
(Annabel Arden)

Writers and revue

As soon as I knew there was such a thing as an alphabet, I was
rearranging it for my pleasure.
(Denise Coffey)

Women comedy writers are not easy to call to mind. As there is no
proven genetic reason for women being less able to write comedy
than men, there must be other reasons for their reluctance. This
chapter looks at some women comedy writers, and attempts to find
out why apparently so few women write for public consumption.
Particular attention is paid to the 'satire boom' of the 1960s,
graduate humour and revue – areas of comedy conducive to the
writer/performer.

Some women find it easy to write and to be accepted as writers,
some find it difficult, and others, like Denise Coffey, find that
writing comes so naturally to them that they never give it a second
thought. Some of the writers we look at incorporate humour into a
more serious scheme of work, some avoid the old structure of gags
and punchlines, preferring a style that is cumulatively funny,
building towards a comic dénouement rather than bombarding the
audience with funny lines. But there are many women, especially
those involved in commercial sketch-writing, who recognise and use
the power of the old gag format. In these cases the actual structure
of a joke or sketch is of utmost importance, and learning how to
write good jokes can be a gradual process. It can take a long time to
realise that a joke isn't working simply because a word is out of
place. For the stand-up comedian delivery is all important and it
can take years to perfect the structure and timing of an act. The
writer has to imagine the delivery of a piece and then hand it over
to be interpreted by the performer, a process which can be both
exciting and frustrating. For writer/performers it is a constant
process of trial and error; even when a joke seems to work on the
page, it can lose everything in delivery.

178

Children generally are not much encouraged to write creatively, nor are they encouraged to see television, film and theatre as an art form at an early enough stage in their lives. They indulge in television fantasy without learning to separate it from reality. They are not taught that a television programme has form and context on the written page, and that the screen image is merely a construction of the written text. The origins of the final product in film and television are mystified. Programmes appear, a writer is credited, but generally, in the mind of the viewer, the actors 'write' their own text. Thus the writer is pushed further out of focus. The final credits of *Hancock's Half Hour* are interesting because they actually show photographs of the writers. It is important that children learn to distinguish between fantasy and reality in the media. Fantasy should not be destroyed, but its origins should be recognised. We should be taught, and teach, a 'willing suspension of disbelief' (Keats) rather than be coaxed into believing a fairy tale. In this way, more people might understand the need for writers in film, theatre and television, particularly as the latter is fast expanding. Comedy in particular has too few people writing good material. Consequently the same writers are consistently under pressure, and the standard of writing inevitably drops. The dearth of writers in general must in part be due to the fact that being a writer is never posed as a career option:

When you're little you don't think about being a scriptwriter . . . it's not something that your career service at University equips you for. It's always personnel or something.
(Andrea Solomons, scriptwriter)

Damage can be done when schooling starts to determine a child's sexuality in terms of traditional expectations:

In my childhood, meals, comfort, guidance and one or two smacks were provided downstairs, while upstairs, imagination ran amok. It was a happy, workable arrangement. To stretch an analogy, it was like writing should be. Meanwhile school taught Beginner's Reality, Intermediate Boundaries and Advanced Narrow Thinking.
School said Clever Girls became nurses, teachers or worked in offices. Oh, and incidentally, ran homes too.
They did not become nuns/vets/comediennes/artists/detectives/lifeguards and they certainly did not work on trawlers. And I know that was back in the sixties, but when I was a teacher (Dear Reader, I did what School taught me) the girls told me at eleven they were going to be airline pilots/army captains/cartoon

artists/and at sixteen left to become shop assistants/hairdressers and work in offices.

'Can't' and 'Don't ruled everywhere except in the upstairs of our houses.

(Bryony Lavery, 'But will men like it? Or living as a feminist writer without committing murder', from *Women and Theatre: Calling the Shots*, ed. Todd)

Many of the women we interviewed said that they were not brought up to believe that they were funny or witty. If they came from a family with brothers, often the brothers were encouraged where the sisters were not. This, coupled with the mystery shrouding the occupation of being a writer, has made it more difficult for women to consider comedy writing as a valid form of employment. The comic novel is an area where a woman could write freely and privately, without exposing her particular style and thoughts to the immediate criticism that stage comedy encourages. The element of secrecy and privacy has already been mentioned as an attractive aspect of the novel. A comic script, whether it has been written by the performer, or for someone else, is valueless until performed. To give a piece of script over to performance can be a nerve-racking business; even more frightening is the audience's response to the piece. Having material rejected can be hurtful. For some men this process seems to be a challenge:

. . . they don't seem to worry that they're not writing particularly good stuff, but a woman just wouldn't have the confidence in that area. You are putting yourself on the line. I worry if I write rubbish.

(Alison Renshaw, scriptwriter)

There has never been much focus on women playwrights – and, as far as most people are concerned, (perhaps with the exception of the seventeenth-century playwright Aphra Behn, who is currently the favourite token woman of English Literature) nearly all the classics are thought to be written by men. It wasn't until the Actresses' Franchise League, and the Women Writers' Suffrage League were formed in 1908 to campaign for the vote for women, that women began to produce their own plays on their own terms, or that a women's theatre of any strength really existed. Women's growth as theatrical writers has been arrested. Until relatively recently, the concept of the comedy scriptwriter may not have been common. The music hall acts were more likely to purchase songs from songwriters, and make up their own patter in between. Marie Lloyd was famous for her dirty jokes and innuendo, and it is assumed she made them up. Vesta Tilley's father wrote her act, but she was something of a puppet performer, and invented visual business rather than verbal gags. The music hall artists, like the variety artists who followed in their wake, would probably have defined themselves as 'acts' or 'turns'. That they originated (or stole) the material would simply have been part of the whole process of being this sort of performer. They would develop an act rather than write one. Many of the women who brought their acts from music hall to radio often provided their own material, sometimes working from improvisation, 'making up' their act as they went along. This method of creating comedy has been enjoyed by women in all areas of comedy, who find it an unpressured way of working. Distinctions are often made between the origin and content of male and female humour. A contemporary theory is that:

Humour is like an orgasm, and male humour is like a male orgasm – bang, bang, punchline – and everything's very jerky. Whereas female humour is much more cumulative – it goes on and on and you may have a big laugh at the end or you may not.
(Lip Service, cabaret double act)

For many women there is some truth in this, and many feel their humour lies in the slow build-up rather than the quick gag:

Women's humour is almost whispered. It's like sticking a pin in a balloon rather than sitting on it.
(Maggie Steed, actor)

Women often feel that they don't 'recognise' conventional jokes:

I've never been able to laugh when someone's screaming 'joke' at me. It's often men who'll say to you, 'I must tell you this great joke, because it will really amuse you,' and your heart sinks because you know you won't get it . . .
    Women slip the humour in, and it's all part of the context.
(Helen Lederer, *Sunday Times Magazine*)

Many women have talked of the sensation of women laughing together, sharing a common language about experiences and memories, a communal joke session while men are out of the room, a humour of understanding. Playwright Christina Reid on Belfast women:

Men were cosseted and pampered like children, but once the men were away to the pub and the women were on their own with the kids, they were so bawdy about the men. They assumed the kids were deaf dumb and blind and didn't understand what they were talking about.

There are certain areas that some women will talk and joke about (bodily functions, sex, men) that they would not dream of discussing in the presence of men. However, this separation of the sexes may be seen as the female equivalent of 'laddish' humour. Is there any difference between men making jokes about big breasts and women making jokes about small penises? Both are forms of sexism, both endorse stereotypes and at bottom line, both areas are as invidious as each other. What makes the man-bashing of Jenny Lecoat more legitimate than Les Dawson's mother-in-law jokes? The simple answer is that women have always had jokes publicly made against them, and have traditionally suffered this kind of oppression. By making fun of men, women are merely redressing the balance – it is the same mixed logic which operates in revue, sketch-shows and cabaret. It is all right to mock an upper-class person and use an upper-class accent but it is currently unaccept-able to use a working-class or regional accent that might appear to be making fun of the working class – a traditionally oppressed sector:

> I still find it impossible not to observe differences in speech and thinking, but now one is no longer supposed to realise there are differences. There was a brief time after my initial success on the stage when any sketch I did in a cockney or rustic accent was criticised by the new young journalists for being patronising to the 'lower classes'. The fact that eighty five per cent of my sketches mocked the upper classes was not noticed.
> (Joyce Grenfell, *Joyce Grenfell Requests the Pleasure*)

This opinion represents the dual standards employed in the name of consciousness-raising. Whether it is a legitimate reversal or not, many women state the case for redressing the balance in their work. Male comics have been prioritised for many years, just as the middle class has dominated the working class. This tradition needs changing and the brief of the early 1980s alternative comics was to do just this. At the Comedy Store (the venue where the new-wave comedy first started) comics were gonged off stage if material of a racist, sexist or reactionary nature was used. The effect of this comedy, though far reaching, has not reached far enough, or has been misconstrued and regurgitated for mass consumption. Gender-specific comedy (i.e. women talking about periods, sex, childbirth, etc.) is fast losing its appeal and immediacy. Despite the belief that women laugh together and at different things to men, there is also the widely held opinion that there is no fundamental difference between male and female humour, and many women in comedy are reluctant to define their humour in terms of their sex, believing that humour is individual. Ultimately it's impossible to know whether there is a significant difference between male and female humour, because, as Victoria Wood put it 'I don't know. I've never been a man.' However, we spoke to Adele Anderson of the female group Fascinating Aïda, who underwent a sex change a few years ago, and asked whether she felt that there was a difference between male and female humour, having had access to the secret jokes of both sexes:

> I've never found male humour, i.e. 'tits and bums' humour, funny. I've always found that distasteful.

Although objecting to traditional male humour, Adele Anderson initially employed a more male aggressive stance within the group, feeling afraid of exposing a more traditionally female vulnerable side:

> Yes, I did feel very aggressive because I thought that attack was the best form of defence, which of course, isn't true. I was very worried about being vulnerable because I felt that if I did open myself up then I would be torn to pieces. The public have sensed that, rallied round and been my strength.

Fascinating Aïda are directed by Nica Burns, who runs the Donmar Warehouse Theatre in London's Covent Garden. The all-female element is one of the group's strengths and the trust that is built up makes them the best critics of each other's work. Adele's initial approach to the group exemplifies the dilemma of many women who are trying to compete with other writers and performers in a 'he who shouts loudest gets heard' situation. This causes some women to adopt an ostensibly male approach in their work, forsaking methods more natural to them for ones they feel they should adopt in order to get material accepted. Of course Adele Anderson's opinion can be seen as purely personal. We must consider women's comic writing and humour as individual expressions, but also expressions which have many common threads.

It is restrictive to lump women together and ascribe them a particular sense of humour. Eleanor Bron pinpoints the dangers involved in exposing the old structures without having powerful enough substitutes:

> Comedy relies on structures you either comment on or destroy, or point out their absurdities. But these structures are being

Fascinating Aïda – l. to r. – Adele Anderson, Dillie Keane and Marilyn Cutts (Marilyn Cutts left the group in March 1986 and has since been replaced by Denise Wharmby).

disrupted now, and nobody knows how to comment, so they stick to the old stereotype. The feminist will probably become a stereotype like the rest.

Dillie Keane bears this out:

Women comedians tend to fall into three camps for me. There's the 'dinky-do' acceptable face of women's comedy of which Diane Keen or Felicity Kendall is the apotheosis. It's that perky, attractive, not very bright, not very witty, 'oops – we've done something a little bit funny'. It's very dainty but it doesn't serve women well, because it's so squeaky clean, so hygienic. Then there's the 'bash-'em-over-the-head-I-want-to-talk-about-thrush-and-menstruation' which is equally painful, unless it's really clever, and I haven't yet seen anyone who's really carried it off – except perhaps this year, Jenny Lecoat. Or there are the few who really know and use themselves, who are messageless: Joyce Grenfell and Victoria Wood. I think that more women like that will further women's comedy much quicker than – 'I'm going to talk about vaginas.'

When we visited Irene Handl, she was more interested in discussing her writing than her acting. Her books *The Sioux* (republished as *The Great Purple Dream* in 1965) and *The Gold-Tipped Pfitzer* are both bestsellers, and she also writes comedy sketches. Her sketches show an acute sense of the absurd, but they are also poignant:

(A middle-aged lady meets a young Frenchman in the park)

She: Hullo. I've been watching you. I say I've been watching you feeding the birds. I think you're marvellous. Aren't they sweet? I don't know how anyone can be cruel to dumb animals, do you? I think it's worse than murder, because they can't speak. Excuse this somewhat crude attire, won't you? I was catchin' up with my sunbathin', hasn't it been gorgeous.

He: (French) Beautifool weather we are having.

She: Yes, of course I tan a lot faster in a bikini, you know – but where's the use of frightening everybody to death? (*Nervous laugh*)

He: My goodness, you would not frighten me, because, when I saw you first, I say to myself, my goodness, what a beautifool woman. I would so very much like to know such a woman of beauty.

She: Oooh, now I call that truly gallant. Shall I get up and take a bow? (*Giggle*)

He: (*Laugh*) Please take one, by all means.

She: You come 'ere often, do you?

He: Well, I come here quite often, as I say, to feed these birds, because I love the open air, and . . .

She: Well, it's very nice, isn't it? I mean, it's private without being insulated, if you know what I mean. I can see you're like me. I will not go into a public park and mingle with the hoi polloi.

He: I quite agree. I like to keep myself to myself.

(From *Shadows on the Grass*, originally performed by Irene Handl and Peter Sellers, in *Frank Muir Presents the Book of Comedy Sketches*)

Irene Handl excels at the character study. The genre is always at best when humour is created from idiosyncrasy. In the old-style revue, it provided a welcome solo spot amongst a number of sketches where the woman was employed as a 'feed'. Hermione Gingold often wrote for herself:

> Of course you will find it difficult to buy a bicycle in war-time, but if you follow my instructions you will be able to make one for yourself.
>
> First of all you will want some wire for the wheels. Any sort of strong wire will do, but I advise you not to go touching the telegraph wire or you will get into trouble.
>
> Next you will want a bell and a lamp, but I advise you to get these ready made.
>
> Now remove some wheels off an old pram, or it will save you trouble if you remove some wheels off an old bike; and why not remove the handles off it at the same time? You will be silly if you don't.
>
> Now perhaps some of you young ladies have a boy friend. Don't be too shy to ask him to come round some night and help you to adjust your mudguard. And perhaps he will put a spoke in your wheel at the same time.
>
> The peddler can supply you with pedals. Or you can wrench some off an old piano. Won't someone be surprised the next time they sit down? And if they're cross at first never mind. Just laugh and tell them that they can play the piano without pedals but you can't ride a bike without, and then they will laugh too – I hope. Be unconventional, don't bother with brakes.
>
> (From 'Bicycling' in *Frank Muir Presents the Book of Comedy Sketches*)

Both Handl and Gingold could suggest mild double entendre, and Gingold often played the innocent, making unconsciously rude suggestions. This is part of their charm, but also part of maintaining an acceptable feminine image. In the monologue quoted, Gingold directly addresses the audience, and carries on a one-sided conversation with them. Nellie Wallace is reputed to have said of Joyce Grenfell (backstage during a wartime concert) who was on stage delivering a monologue:

> What does she think she's doing out there on her own talking to herself?
>
> (From *Joyce Grenfell Requests the Pleasure*)

This illustrates the basic difference in the style of writing for the stand-up comedian, who generally addressed the audience directly, and for the monologuist who might employ this technique of the 'invisible person'.

Revue has long been a prime area for the writer/performer. Its formal definition is:

> A hybrid form of theatrical entertainment consisting of a rapid succession of short items – songs, dances and sketches – often with a vaguely topical or satirical basis.
> (John Russell Taylor, *A Dictionary of the Theatre*)

The first revue appeared in about 1893, and the majority of London revues up to the 1920s were presented by André de Courville, André Charlot and Alfred Butt. Less popular through the 1920s, revue returned during the interwar years, and later, as the Intimate Revue. It was this era that attracted many major stars: Jessie Matthews, Gertrude Lawrence and Beatrice Lillie were among the best-known performers; Noel Coward and Herbert Farjeon among the writers. The revue format became more popular in the 1950s, with writers such as Harold Pinter, N.F. Simpson and Peter Cook as contributors, but it was the 1960s that put modern revue on the map with the 'satire boom' which erupted on to the theatre scene with *Beyond the Fringe* (1961):

> It altered the face of revue forever. The old-fashioned revue, brilliant as the form was, dealt in many ways with inconsequential things, social mores; whether you held your little finger out at the right moment, or whether you put your foot in it at a family gathering or misbehaved at the bridge table . . .
> Here were four young men dealing with greater issues: the Bomb, the Second World War, disease, the projection and apprehension of God. They catapulted entertainment into more profound areas. At the same time a programme called *That Was the Week That Was* was shooting satire at the establishment every week, shocking us into reassessing our own beliefs. Suddenly there was no place for the dainty glamorous revue and this has persisted. Indeed only a short time ago, a very great revue artist, Beryl Reid, tried to bring back the other formula of revue, and she wasn't successful. I said then, 'If she can't do it, nobody can.'
> (Patricia Routledge)

Latterly, revue has largely become the domain of university groups at the Edinburgh Festival Fringe. The ones that unfailingly pull in the biggest crowds are those from Oxford and Cambridge Universities. Although the Oxford revues are very successful, it is their Cambridge counterparts, the 'Footlights Club', who have the reputation which secures them full houses wherever they go. Each year people flock to the Footlights summer revue, or Mayweek Show as it is called, hoping to see the next John Cleese or Jonathon Miller, both of whom were once in the Footlights revue. The list of now-famous ex-Footlights people is, admittedly, impressive: John Cleese, Jonathan Miller, Eric Idle, Graham Chapman, Bill Oddie, Bamber Gascoigne, John Bird, John Fortune, Peter Cook, Humphrey Barclay, Trevor Nunn, Graeme Garden, Jonathon Lynn, Richard Eyre, Michael Frayn, John Lloyd, Douglas Adams, Griff Rhys Jones and many many more. Women who have since become well-known are fewer but impressive: Eleanor Bron, Miriam Margolyes, Germaine Greer, Julie Covington, Jo Kendall, Sue Limb, Maggie Henderson, Sandi Toksvig, Jan Ravens and Emma Thompson. The Footlights Club has a long and somewhat misogynistic history, which is worth examining because of its effect on British comedy.

The first Footlights production *Bombastes Furioso* was put on in June 1883 and is described by Robert Hewison in his book *Footlights! A Hundred Years Of Cambridge Comedy* as 'a popular burlesque of heroic tragedy'. It had no women in it (women were not considered to be proper members of the university) but this was more than made up for by lots of men wearing women's clothing. Once the Club was established it built up a tradition of Christmas pantomimes and summer shows which attracted attention from townspeople, students and eventually from the London theatre world, thanks to the undergraduate Jack Hulbert, who was taken on by London Theatre producer Robert Courtenidge in 1913. Hulbert later married Courtenidge's daughter Cicely and together they formed a musical-comedy double act. The summer shows developed into Intimate Revue – and, in 1932, the first women, Naomi Waters and Anna Lee, were admitted to the summer revue – *Laughing at Love*. Sadly the show was a flop. The university was disappointed because of the lack of polish, and the townspeople were disappointed because:

> They liked seeing undergraduates dressed up as girls and playing feminine roles.
> (Albert Robinson in *Footlights! A Hundred Years of Cambridge Comedy*)

So much for the typical Cambridge audience. The show's failure was attributed to the inclusion of Waters and Lee so the 1933 show was called *No More Women*. The title song bears witness:

There are no women in the Footlights show
There are no women here
They were awfully pleasant little girls to know
So we tried them out last year
But we've no more women in our May Week show
As will presently appear,
Last year they were a flop,
So we thought we'd better stop,
So we've no more women here.
(*Footlights! A Hundred Years of Cambridge
  Comedy*)

Interesting. Footlights cultivated theatrical camp as part of its identity, and the tradition of drag was long perpetuated after 1933. The club became increasingly professional in concern through the late 1940s and into the 1950s. Eventually camp disappeared and was replaced by a more surreal humour. The 1956 show *Anything May* reflected the darkening political scene (the Suez Crisis was looming) and the increasing disenchantment with the image of the Cambridge undergraduate punting down the Cam with a boater on his head and a magnum of champagne in his stomach. As the New Left and the Campaign for Nuclear Disarmament gathered momentum, they affected the revues of 1957 onwards. *Zounds*, the 1957 Footlights revue, was so radical it reintroduced women. Dorothy Mulcahy, a Girton College undergraduate, and Ann Jones, an actor-dancer, were a success:

The girls, Ann Jones and Dorothy Mulcahy, are an innovation. Footlights have been all-male for twenty-five years.

Miss Jones and Miss Mulcahy brought to the show tiny voices and the kind of rugged determination to triumph that once made memsahibs what they were.
(*Cambridge Evening Standard*, Footlights Archives)

Unfortunately, the boys of 1958 were not as taken by the girls' 'memsahib' potential as the reviewer, and so once again they were ousted. The 1959 Revue, *Last Laugh*, directed by John Bird, took imminent nuclear disaster as its theme, and Eleanor Bron, the first woman to make a major contribution to Footlights, was in the cast. Eleanor Bron, who later became well-known to television viewers in *Not So Much a Programme More a Way of Life* (1964), provided a prototype for women in the Footlights Revue. She was a far cry from the demure or dumb female of contemporary comedy, and her quirky humour was not dependent on being a feed to the men.

Footlights does have a tendency to promote the virtuoso rather than the ensemble, and it can rely on an individual to maintain its reputation. Audiences look out for the individual and this honing in on one performer, in effect this 'star-search' seems to have benefited women less than men. With the exception of the 1981 Mayweek show, *Electric Voodoo*, which had four women and two men in the cast, men have always been in the majority in the shows. This is often to do with the proportion of women to men who audition for the show, rather than overt sexism in casting.

We asked some of the women who have been involved in the club about their experiences. Miriam Margolyes:

> I was at Cambridge in the sixties (1960-1963) and I was there with all the people who subsequently became very famous: the Monty Python people. I loathed them and they loathed me. They didn't think I was funny and they weren't interested in whether I was funny or not. In those days, women were just not. I think women were meant to be frilly, and I wasn't frilly then, nor am I now. You see they're not actually interested in women. They play all the women's parts, and they play them in bold caricature. The only one who's allowed women any prominence is Cleese in *Fawlty Towers*.

Emma Thompson (Footlights 1980-1) felt that she received a lot of attention through Footlights and, despite the difficulties of being in a minority, it gave her tremendous opportunities. The 1981 Footlights Revue *Cellar Tapes* was particularly successful, winning the Perrier Award at the Edinburgh Festival and later transferring to television. She has since worked as a stand-up comedian, on television in *Al Fresco*, *Saturday Live*, *Tutti Frutti* and in the West End show, *Me and My Girl*. She is reluctant to talk about women in comedy, feeling it to be an over-analysed area:

> People are always asking us about it and a few years ago I used to say 'well, it's been really difficult because of blah, blah and blah.' but now I think the best way is to shut up and get on with it. I hate talking about comedy, I hate analysing it, it disappears into thin air.

Eleanor Bron had her own thoughts on the lack of women in revue:

> There are very few women in revue because it's a very special category. Women have to be grotesque (or think they do), they have to be fluttery or vapid, or dumpy or odd-looking. Women in comedy tend to compensate for not being beautiful.

Despite others' affirmations of her own looks, she still feels

Emma Thompson and Stephen Moore in *Up for Grabs* (a Limehouse Production for Channel 4 – photograph by Laurie Asprey)

awkward, gauche and self-conscious. This concern about personal appearance has frequently been cited as one of the major difficulties for female performers, and yet this very self-consciousness can lead to much female humour. Eleanor Bron joined The Establishment, a comedy club set up in 1967 by Peter Cook in Soho. The club was the trendiest night spot in town and a fertile atmosphere for comedy. Although the volume of material Eleanor Bron performed was limited, her monologues were outstanding. Lady Pamela Stitty, a very nice but very stupid Tory lady, was one memorable character she played. Improvisation is another of Eleanor Bron's strengths, and the sketches she improvised with John Bird and John Fortune were successful and innovative. Roger Wilmut in his book *From Fringe to Flying Circus* writes of her:

Bron in particular showed herself to be an excellent actress, the mistress of the subtle inflection and expressive pause.

Eleanor Bron felt that she differed from the men in the Establishment:

They had very strong political voices and were well informed – I didn't know enough to make a comment. My work was social not political. Being Jewish, female and living in class-ridden England, I chose to evade overt feminism and other political stances and keep my independence.

The Establishment introduced taboo subjects through comedy: sex, previously the domain of the dirty joke, became acutely funny thanks to observations of comedians Bron and Fortune. Their improvisational ability, influenced by the Americans Nichols and May, recurred in the Bron-Fortune television show – *What Did You Say This Thing Was Called, Love?* (1968) and their series *Where Was Spring?* (1968/9):

> *Is your marriage really necessary?*
> A couple in bed the morning before the wedding:
>
> Bron: Did I tell you Mummy phoned last night? She's so sentimental. She was very worried.
> Fortune: Why?
> Bron: Oh, she said she didn't like the idea of my spending my 'last night' alone. (*They laugh*). If she could see us now! I've heard so many of my friends who've been living together say that as soon as they decided to get married, everything went wrong . . . but it seems to have made us much better. Hasn't it?
> Fortune: Mm. Much.
> Bron: Mm. Do you want to see my wedding dress? I'm going to try it on!
> Fortune: Hey! I thought it was supposed to be unlucky to see the bride in her dress.
> Bron: Silly. That only applies to the groom.
> Fortune: Oh yes.
> Bron: It is a bore. I wish we could have got married on the same day.
> Fortune: Never mind. At least I'll be there. Besides, I wanted to be Edward's Best Man. I couldn't do both.
> Bron: He insisted on a white wedding, you know. I was surprised.
> Fortune: Ah well, it's all for the best . . .
> Bron: All for the best man, actually. (*They laugh*). It's worked out terribly well, hasn't it?
> Fortune: Well of course. It's what I said: if we hadn't decided to get married we'd never have stayed together. We were going from bad to worse! Physically and mentally: it was humdrum, man. That's the only word for it. We might just as well have been married . . . Now – well! We'll have all the excitement: the danger,

Eleanor Bron

the thrills, letters, clandestine meetings . . . All the advantages of
Adultery.
(from *Where was Spring*)

Eleanor Bron appeared in the pilot programme of the new
satirical television programme *That Was The Week That Was*
(1962), hosted by David Frost. She did not take part in the series,
however. Millicent Martin appeared as the only woman in the new
cast. Martin was an impressive member of an impressive team
which also included David Kernan, Roy Kinnear, Willie Rushton,
Kenneth Cope, Lance Percival and Bernard Levin, directed by Ned
Sherrin. The programme was both innovative and acrimonious.
Although Millicent Martin was excellent in the sketches, her main
contribution to the show was as a singer. Music played a major part
in the programmes; each episode began with the theme tune, sung
by Martin with incredible speed and clarity, to different words each
week, rounding up the events of that week. Music was by Ron
Grainer and words were written by Caryl Brahms. Martin also
performed topical songs in the shows. The musical element was
used powerfully rather than just as light relief, and Martin's
distinctive delivery added to the often chilling effect.

Bron was offered the part of Patrick McNee's assistant in the
popular television series *The Avengers*, which she turned down in
favour of developing her own projects. After numerable notable
television performances in the 1960s, Eleanor Bron wrote *Beyond a
Joke* (1972) followed by the series *Making Faces*. Despite the
intelligent, subversive and funny nature of Eleanor Bron's work,
Roger Wilmut (in *From Fringe to Flying Circus*) suggests that the
BBC have been less than enthusiastic and attributes this to the
erudite or 'oblique' areas she tackles. Whatever the reason, it is to
be lamented that she has stopped writing for television light
entertainment. She has concentrated successfully on 'straight' roles
in theatre; she took this path because:

I have a great facility for superficial things, and I wanted to prove
that I could do something else. I didn't want to be over-exposed
doing the same thing – although I know that people seem to like
the same thing over and over again, and it can make you very
popular, I find it limiting. I'm a minority taste and I have to
take the consequence of changing tack.
(Eleanor Bron)

Eleanor Bron feels that the situation for women in light
entertainment has changed, and that women such as Julie Walters
can move easily from straight theatre to comedy and back again
without being typecast and she entertains the possibility of

returning to comedy. The problem of typecasting is an occupational hazard for women in comedy. Funny women are at such a premium that their comic ability can sometimes limit them to the confines of the field.

This argues the case for more women writers, or at least for writers who can write thoughtfully for women. Germaine Greer discussed the difficulties of female comedy writing through references to her own experience in Footlights. Germaine Greer came from Sydney University to Cambridge in 1964 to do a PhD, and appeared in the 1965 revue *My Girl Herbert* and the 1966 revue *This Way Out*. She said that comedy came naturally to her and that she did the cabaret at school dances because:

> If I didn't do cabaret, I'd have to dance with some boy who was three foot shorter than I was, and had his face in my waist.

At Cambridge she joined the Footlights because she wanted to be noticed:

> . . . the whole thing about Cambridge then and probably still is that you have to compete with people in a silly image-building way. You've got to become a local celebrity. If you were an Australian, you didn't go to one of the great schools and your academic performance is as yet unknown, they just think you don't exist. I just couldn't get used to being cut and ignored by people I had met not just once but several times. I'd always been a minor celebrity in other universities, and I thought 'this is not good'. We knew that Footlights was going to take women members. They used to use women in the Footlights Revues but they used them as props, stooges in the men's stuff. Jo Kendall was the stooge before us, and she played all the female parts.

Germaine Greer was one of the first women admitted to Footlights. Her entrée was via a smoker: an informal cabaret held in the Footlights Clubroom, where performers can try out new material in front of a rowdy audience, usually in the hope of being selected for the Committee or for the summer show. Women had for years been barred from attending them:

> I did a sketch loosely based (actually it was quite tightly based) on one of Barry Humphries' performances, about how to get the Australian accent. He used an egg-slicer which you put in your mouth and then you got the accent. I did all this and it was really quite funny – and it did appear to them that I had written it myself – which I'm sure I had – I could barely remember what Barry had done with it, and besides, in the best traditions of

195

comedy, you take somebody else's material.
(Germaine Greer)

She disputes the suggestion of male opposition to female writing:

The men around us would encourage us to be as outrageous as
we could. They would have loved it if we'd written our own
material, I'm sure, provided it was funny.

However, Germaine Greer did not write for herself:

I did very little of my own stuff. Couldn't write it. Tried. Wasn't
funny. I could turn the worst line in the world into a funny line
just by thinking of a way to do it, pointing it or whatever, and I
could make any song funny, but I couldn't write the funny things.
It's like women performers of music. Callas can take
undistinguished 19th Century Donizetti and turn it into
something amazing, but she obviously never wrote a line of
music. And I don't know what that's all about. I think it's
something really basic. It starts with the beginning of your
personality, when you're a little girl and you work on other
people's material right from the time you're born. There's an
extra element of arrogance that's missing, that boys get to very
easily, and I think girls simply don't. I wrote a book about it, *The
Obstacle Race*. Why is it that women work in a small compass?
Why is it that they'll copy other people's work and make them
look better than they did originally? Why is it that when suddenly
faced with a huge wall and told to paint the 'Last Judgment' on
it, they just cave in?

Dr Greer discussed the psychological aspects of physical presentation:

One of the real problems about women in comedy is narcissism.
You've got to be prepared to make yourself look ridiculous, and
lots of women find that very difficult to do. I had a big
advantage, I was tall; Pamela [Stephenson] has a disadvantage of
being amazingly good-looking in a totally unconvincing way. It's
amazing. Her face looks like she bought it somewhere.

Germaine Greer was often picked out as the one member of the
group who should become professional; she and her female
colleague were a success:

The best performers, Miss Buhr and Germaine Greer, two very
adroit comediennes, for some odd reason are not given nearly
enough to do.
(*Oxford Mail*, Footlights Archives)

Germaine Greer (second from right) and the Cambridge Footlights

The assumption is that the women should be written for, and this question of women's contribution to the revue crops up time and again. Germaine Greer was one of the few women who braved smokers. Prior to the acceptance of women on to the Committee in 1965, there can have been little incentive to do smokers if there was no hope of taking part in the workings of the club. It was thanks to Footlights president (1965) Eric Idle that women were admitted to the Committee:

> I think it is degrading and fantastically backward looking that women should not have the same opportunities at University as men, and it is rather sad that Footlights lag even behind the Union in this.
>
> (Eric Idle, letter to Footlights Senior Treasurer, 1964, Footlights Archives)

Idle argued that it should not be assumed that women could not be funny, because they had never had a chance or really been encouraged to do revue. And so the drag element in Footlights faded out:

> . . . there was no need for drag – Germaine did all that.
> (Eric Idle, *Footlights! 100 Years of Cambridge Comedy*)

And Germaine Greer felt no opposition to being funny:

> They never saw me as any kind of sex-object. I was never a woman to them really. There's a whole sort of special 'wetness' about Cambridge. These boys were 18, 19, 20 – they didn't even masturbate – I don't know what they did. They had an idea of what a woman was like, it was probably Susan Hampshire, and if you weren't Susan Hampshire you didn't exist.

But she pointed out:

> What's extraordinary of course, is that they didn't write for women, but they wrote for themselves as women. All those boys are full of woman-hatred. They're afraid of women, and they dislike them. But in that I just think they're typically British.

Writer Sue Limb experienced similar problems with trying to be accepted as a funny woman:

> The women in Footlights were always very peripheral, always token. They were not really taken seriously as sources of comic material in their own right . . . so Sarah (Dunant) and I were so fed up with this stereotyping, we prepared a sketch. We didn't have a sex, we were just little creatures – and it wasn't a bad sketch either – but the other members of the revue team just sat and watched it in stony silence, and we felt all our confidence drain away, and they said 'Well, nice idea, but women just aren't funny on their own like that.' And that was that. We came up against a blank wall. And this was odd, because I was at Cambridge at the time when women started to do all sorts of interesting things like direct plays for the first time – remarkably late if you think about it – but there was this resistance against them. They could do monologues occasionally, they could be any number of a whole range of stereotypes, but you didn't really have much success if you tried to do anything that didn't depend on the traditional misogyny.
> (Sue Limb, Footlights Revue 1972)

In bringing up the important changes in women's perception of themselves in the early 1970s, Sue Limb suggests a reason why women shied away from Footlights at this stage:

> When feminism really began to get going, the women who were
> talented and inspired and great comic geniuses didn't want
> anything to do with the traditional male establishment which
> included the BBC above all else, and I think they went
> 'alternative'. They joined feminist revues. They wanted to make
> their own comic talent work and support their political views.
> And this is perhaps why the Light Entertainment department of
> the BBC has remained unvisited by women writers.

Sue Limb does not believe that she writes specifically for women
or as a woman, but she does reject what she sees to be the more
aggressive world of sketches and punchlines. She prefers to write
without any obvious jokes but with an endemic humour. She feels
that this is what women can contribute to comic writing.

Many women have had to work extremely hard to get to
University. Not just academically, but to prove themselves to be
rational, sane people, 'head girl' material who are able to cope. And
at University, in a situation where there are many more men than
women, they have to work doubly hard at maintaining that status.
This makes self-exposure very difficult. To then go on stage at a
smoker, or equivalent, with something you've written yourself, and
to be ridiculous, is to risk blowing all those years of hard work.
And then if it's not funny, you've blown it completely. It isn't easy
to pick yourself up after failing in a male-dominated atmosphere.
Women seem to be allowed fewer chances to fail:

> If a man goes on stage and bombs, it's OK and he's one of the
> guys; if a woman fails, it's tragedy.
> (Kit Hollerbach, stand-up comedian)

Jan Ravens put paid to much theorising about women in
Footlights when she became its first woman president in 1980:

> Once I did it, I thought, 'It's amazing that they haven't got a
> woman to do this before because really it's a fucking slog.'
> (Jan Ravens)

She remembers that being the first woman President of the club
was a tremendous pressure, but she is very unassuming about her
place in comedy history. There has been one other woman president
of Footlights: Cathy Crewe (1984). She pointed out that there are
still few women interested in being in Footlights, and that those
who are keen are often reluctant to write. The attention we have
paid to Footlights may seem disproportionate, but the effect the
Club and its ex-members have had on British humour is huge. In

Jan Ravens – 'I hope this isn't too "Hello loves, I'm an actress".'

Sandi Toksvig was in the 1980 Footlights revue *Electric Voodoo* (the cast included Jan Ravens and Sheila Hyde – now a stand-up comedian); she later got together an all-female revue, *Woman's Hour*, with Jan Ravens and Emma Thompson. She is now well-known to television viewers as Ethel on the Saturday morning programme *Number 73* and she is also a prolific comedy writer.

this respect it acts as a microcosm of the larger world of light entertainment.

In 1985 Platform, a co-operative drama group, was set up in Cambridge and put on an all-female feminist revue. They discovered that their most successful work departed from the accepted sketch format: they used movement and 'a non naturalistic mode of approach'; the sketches which were least effective were those which clung to a traditional format (i.e. court-room scene, political meeting):

> It struck me that perhaps the myth of women not being as funny as men was due to the fact that they were just trying to imitate a style more suited to men than women.
> (Maeve Murphy, Platform member)

It is good to see women re-emerging and trying to work out their style of humour on their own terms. Although revue itself is not an innovative format, and at worst university or college revues are arrogant and unfunny, at best they can be accurate and incisive and challenging for those involved.

The Millies is a predominantly female comedy-singing group whose first show, *Cover Girls*, was revue based. The Millies met in Cambridge. Caroline Leddy, Donna McPhail, Jo Unwin and Richard Vranch joined up in 1984 to put on a show in the Footlights Clubroom. As The Millies they have been touring London and the provinces ever since. They classify themselves as a theatre group rather than a cabaret act and they present a narrative show punctuated by excellent songs. They write all ther own material, and are rare among comedy groups, having only one man; a reversal of the traditional revue situation. They were particularly interesting on this subject. Richard Vranch, the 'token' man:

> There are two ways in which I get a raw deal, and I'm sure you've heard the same from women in the minority of one in a male group. One is that people think you've just been hired in for the gig. Secondly they don't give you any credit for having any writing talent, especially as it's a 'womeny' show.
> (Richard Vranch, The Millies)

Jo Unwin felt that the situation for Richard Vranch as the only man was worse than for a woman in an equivalent position:

> Whereas with Richard we've got the advantage because I think a lot of people find women more interesting on stage.

The Millies attribute their success in part to the relative novelty of being a predominantly female comedy group:

The Millies (l. to r.) Jo Unwin, Richard Vranch, Donna McPhail and Caroline Leddy.

. . . there's a big buzz about women in comedy, I think people are very interested and want to know about it. And although it's early days for us yet, I still think that everybody is very interested in seeing funny women on stage.
(Donna McPhail)

They avoid any overtly feminist statement, because, as Caroline Leddy put it, their strength as funny women should come from performance by: 'making so many statements just by avoiding making statements'.

A collection of ex-Footlights members joined with Terry Jones, Michael Palin and Terry Gilliam to form *Monty Python's Flying Circus*. Their first television show went out in 1969. They exploded the accepted sketch format by voyaging into a strange surrealistic land of cartoons, warped satire and oddity. Germaine Greer remembers their impact:

> The great thing about them is just that they were plain ridiculous. We'd had far too much of TW3 (*That Was The Week That Was*) and finally when we saw Terry Jones playing the piano in the nude it was a relief to be able to belly laugh. But that's my favourite sort of comedy.

Their use of women, however, was somewhat less extraordinary and original. Carol Cleveland joined Monty Python very much as the female 'feed'. She had worked as the glamorous stooge in television comedy with Ronnie Barker, Ronnie Corbett and with Roy Hudd. She has never found her looks a handicap in comedy:

> Somewhere along the line, someone thought I had a sense of humour as well as being glamorous because when the Pythons were starting their series, someone at the BBC suggested me. They wanted a glamorous lady, who could also be funny.
> (Carol Cleveland)

Cleveland, although regretting that she did not write her own material felt that her comic ability was put to good use with the Pythons, despite the fact that:

> I could respond to their way of thinking, but I couldn't actually think the way they did. I was prepared to do whatever they asked me, and the fact they realised this was why they kept me on. And I found that I enjoyed being absolutely ludicrous.

She says that she has been criticised by feminists for her apparent acquiescence to female stereotyping, but she argues her case:

> I think that being glamorous and funny is the best combination there is. And I think that's why what I did in Python was successful. Had I just been a sex object, and just stood there in bra and panties and not opened my mouth then I think possibly I would agree with with the feminists who'd say I'd been exploited in some way. But I was able to combine that with a good sense of humour and a sense of the ridiculous and I was quite prepared to stand there and look sexy and yet still get a custard pie in my face. I think if you're a glamorous women who's prepared to

Carol Cleveland and Michael Palin in *And Now for Something Completely Different*

make a fool of yourself, then you've got it made as far as being a comedienne is concerned.

Actor and writer Connie Booth was also an occasional member of The Monty Python team. Although she did not write with the team, she later joined John Cleese to become half of one of the most successful writing partnerships of recent years. In 1975 the first series of *Fawlty Towers* went out and has subsequently been acclaimed as one of the most brilliant comedy series to be shown on television. The series (of which there were only two) displayed the perfect fusion of imaginative plot and character delineation, as common frustrations mingled with the absurd in each episode. Cleese has remarked that his contribution to the series was mainly to the comic construction whilst Connie Booth developed the characters. It is not widely recognised that Connie Booth played such an essential part in the construction of the series. Whether this is because of Cleese's fame and the fact that the character he played in the series, Basil Fawlty, was essentially comic whereas Connie Booth's character, Polly, was essentially 'straight', or because people are generally reluctant to accept women writers, it is difficult to tell. Whatever the reason, it is a common problem among mixed writing partnerships.

The assumption that women do not write comedy scripts was one with which Lise Mayer, co-writer of *The Young Ones* television series, has also had to contend. She started writing for Rik Mayall's Kevin Turvey in the television series *A Kick Up the Eighties* and later she joined with Rik Mayall and Ben Elton to write a pilot television programme of *The Young Ones* for the BBC. She remembers the impetus for the programme being charged by an anti-'Oxbridge' feeling:

> We were much more angry, much more arrogant when we made the pilot of *The Young Ones*. It coincided with the fourth series of *Not the Nine O'Clock News*. Although we were all Python fans, there was so much comedy being dominated by the ex-Footlights people and the Oxbridge Mafia, and it had all been revue. Stand-up and sitcom seemed quite a different thing to do. (Lise Mayer)

Lise Mayer is a writer of the post-Python generation and her humour is reflected in her writing: *The Young Ones* is fast and iconoclastic, and she says of herself 'I like jokes that make you go "Ugh!"'

But she did feel that she had been treated differently through being the only female writer of *The Young Ones*:

Lise Mayer (centre) and 'The Young Ones' Chris Ryan, Rik Mayall, Adrian Edmonson and Nigel Planer

People would say 'Oh, did you think of the costumes?' Not only that, people who've worked at the BBC – who should've known better – would say 'she "helped" write it.'

We asked her how she countered this sort of comment:

You don't really, you just think 'I'll show you, you bastard.'

She felt that it had only occasionally been useful to be a woman writer:

I don't think writers are treated terribly well. But you can never tell whether it's because you're a writer or because you're a woman. You can only go on your own experience.

She felt women were less prone to isolationist competitiveness:

Maybe women have much more of a collective identity than men. Certainly in terms of friendships women have a feeling of being women, and they feel for other women in similar situations, whereas men tend to be much more isolated because they don't share their feelings with other men to the same extent. And all the male goals are competitive things about being better than everybody else and not siding with the underdog.

Many women encounter conflict between their more humane side and the side that feels they must push themselves to get on. Lise Mayer suggests that women should move more into areas of production, something which she hopes to do. Scriptwriter Vicky Pile, now working in production at the BBC, has also written for numerous television and radio sketch-shows, including *Spitting Image* and *Rebellious Juke Box*. She got into mainstream comedy in 1980, writing for *Not the Nine O'Clock News*. There were a lot of what she terms 'Two Ronnies' style sketch-shows being made at the time and although she didn't find them particularly funny, she was able to emulate their style in her own writing:

> In a naïve way I'd never made an association between being a female, and not relating to it (the humour). I suppose in a typically female way I thought 'oh, it must be me.'
> (Vicky Pile)

She also wrote for the all-female comedy show, *Revolting Women* (1981):

> *Revolting Women* came up which was the first programme by the BBC (I think I'm right in saying) which asked specifically for women writers. And I think if that programme hadn't been there I wouldn't have got started.

The show was slammed by critics, and although Pile admits it was 'a bit of a disaster' she explained why:

> Because of the weight, the emphasis, that was put on the programme. All the women were desperate to unload ten years of trying to get their words out, and put them into this half-hour programme. There was too much trying to be done in too little time . . . it was fraught with personal battles, everyone had an axe to grind. And I don't think it should have been like that. We should just have been stepping in to make a comedy programme, and the fact that we were women should have been almost incidental.

The show did not run smoothly:

Revolting Women – on the floor – Philip Bird; (l. to r.) Linda Broughton, Linda Dobell, Jeni Barnett (centre). © BBC Enterprises 1981

There was prejudice right from the start. Again, I was so green, I'd never encountered such blatant sexism until then. I think, because we'd gone in waving banners, some of us, the press was going to be bad from the start. So there was no help, very little money, everything was put in our way. Had it had another series I think it would have been really good. With a slight change of personnel, it would have been great.

Here, once again, are the disadvantages of being the 'first woman'. Vicky Pile feels that shows such as *Revolting Women* and *Watch the Woman* should just be two of many programmes by and for women; thus, such shows would be under less pressure and could progress and develop naturally. Although she went back to writing formula comedy, Vicky Pile now knows that what makes her laugh is:

. . . not just the line or the delivery of the joke but the performance, the concept behind it, and the character.

She finds that women are the best proponents of this style:

I find it easier and more interesting to write for women these days . . . I really do want to write, but I want to write what I want to write, and to be in a position where it's accepted.

209

Get yourself a trauma by Vicky Pile (from Channel Four's *Coming Next*)

Girls! Have you got a weight problem? Maybe I can help. You may find this hard to swallow, but a short while back I was a ten ton truck – some hellava broad broad if you know what I mean. I only had to breathe in at a party and I could suck up the whole buffet quicker than a hoover on heat. Talk about fast food? I could put away 6 half-pounders before you could find the opening in your face.

Sick? I wasn't sick – The only thing wrong with me was total happiness – yup . . . total blinding happiness. I didn't get embarrassed swigging cocktails by the pint, I didn't care that my tits were so low slung I wore hipsters instead of a bra . . . and I was forever tucking my waistline into my boots. I just DID NOT CARE! And people LOVED me! But I never let guys get too serious, in case they cramped my eating style – you know, dinner for two is so much better eaten by one. But anyway, then something happened that totally changed my life . . .

It was one of those hot, sticky summer days when you've got rivulets of melting chocolate running all over your body – I was trying to suck it out of my pockets with a straw, whilst backing out of the garage – and I ran straight over my own kid brother. And his guide dog. Squashed them flatter than a strawberry pancake. Well, I could not eat a thing . . . for at least two hours. BUT THINGS GOT WORSE. I met Gregory, a man in a million . . . I knew I loved him more than the last bite of a Yorkie bar. And he hated my guts. All of them. I had discovered D . . E . . P . . R . . ESSION. My first TRAUMA.

Girls, forget faddy diets, forget exhausting exercise . . . get yourself a trauma, and your excess fat will disappear faster than a King cone in a microwave. Within 2 weeks I had a figure like a giraffe's neck (the spots wear off after a while) and at last I was just like other girls – I too, could look nauseous in the presence of french fries, I too, preferred chewing the corner of my pillow to a turkey leg, I too, was utterly miserable.

So take a tip, girls, if you've got a weight problem, start worrying. You can make yourself pretty goddam unhappy if you try – Break up your marriage, find a man who'll beat you up weekends, or take out a mortgage you can't pay back. Get yourself a trauma, and cry away those calories.

Scriptwriter Alison Renshaw also spoke of the need for more women in light entertainment at every level of performance, writing and production. She expressed anger at women who believe that their material is rejected because male producers don't find it funny, and cited a case, at a lecture given by writers Ray Galton and Alan Simpson (*Hancock's Half Hour*), where a woman got up and complained of this kind of sex-discrimination:

> And I felt like saying 'No! You're wrong. You write stuff that's good and funny and accessible to everyone. You don't just blame the fact that your writing is in a feminine tone. That's wrong. You've got to write good, solid material.

Radiation Newsreel by Alison Renshaw, transmitted on Weekending 9.5.86 at the time of the Chernobyl Nuclear Reactor disaster.

(Music: Pathé Newsreel style)

News reader: Look out, here it comes again, that nasty old commie radiation cloud is back, but has it put the wind up Mr and Mrs Ordinary Britain – no sir. The plucky Brits are going about their daily business without a care in the world. Why, a little bit of radioactive rain isn't going to stop them shopping for essentials . . .

Man: 2 litres of iodine please.

Shopkeeper: You'll be lucky, I've just sold the last lot to the vicar.

News reader: People have been reassured by the experts that there's no danger to health. But just to comfort a few worried mums and dads our quick thinking government has set up a hot line only five days after the cloud first reached Britain's shores . . .

Mum: Hello, can you tell me if it's safe for my Tommy to drink the milk?

Expert: (*Patronizing*) Quite safe, Mrs.

Mum: And can you tell me the radiation level in milk please?

Expert: Well, would you like it in rems, Rads, Becquerels, Cuvees, Roentgens, or Sieverts.

Mum: Oh well, Roentgens sounds nice.

Expert: Ah sorry, I haven't got the level in Roentgens. You'll have to have Becquerels. And they're only twice the normal level.

Mum: And what is the normal level?

Expert: Ah, half the level at the moment.

Mum: Thank you, you've been most helpful, and I'm totally reassured.

News reader: The government message is: just ignore it and it'll blow away. Why be concerned about something you can't see, smell and haven't got the brains to understand. So well done you Plucky Brits, why worry about something that won't kill you for 30 . . . well maybe 20 . . . years.

Abi Grant, who writes for television – *Spitting Image*, *Now Something Else* – cited Victoria Wood and French and Saunders as women who have achieved popular appeal with a minimum of compromise. French and Saunders worked collectively with the Comic Strip, where it was never assumed that because they were women they didn't write. They branched out on their own to write the television series, *Girls on Top*, together with Ruby Wax and which originally included Tracey Ullman in the cast. The programme combines the writing and performing styles of Ruby Wax, who is originally from America and whose comedy is based in a very specific up-front rapid delivery, the more accumulatively funny tauntings of Dawn French and Jennifer Saunders and the pert connivings of Tracey Ullman's character. The series represents a very positive move forward for women on television and it is to be hoped that it paves the way for more programmes of its kind.

Cell net car phones by Abi Grant

(*Shots of smart young executive driving along motorway*)

Voice/over: Attention all businessmen, new from British Telecom and available now – the Cell net Car Phone. With new Cell net you can at last hold that important conversation with your boss in Japan . . .

(*The phone has rung. The Businessman takes hands off steering wheel to answer it.*)

V/O: . . . whilst driving into the back of another car.

(*Car hits one in front and lurches.*)

V/O: Yes, now you too can drive off roads . . .

(*Cut to photo of smart car driven off road into ditch.*)

V/O: . . . into lamp-posts . . .

(*Shot of car wrapped around lamp-post.*)

V/O: . . . Even reverse over small children and still be able to make that important call.

(*Cut to shot of Cell net phone.*)

V/O: So why not be really in with the in-crowd and get a Cell net phone fitted into your car. Available only from . . .

(*Cut to end bit of Telecom ads with finger coming down and pressing button.*)

V/O and Caption: British Telecom . . . The Power Behind the Accidents.

(*Sounds over voice of young businessman as ringing phone is picked up*): Hello? Hello? I'd like to call an ambulance please . . . . .

This sketch was originally broadcast in the programme *Spitting Image* made by Central Television in association with Spitting Image Productions ltd.

Medallion man by Andrea Solomons, broadcast on *Three of a Kind*

Bar. Tracey Ullman sitting at table, reading book. David Copperfield (wearing open shirt, medallion, i.d. bracelet, flares, etc.) comes and stands over her)

David: Haven't I seen you somewhere before?
Tracey: Yeah, you've been staring at me for half an hour.
David: Can I sit down, babe?
Tracey: I doubt it, in those trousers . . .
David: Oh, groovy. Yeah, what a girl!
(*Sits down in discomfort. Leans over.*)
David: So, what are you having, dream child?
Tracey: A lot of aggravation . . .
David: Hey groovy. Barman! Two martinis!
Tracey: One with ground glass in it please.
David: Hey, those pretty lips of yours could be put to much better use. How about showing me what they can do?
(*Tracey blows raspberry at him.*)
David: Yeah, nice sound. Come on now, babe. You and me. Me and you. We could work magic together.
Tracey: We could work magic?
David: Yeah.
Tracey: Well, let's start with your disappearing trick.
David: Babe. Easy now. Look into my face.
Tracey: How can I? You're sitting on it.
David: Look, all I want to do is have a nice time. We could go back to my pad, turn the dimmer switch down low, pop on a Tony Christie LP and swing, swing, swing . . .
Tracey: Oh, I'd like to see you swing.
David: Hey, hey, hey, so what do you say?
Tracey: Get stuffed.
David: Hang loose, babe. I'm the company's number one rep . . .
Tracey: Short for reptile?
David: No, you're talking to money here. You're talking to ten thou plus commission and petrol. You're talking to a Ford Sierra with

heated rear window. You babe, are talking to a circular bed and a sunken bath.

Tracey: And you are talking to a brick wall, so shove off.

(*Lenny Henry appears in a suit and tie*)

Lenny: I'm the manager, miss. Is this jerk bothering you?

Tracey: Yeah, he really is.

Lenny: O.K. mate, hop it. Out.

David: Yeah? What are you going to do about it? . . . O.K.!

(*David exits*)

Tracey: Phew, thanks. It's lucky you came over.

Lenny: (*sits in David's seat*) Yeah, it's your lucky night tonight, all right.

(*Sits down and rips off tie to reveal medallion*)

Girls on Top is reminiscent of one of the early television shows to feature women: *The Liver Birds*. The Liver Birds was set in Liverpool where Beryl and Sandra share a flat. The series was one of the most popular shows of the 1970s and was originally written by Carla Lane and Myra Taylor, though Carla Lane wrote the following one hundred episodes on her own. Carla Lane remembers that it was very easy to get the show on television, because of the newness of the idea and the ripeness of the market. She told us that she had never felt or been expected to be a mouthpiece for women, and her work has always been about 'relationships' rather than 'issues'. She enjoys writing for women because she feels they are much more honest than men. Her interest is in passions among men and women and she has a fascination for the 'breaking of bonds'. We asked her why she thought there were so few women comedy writers, and her view was that it was because women were too busy with domestic and emotional concerns that don't seem to affect men. We then asked if this criterion also applied to women comedy performers, but she felt that the main problem there was that women don't like to look unglamorous. She felt that pity was an essential ingredient in comedy, and that an audience have to feel sorry for comics. She attributed the success of Polly James (Beryl in *The Liver Birds*) to her ability to look ridiculous, and said that this was also the appeal of contemporary women comics, such as French and Saunders:

I love them. They really do appeal to me. They're very real. You can imagine them sitting in a room with a coffee having their conversations.

(Carla Lane)

214

There are of course many fringe and professional groups who construct plays through improvisation and through collective writing, where often the writer is a member of the cast. This is a particularly fruitful area of work, as each person has a say in the kind of part they play. It also helps to dissolve the idea of the writer as an 'artist in a garret', a figure who sits in creative bliss as the characters flow forth on paper. Instead the cast are encouraged to see how parts are constructed and to recognise the pressure that is on a writer to deliver the goods. In a theatre company such as the all-women group Siren, a member of the company takes on the writing whilst also acting in the plays. Tasha Fairbanks is an accomplished writer, who, also works as a writer outside the company. Such situations help to bridge the gap between writers and performers that can so often widen in rehearsal. Many writers said that their ideal working condition would be to sit in on each rehearsal and change the script to the requirements of the cast and director. Many performers also felt that this would be a perfect working situation, as they had sometimes felt worried by a script, but had no constructive outlet for their feelings. Maggie Steed spoke of the situation of working on the programme *Shine On Harvey Moon* for television, where the cast freely suggested ideas and script changes. This is not always a successful situation because just as good writers don't necessarily make good performers so good actors may not have a flair for writing. But it is always worthwhile having a situation where suggestions can be put forward. Television is notoriously unsympathetic to writers, as one constantly hears horror stories about writers not being consulted about script changes, and material going out on television which bears little resemblance to the original. There is a definite case for closer liaison between writers, directors, performers and producers.

Bryony Lavery, who has worked with women's theatre groups including Monstrous Regiment, on shows such as *Female Trouble* and *More Female Trouble* and also for the National Theatre of Brent, *Revolting Women* and Pamela Stephenson, spoke of the specific problems of being a feminist writer:

> You're pretty sure that if you say you are a feminist comic, you are going to have to prove that you're funny. To most people there is the feeling that feminism is humourless which of course is the usual fiction, like 'women talk more than men', 'women are less funny than men', and it's all part of a huge propaganda. Humour is a weapon and if we say that women are not funny, they can't use that weapon.
> (Bryony Lavery)

She is committed to writing for women:

I have a physical preference for writing for women and I have a theatrical preference for writing for good improvisors.

She has always used comedy as a form of serious expression in her work. She, like Vicky Pile, worked on *Revolting Women* and felt that it was a nice idea that required 'more time, more money and more thought'. She strongly believes that battles remain to be fought and won:

I do think women are funny but they're not paid for it at the moment. There are hilarious women in every office, in every kitchen, in every theatre in the country, and a reasonable number who could be good professional comedians.

Scottish writer Rona Munro (writer in residence at Paines Plough, the London Writers' Company) started writing sketches for *Not the Nine O'Clock News* and other television sketch shows, and realised that she wasn't suited to that style of humour. She then received a commission from the Traverse Theatre, Edinburgh, to write a play, *Fugue*, and has been writing plays for theatre, television and radio ever since. Like Bryony Lavery, she has suffered from being bracketed as someone who only writes about 'women's issues':

I'm a feminist, but I think that when people say you write about 'women's issues' they're shoving you in a little pigeon-hole which means that they'll come and look at you and assess you, with a 'I've been right-on and seen something about feminism and OK I can forget about it now' attitude instead of acknowledging that someone's writing about the preoccupations of half the human race.
(Rona Munro)

Piper's Cave, by Rona Munro
Jo meets Alisdair while she is out walking in the hills:

Jo: Are you a tramp or something?
Alisdair: What if I am?
Jo: Nothing, you just seem a bit out of the way that's all.
Alisdair: A bit out of the way for what?
Jo: Everything.
Alisdair: For a brain surgeon this might be something of a
    backwater, a nuclear physicist might find he had a few

communication problems. For a tramp it's just the job. Tramp?
What kind of label is that? Talk about snap judgements. How about
calling me a hermit, a philosopher of life, a recluse. Could you get
your tongue round that?

Jo: A recluse?

Alisdair: That's the way. Reclusive and exclusive, Alisdair MacKerral
is ex-directory. (*He drinks.*) What do you do?

Jo: I work in a chemist's.

Alisdair: Not out here you don't, unless you're selling dandruff
shampoo to the seagulls.

Rona Munro spoke of the differences in the way that male and
female writers are perceived:

> It seems to me that women are much more identified with their
> work than men are. A man can write something and people don't
> immediately start speculating about their personality or their beliefs
> or what they stand for, or even if they do, it's in a much more
> objective way, whereas people seem to demand that women
> represent their writing in a much more personal way. You're that
> much more vulnerable.

Rona Munro cited Liz Lochhead, a Scottish writer with a comedy
bias, as a major influence on her work. Currently writer in residence
at Edinburgh University, Liz Lochhead has written six plays for
theatre and five books of poetry; her work is increasingly popular in
Scotland and England. She has recently started a double act with
Elaine C. Smith (who was in the television comedy series *Naked
Video*) called Nippy Sweeties. Her most recent collection of poetry,
raps and monologues – *True Confessions & New Cliches* – shows
her particular style of written and performed observation deals with
the everyday problems of women in a humane and witty way.

True Confessions by Liz Lochhead
(*Rap*)

Wanna know anything 'bout being a woman?
Well, better just ask us.
I know her dramas, her traumas, and her fiascos
I know her sober
(but I know her better pissed)
I know her acid trips,
her abortions, and her analyst

I know the Story of her Life –
each ironic twist.

She lent me her copy of Anais Nin
and we discovered we were Sisters Under the Skin.
Oh, I know her inside out –
thanks to the sessions
of all-and-sundry, dirty-laundry
True Confessions.

Our conversations range from the Arts to Child Psychology
From World Affairs and Who Cares
To Avant-Garde Gynaecology.
I know her trouble with her nerves
and the trouble with her mate;
What she did with her brother when they were eight;
And Should-she-love-him? Should-she-leave-him?
What-were-their-Chances?;
the night she was almost tempted by lesbian advances
I know about the strange stains she found
on young Sebastian's pyjamas;
her Wild Night with that waiter
on her trip to the Bahamas;
I get the dope on each High Hope;
on her fainting spasms;
the ins-and-outs of her orgasms.
How the Pill gives her Headaches;
her cramps with the coil;
how My-Man-once-made-this-pass-at-her-at-a-party-but
She Was Too Loyal.

Oh, we spill the beans and we swill our gin
and discover that we're Sisters Under the Skin.
Oh, I know her inside out –
thanks to the sessions
of truly hellish, unembellished
True Confessions.

Jill Tweedie, journalist and author of the television sitcom *The Fainthearted Feminist* (discussed in the chapter on television) spoke of the need for women to write more comedy:

> Comedy is one of the ways of getting people to swallow bitter pills, and that's why I think it's very important.

She, like writer Sue Townsend, moved from the more solitary

area of novel-writing to adapting work for television. Townsend's *Secret Diary of Adrian Mole aged 13¾* was a massive success as a novel, a stage musical and a television series. Sue Townsend recently joined up with writer Carol Hayman to write a series for Yorkshire Television, *The Refuge*. Hopefully, their work will encourage other women writers and novelists to move into scriptwriting.

In Belfast, playwright Christina Reid did not write for public consumption until 1980, when her play *Did You Hear The One About The Irishman* won the UTV Drama Award. She followed this success with *Tea in a China Cup* (1982). Her play *Joyriders* (1985), set on a Youth Training Scheme in a former linen mill in Belfast, played to packed houses in London and Belfast in 1986. She uses comedy at the most unexpected moments in her work, maintaining the belief that humour can thrive in the most intolerable conditions. Like Charabanc Theatre Company, she felt that her writing was more concerned with the political situation around her than specifically with women, but her perception of the female relationships between friends, mothers and daughters is particularly well defined in her work:

> The Church is still very powerful here so women's roles are still very clearly defined.
> (Christina Reid)

She compared the self-referential qualities of Irish and Jewish humour, saying the best 'Irish' jokes she hears are the ones from her children – 'Join the RUC and come home to a real fire.' Like Rona Munro, Christina Reid does not write comedies as such, but it is through humour that she makes some of her most important points, and it is because of the humour that her moments of poignancy are so powerful.

Victoria Wood is a writer/performer who combines a traditional stand-up style with a more sustained comedy of recognition in her character work. The conciseness of her writing is a great strength. She conjures up a totally unexpected image from a monologue or sketch which employs an ostensibly mundane style. She uses 'type' to arrest the viewers' attention and to familiarise them with the source, and then she disrupts the pattern with unpredictable and often surreal images. She takes an everyday situation and then takes it one step beyond. Victoria Wood's cv is impressive. Best known for her series *Victoria Wood as Seen on TV*, she has worked extensively in other media. Her stage play *Talent* (1978) won the Plays and Players and Evening Standard awards for most promising playwright, and was televised in 1978. She has also won a Pye

Colour TV Award and an award from the Film and Television Festival of New York. Her sequel to *Talent* was *Nearly a Happy Ending* (1980) and her stage musical *Good Fun* was premiered at the Crucible Theatre, Sheffield. Her third television play *Happy Since I Met You* was shown in 1981 and was followed by the television series *Wood and Walters*. She has a one-woman show which she recently toured, and she won two BAFTA Awards, for best Light Entertainment programme and best performer for *Victoria Wood as Seen on TV*. She has also written a screenplay *The Natural Order* and two books *Lucky Bag – The Victoria Wood Songbook* (1984) and *Up to You, Porky* (1986), a collection of sketches and monologues. She wrote her first sketch whilst in a revue at the Bush Theatre, London, *In at the Death*. In the cast were Snoo Wilson, Ken Campbell and Julie Walters. She now writes all the scripts and the music for her theatre and television shows. She likes to maintain as much control as possible over her work and the way it is presented:

> That at least makes you responsible, and if it's bad then I'll still stand by it . . . but I do like to be in charge.

She has never felt under any pressure to change what she writes:

> I've just done what I wanted. Nobody's ever wanted me to do anything different. The only pressure I've ever felt was about what I should wear. Nobody's ever tried to change the material.

Of course there is now a tremendous pressure on her to make her next piece of work as good if not better than the last. But the pressure is not because she's a woman. It would be the same for any comedy performer of her stature. Her style is distinctive, it is about ordinary people and the ordinary things that happen to them, but it is written wtih an extraordinary perception of irony and the comic turn of phrase. Her humour often looks at the specific comedy that comes through the language and accents of the north of England.

> It's a very nice place to come from for the language, for the way you can phrase things and for those particular women you might write for, like Pat Routledge; Alan Bennett writes in the same way. I just love the way people talk . . . the northern way of expressing yourself is different to anywhere else, and it's just nice to play with that.

She avoided watching much television for a long time in case she was influenced by it. She is an original, although similarities between her work and that of Alan Bennett have been commented on:

Writers such as J.B. Priestley, Alan Bennett and Victoria Wood are writing of what they know at first hand: the opinionated expression of moral and social indignation. It's the Pharisaical tract: one is not as other men are. When it is so acutely observed, it is *very* funny.
(Patricia Routledge)

We asked Victoria Wood why she wrote mainly for women in her television series:

I think I just find it easier to write women's parts. That's why there are so many men writers and so many more parts for men, because they find it easier, and I find it easier to write for women. I'm trying to do a few more men this time to even it up a bit, and also to give me a few ideas. But it's also a natural thing. If you think of a character it tends to be a woman. I think if I wrote a lot of men they'd tend to fall into 'Businessman' 'Carpet Salesman' and I'd hate to do that.

In saying this she illustrates how the male-female imbalance of comedy is perpetuated. She is also an example of how this particular status quo can be disrupted.

Kitty: One by Victoria Wood

(Kitty is about fifty-three, from Manchester and proud of it. She speaks as she finds and knows what's what. She is sitting in a small bare studio, on a hard chair. She isn't nervous.)

Kitty: Good evening. My name's Kitty. I've had a boob off and I can't stomach whelks so that's me for you. I don't know why I've been asked to interrupt your viewing like this, but I'm apparently something of a celebrity since I walked the Pennine Way in slingbacks in an attempt to publicise Mental Health. They've asked me to talk about aspects of life in general, nuclear war, peg-bags . . .

I wasn't going to come today, actually. I'm not a fan of the modern railway system. I strongly object to paying twenty-seven pounds fifty to walk the length and breadth of the train with a sausage in a plastic box. But they offered me a chopper from Cheadle so here I am.

I'm going to start with the body – you see I don't mince words. Time and again I'm poked in the street by complete acquaintances – Kitty, they say to me, how do you keep so young, do you perhaps inject yourself with a solution deriving from the placenta of female gibbons? Well, no, I say, I don't, as it happens. I'm blessed with a robust constitution, my father's mother ran her own abbatoir, and I've only had the need of hospitalisation once – that's when I was concussed by an electric potato peeler at the Ideal Home Exhibition.

No, the secret of my youthful appearance is simply – mashed swede. As a face-mask, as a night cap, and in an emergency, as a draught-excluder. I do have to be careful about my health, because I have a grumbling ovary which once flared up in the middle of *The Gondoliers*. My three rules for a long life are regular exercise, hobbies and complete avoidance of midget gems.

I'm not one for dance classes, feeling if God had wanted us to wear leotards he would have painted us purple. I have a system of elastic hoops dangling from the knob of my cistern cupboard. It's just a little thing I knocked up from some old knicker waistbands. I string up before breakfast and I can exert myself to Victor Sylvester till the cows come home.

There's also a rumour going round our block that I play golf. Let me scotch it. I do have what seems to be a golf-bag on my telephone table but it's actually a pyjama-case made by a friend who has trouble with her nerves in Buckinghamshire.

Well, I can't stop chatting, much as I'd like to – my maisonette backs onto a cake factory, so I'm dusting my knick-knacks all the day long.

And I shall wait to see myself before I do any more. Fortunately, I've just had my TV mended. I say mended – a shifty young man in plimsolls waggled my aerial and wolfed my Gipsy Creams, but that's the comprehensive system for you.

I must go, I'm having tea with the boys in flat five. They're a lovely couple of young men, and what they don't know about Mikhail Barishnikov is nobody's business. So I'd better wrap up this little gift I've got them. It's a gravy boat in the shape of Tony Hancock –they'll be thrilled.

(*She peers round the studio.*)

Now, who had hold of my showerproof? It's irreplaceable, you know, being in tangerine poplin, which apparently there's no call for . . .

(*She gets up and walks past the camera.*)

There's a mauve pedestal mat of mine, too.

Victoria Wood has achieved the popular appeal that many people would not normally credit to a woman. She shows that there need be no difference in appeal of male and female writing, shows that women can achieve total control over their work, and that they can become top comedy writers and performers. Apart from the obviously high standard of her work, we cannot say why it is that Victoria Wood has reached the position she is in. By remaining unassociated with other contemporary movements in comedy, she has created her own style and form, and it is her refusal to compromise as well as her ability, that has led people to place their professional trust in her. She is one of the country's top comedians, She has control, she has popular appeal, but most of all she is very funny. What better role model can there be?

WHO OR WHAT MAKES YOU LAUGH?

Woody Allen, Alan Bennett, Victoria Wood, Les Dawson, Patricia Routledge, Beryl Reid, Jonathan Miller, *La Cage Aux Folles, The Producers*, re-runs of *Bewitched, Lucy, Bilko, Cheers*, Robert Lindsay in *Me and My Girl, The Young Ones*, Billy Connolly, Nichols and May, Python and Fawlty, Jewish people when they see me, my mother, John Mortimer and Clive James, Linda Agran, Mr Rosenthal senior and junior, jokes, Joyce Grenfell, Alistair Sim, Denis Healey, and Willy Whitelaw being interviewed outside with the wind blowing, Dorothy Parker and Neil Simon. For a Jewish girl, I've got a catholic taste.
(Maureen Lipman, actor/writer)

Leonard Rossiter, Tony Hancock, Eric Morecambe, Gene Wilder, Walter Matthau, Lily Tomlin, Judy Holliday, Lots!
(Frances de la Tour, actor)

Woody Allen, *Cheers, Taxi*, things with pace that don't hang around.
(Vicky Pile, scriptwriter)

Victoria Wood is excellent. And Julie Walters. She's brilliant.
(Faith Brown, impressionist)

Python, Laurel and Hardy, Joyce Grenfell, Margaret Rutherford, Alistair Sim, Alec Guinness, *Animal House*, Steve Martin, Robin Williams, Alexei Sayle, a combination of the intellectual and very silly, Ealing films, *Soap, The Mary Tyler Moore Show, Bewitched, Bilko* . . .
(Lise Mayer, scriptwriter)

Whatever touches you in your life, locally.
(Denise Coffey, actor/writer/director)

I love filth.
(Su Pollard, comedian)

Watching Joan Rivers is like watching spiders copulate.
(Germaine Greer, writer)

Mike Nichols and Elaine May, Jaques Tati, Charles Chaplin, Lily Tomlin, and Bette Midler.
(Eleanor Bron, actor/writer)

Recognition and familiarity. Lily Tomlin, Rita Rudner, Julia McKenzie, Denise Coffey.
(Jennie Campbell, radio producer)

We make each other laugh. We're like a mutual masturbation society.
(Charabanc Theatre Company)

Victoria Wood – I think she's hysterical.
(Judith Jacobs, actor)

George Cole.
(Elsie Waters, actor)

Pat Routledge makes me laugh whatever she does.
(Miriam Margolyes, actor)

Comedy is intangible. I don't know why people laugh.
(Beryl Reid, actor)

Victoria Wood, Alexei Sayle.
(Emma Thompson, actor)

Victoria Wood is marvellous, and Julie Walters. They're so accurate.
(June Whitfield, actor)

I love Victoria Wood. I think she's marvellous. She just hits it each time.
(Nerys Hughes, actor)

My mammy.
(Marie Jones, Charabanc Theatre Company)

My favourite comedy performer would have to be Victoria Wood. The work she does is truly funny and it isn't anything to do with the political or social, class, race, or sects.
(Helen Atkinson Wood, actor)

Arthur Marshall.
(Victoria Wood, writer/performer)

Television

... and the taxi driver said, 'You're Kitty aren't you?' and I was in heavy disguise in my specs and winter hat, and I said 'Yes, I'm afraid so' and he said 'what are you afraid of? My wife laughs at that even when it's not on.'
(Patricia Routledge)

Television is a monster among media: it dominates despite its relative youth. In 1985, 18,715,937 licences were sold (*BBC Handbook*, 1985) and most people spend more of their time watching television than they do listening to radio or frequenting cinemas, theatres or cabarets. For many performers, too, television dominates the employment horizon and securing regular television work is an important goal. In the nineteenth century live work was the only option for comic performers, but with technological invention and expansion, many performers want and expect to work in various, if not all, media. The patterns of work among the women we interviewed certainly reflect this tendency. Even if they are particularly skilled in, and suited to, say, live performance, television work is highly valued because it offers national exposure, high salaries and the stamp of success. These attractions outweigh the fact that some television work is of poor quality and allows performers little control over the product.

In 1985, 7 per cent of the BBC's output was Light Entertainment (BBC publicity office). On average about thirty hours a week are taken up with Light Entertainment and music on ITV and Channel 4. This is just over 20 per cent of the total number of hours for all programmes (Independent Broadcasting Authority information office). Although the IBA figures cover quizzes and chat shows, variety and comedy nevertheless fill a significant proportion of the television schedules. You are more likely to have seen the women discussed in this book on television than in any other medium. The actual ratio of women to men in television is, however, relatively small. As the European Broadcasting Union stated in their Review of July 1986:

> Women appear distinctly less often, are on screen for a shorter time, have less opportunity to say anything, are interrupted more often when speaking and their outward appearance plays a disproportionate role.

Fair representation of women is not simply a question of numbers. The roles which women in light entertainment are expected to play are also significant. Both branches of the department – variety and situation comedy – are often accused of presenting women as stereotypes. Maureen Lipman described the trends in sketch shows: 'A token female usually exists in sketch shows for glamour or "old-bagness" ' and Eleanor Bron said about situation comedy:

> Women are limited in their comedy: they have to be grotesque or flighty, their parts are always directly to do with being a woman. In *Last of the Summer Wine* the men are characters but the women are either sex objects or harridans.

Stereotyping is also highlighted and analysed by critics of situation comedy. In their article on *The Gender Game* (BFI dossier *Television Sitcom*) Andy Medhurst and Lucy Tuck argue that women in situation comedy are stereotyped as 'the dragon-like mother-in-law' or 'obliging busty secretary'.

Having isolated stereotypes Tuck and Medhurst admit that stereotyping is necessary:

> Sitcom cannot function without stereotypes. In a space as brief as a thirty-minute sitcom, immediacy is imperative, and to find a character immediately funny, that character must be a recognizable type, a representative embodiment of a set of ideas or a manifestation of a cliché.

Su Pollard, who plays Peggy in the highly successful sitcom *Hi-de-Hi* agrees, and believes that men are just as stereotyped as women:

> Women say they're stereotyped in comedy, but so are men. You're all stereotyped in a way. Any part you play, there is somebody in the world like that.

While Su Pollard perceives stereotyping as essential to the success of the sitcom, performer Sheila Steafel is less enthusiastic:

> I think that TV light entertainment and sitcom are very two-

227

dimensional. You know what's expected, you know more or less how many episodes and you know they're bound to be cardboard people.

As with the stand-up comic, the question of stereotypes in television is everpresent and complex. Some believe they are insidious, some necessary; some believe that men are equal victims of stereotypes, others that women are in fact treated differently: given less significant and more limited roles. In terms of women's position in society, does television help to maintain a dominant ideology which prevents women from being depicted as progressive, subversive, and innovative? This chapter addresses itself to these questions.

Situation comedy and variety, though distinct, have a lot in common and shared roots. Variety is a natural television extension of live performance. It has historical links with variety and revue and their antecedent, music hall. The situation comedy developed from variety and radio sketches, which centred around constructed characters, rather than individual personalities, as the music hall had done. Tom Sloan, in a BBC lunchtime lecture, spoke of the influence of 1930s American comedy:

> . . . it consisted of a resident cast, headed always by a well known entertainer, who played farcical comedy, in which recognisable characters like the next-door neighbour, the country philosopher, the newly married couple, the screwball comedienne and, in less complicated times, the white folks' idea of the comedy coloured servant – all played their part.

The war and the US Forces Network brought the genre to British listeners and it slowly developed from the deliberate theatricality of the variety sketch to longer pieces which, though they were still clearly joke-orientated, nevertheless introduced a greater degree of realism.

The situation comedy is one of the few forms to have been created by television, and Terry Lovell, in 'A Genre of Social Disruption' (in BFI dossier *Television Sitcom*) describes it as 'a celebration of television'. Because of the three-dimensional naturalistic possibilities of the medium, the situation comedy purports to present a a greater degree of 'reality' than the sketch or monologue can: it has a recognizable setting, with more or less rounded characters and a storyline. Tony Hancock was an early and fervent proponent of realism in television comedy. He and his scriptwriters, Galton and Simpson, achieved this end by creating a rounder character than the sketch could encompass and developing a single theme rather than a series of gags. Hancock's thirst for credibility led him to dispense with start-stop recordings and to choose 'straight' actors rather than comedians for the supporting roles.

Hancock may have been clear about what he meant by 'realism' but the term cannot generally be used without clarification. A sitcom may be 'realistic' in that the front room of its set can be like the front room in which our television sits, or a front room we recognize; the characters can have the appearance, and even characteristics of people we know, but this does not mean that the result is 'realistic'. Moreover, the situation comedy may achieve a degree of realism in the milieux it presents while omitting many groups of people and situations from its repertoire of potential scenarios.

Despite the realistic trappings, situation comedy is as prone to ideological limitations as any other genre. The world it presents is neither objective nor arbitrary: writers, producers and programme controllers choose certain milieux, certain characters and story lines. Political and moral parameters are set and the sitcom can become artificial and indeed less relevant than the 'artificial' form of the sketch. John Lloyd, producer of *Not the Nine O'Clock News* and *Spitting Image* explained, in an interview in *Television Today* (24.1.80):

> Comedy is dealing with truth . . . Britain is a messy, confused place at the moment and that is not generally reflected in what we see in much of television situation comedy. Sitcom generally is a monster. It doesn't relate to the world as I see it.

If the sitcom, in the guise of realism, presents an unreal world, how is this world created and how does it function? Francis Wheen in his book *Television*:

> For most of their history, sitcoms have been governed by one rule: the central element is the family. It can have quirks or complications, but it must be a family. A glance at the titles of British and American sitcoms is enough to make the point – *My Wife next Door, I married a Bachelor, Bachelor Father, Father Dear Father, Not in Front of the Children, Mother makes Three, My Good Woman, Bless this House* . . . it can be extended forever.

As traditional families have a parent of each sex, it is undeniable that family situation comedies have offered some fine opportunities for women, and Pauline Collins, Wendy Craig, Diana Coupland, Peggy Mount, June Whitfield and Yootha Joyce, among others, are as significant as their male counterparts. The sitcom has not entirely failed to reflect social change: *Miss Jones and Son* was about an unmarried mother, *Leaving* about a divorced couple entering new relationships, *Solo* about a woman's life alone after the break-up of a serious relationship and *Butterflies* about a married woman contemplating having an affair. These departures into the unconventional are relatively rare, however, and are only risked once the social change in question (divorce, single parenthood, etc.) has been fairly widely accepted. The family dominates and the continual choice of the family as subject matter has a normative effect. It's true that a significant proportion of the population does live in a family unit but family sitcoms suggest that this is the only way that life is lived, rather than being one of many social possibilities.

The depiction of gay or communal households and women living alone, or with other women is relatively rare; lesbians seem still to be totally taboo in situation comedy. The family subject dictates that most women's roles are as wives and mothers, which is not unhealthy in itself, and it could be implied that men are depicted as husbands and fathers. The problem is that women are seen only in these roles and when they are depicted outside the family unit their priority and concern is still their relationship to the potential family unit (as in *Solo*). Men have a wider variety of scenarios, in many of which they are portrayed as independent and unaware of women (hardly surprising, as there are few of them around). Many exclusively male situations have provided subject matter: *Dad's Army*, *Mess Mates* (about a cargo ship), *Firecrackers* (an East End Fire Brigade), *The Dustbinmen*, *Get Some In* (RAF National Servicemen) are just a few of the titles. It's arguable that women have traditionally functioned less in social groups outside the home, but as women increasingly break into new areas of work, we must hope that situation comedy will reflect this trend. Moreover, there are many female situations which have not been used and which have as much potential humour as or any of the male-dominated series.

A few sitcoms which have largely featured women have provided an exception to this general rule. Set in a sewing workshop in the East End, the three series of *The Rag Trade* (1961/62), directed by Dennis Main Wilson, had a very strong cast with many female actors: Esma Cannon, Judy Carne, Sheila Hancock, Miriam Karlin, Toni Palmer, and Barbara Windsor. Sheila Hancock spoke about some of the reasons for the series' success:

> *The Rag Trade* was probably the first time that people had
> genuinely laughed at women en masse; even though we were
> caricatures, at least people got very amused by women. There

Wendy Craig in *Butterflies.*
© BBC Enterprises 1983

were a lot of scenes with us girls chatting among ourselves and maybe the women in the audience identified with that. Men have no idea how women chat together, and all these quite risky jokes we used to have between ourselves, and the sending up of the men and the conning of the men that went on in *The Rag Trade* . . . . maybe women in factories and sewing shops all over the country thought 'Oh God, at last someone's showing that women actually fight back!'

This setting and ambiance were enhanced by the skill of the cast:

It was an extraordinary group of people. Miriam (Karlin) was very strong, and there was this wonderful woman called Esma Cannon who was physically a wonderful comic. She could do all sorts of things with her body, 'little Lil', she was. It had catchphrases that caught on. It was a very good team.
(Sheila Hancock)

The Rag Trade appears to have offered women a key opportunity to be grotesque and funny. Physical beauty was not a priority. This

231

The Rag Trade (l. to r.) Miriam Karlin, Esma Cannon, Rita Smythe, Toni Palmer, Peter Jones, Reg Varney, Barbara Windsor, Anne Beech, Judy Carne, Sheila Hancock. © BBC Enterprises 1961

liberation was reminiscent of Joan Littlewood's approach to female characterisation at the Theatre Royal, Stratford East, and Sheila Hancock equated the two;

> *The Rag Trade* was a bit like that (Stratford East) in as much as we weren't the pretty birds, we were grotesque if you like. I was grotesquely pretty but I sent it up. I certainly wasn't aware of the feminist movement at that stage, but even then I had my tongue very firmly planted in my cheek.

Barbara Windsor felt, in contrast, that even in an innovative series such as *The Rag Trade*, the stereotyping was maintained:

> So I went to the producer, Dennis Main Wilson, and I said to him, ' 'Ere you', 'cos we wanted to work, and all we did was chew gum and go 'Sshh, here comes Mr. Fenner.' So I went and told him. I said, 'You don't need me. You're paying me 40 quid for this show, and I don't know why, you might as well get anyone to do it.' He said, 'No I can't,' he said. 'Do you know, Barbara,' he said, 'whenever I put the camera on any of you girls, you're always doing the right thing.' So then Judy [Carne] said

'Oh, I've had enough, I'm going off to America,' he said, 'Well, you should both go to America,' he said, 'You're too attractive to be funny.' So we said 'What?' and he said 'In this country you've got to look like Hattie Jacques, Irene Handl or Thora Hird.' And he was right. Because when I looked they'd made me look stupid. They made you wear your hair all over the place. And when I see some of the *Carry Ons* I go mental. You could never be just yourself and be funny . . . whereas if you go to America with the *I Love Lucy* and then later with Goldie Hawn, you can. And in the *Carry On* films, Gerald (Thomas, director) said that he could only have one attractive girl with lines, and even then, she had to be 'laid back'. Although I was the girl with 'all that' they always had another one.

The Liver Birds (1969-77) is one of the other rare but excellent sitcoms in which the central figures and central relationships are female. Sandra (Nerys Hughes) shares a flat with Beryl (Polly James) and later with Carol (Elizabeth Estenson). We asked Nerys Hughes the reasons for its success:

Reality, identity and very good writing.

The Liver Birds
The flat – the living-room

(Sandra is sitting on the sofa eating a salad. Carol, in a chair, is just playing around with her meal, which is steak and chips. Her face is covered in thick cream.)

Sandra: You were lucky not to lose your job, Carol.
Carol: I wouldn't care if I did.
Sandra: But that's not the right attitude. Just because you've met somebody you care about you can't stop caring about everything else.
Carol: It's only a biscuit factory – I mean, it's not exactly going to get me in to 'The Woman of the Year' class, is it?
Sandra: It's money, Carol, it's that little brown envelope every Friday.
Carol: Yes, and it's them little brown biscuits every Monday, Tuesday, Wednesday and Thursday.
Sandra: Well at least eat your meal.
Carol: I don't feel like it.
Sandra: Oh now, come on – it's your favourite – cow and chips.
Carol: I'll have it in a butty tomorrow. He takes lovely photographs though, doesn't he – Leonard. There was this blackbird in the park – it was tugging a worm out of the grass.

Polly James and **Nerys Hughes** in *The Liver Birds*: *Anybody here seen thingy?* © BBC Enterprises 1973

Sandra: Ooh, poor little thing.

Carol: They're amazing things them worms, you know. They stretch to about . . . (*holding out her hands*)

Sandra: All right, Carol – I *do* know about the agonising struggle between bird and worm.

Carol: And this little wild flower – he got right down on his stomach to get a picture of it.

Sandra: He's a lovely, artistic, creative man – but he's not worth starving for. Now *eat*.

(from *Oh the Shame of it* by Carla Lane in *Television Comedy Scripts*)

Carla Lane, who wrote *The Liver Birds*, elucidated:

It was the first time that flat-sharing had been written about and the series contrasted the posh well-brought-up girl and the down-to-earth street-wise girl. There was conflict, but in a gentle way.

She felt that when she began the series it was fairly average, but as the characters developed, it became a more poignant and serious. Many of the women to whom we spoke cited *The Liver Birds* as an influence or a favourite programme. Its appeal was widespread, as the semi-emancipated woman – 'free but not free' (Nerys Hughes) – proved a good subject to draw in a post 1960s audience, many of whom were preoccupied with the same kinds of problems as Sandra and Beryl.

The Liver Birds was refreshing because the female relationship at its centre was credible and complex. This saved it from 'cardboard' stereotypes. The scenario – two girls sharing a flat – could be described as stereotypical, but the accurate observation made it relevant and individual. Judy Dench in *A Fine Romance* and Jan Francis in *Just Good Friends* have achieved the same veracity. This is the kind of emotional realism that Hancock sought and it is this, rather than a naturalistic setting, that is the secret of the sitcom's believability. *Fawlty Towers*, for all its ludicrous behavioural trappings, is closely based on experience. The character of Basil Fawlty is based on a Torquay hotel owner but his emotional depth is drawn from the preoccupations of the series' writers, Connie Booth and John Cleese. John Cleese in *From Fringe to Flying Circus*:

> Connie and I have always had a thing about suppressed rage – people who can't express their rage properly, which neither of us can – we always find it very funny to see people getting really steamed up and not being able to 'blast'. That was part of it, and the other part was, there was a certain amount of me in him, and a certain amount of my father. And I suppose, with the suppressed anger, a certain amount of Connie, too.

Fawlty Towers by John Cleese and Connie Booth

Sybil reacts to the disastrous building work on Fawlty Towers, wrought by the unreliable but cheap Mr. O'Reilly, favoured by Basil instead of Sybil's choice of builder, Mr. Stubbs:

Sybil: I am going to make you regret this for the rest of your life, Basil.
(*Basil nods.*)
Basil: Fair enough, I suppose. But I think Stubbs is *partly* . . .
Sybil: (*screaming*) Basil!!!!
(*Basil leaps in the air, lands and withdraws a couple of paces*)
Basil: . . . Yes, dear?
Sybil: Don't you *dare*!!! Don't you dare give me any more of those . . . pathetic lies!!
Basil: Oh! Right.

Prunella Scales in *Fawlty Towers*. © BBC Enterprises 1975

Sybil: What do you *take* me for?!! Did you really think I could believe this shambles was the work of professional builders, people who do this for a *living*?
(*Basil looks at the work*)
Basil: No, not really, no.
Sybil: Why did I *trust* you, Basil?! *Why* did I let you make the arrangements?! I could have seen what was going to happen. *Why* did I *do* it?!
Basil: . . . Well, we all make mistakes, dear.
(*Sybil runs to the reception desk*)
Sybil: I am *sick to death* of you!!! You never learn, do you?! You *never, ever, learn*!!!
(*She picks up the cash box*)

In the lobby
(*Basil is backing off. Sybil pursues him*)

Sybil: We've used O'Reilly three times this year and each time it's been a *fiasco*!! That wall out there is *still* not done!! You got him in to change a washer in November and we didn't have any running water for *two days*!!

Basil: (*reasonably*) Well, he's not really a plumber, dear.
Sybil: Well, *why* did you *hire* him?!
(*Basil chews this over*)
Sybil: . . . Because he's *cheap*!
Basil: Oh, I wouldn't call him cheap, Sybil.
Sybil: Well . . . what *would* you call him?
Basil: (*weighing his words*) Cheap . . . ish.
Sybil: And the reason he's cheap is he's no bloody good!
Basil: Oh, Sybil, you do exaggerate. I mean, he's not *brilliant* . . .
Sybil: Not brilliant!?!?!?
Sybil: He belongs in a *zoo*!!!
(from *The Builders* in *Fawlty Towers* by John Cleese and Connie
  Booth)

Maureen Lipman has similar theories about emotional motivation:

What I've realised over the writing and acting years is that I'm
largely fuelled by anger – maybe that's what's funny.

Felicity Kendall and Penelope Keith in *The Good Life*, Frances de
la Tour in *Rising Damp*, Wendy Craig in *Not in Front of the
Children* all demonstrate that emotional credibility and identification are the keys to success.
Su Pollard, who plays Peggy in the much-loved series *Hi-de-Hi*
explains:

I appeal to the underdog. I appeal to the hopelessness in people.
We've all got that feeling of 'Oh look at this – I'm never going to
get through'. They can identify with the feeling that she's been
knocked back so many times but she's still going to have a go.
They like her because she's potty but she's still got a good heart.
I've got about thirty yellowcoats at home that people have made
and sent to me. It's frightening in one way, when you portray a
character that people can get inside when they're watching
because of course they think that she does exist. There are
thousands of Peggys about, if the truth be known. I think that's
why the programme is such a success – because they're such
believable characters.

The key is recognition. Maureen Lipman:

If the characters are sharply defined, well written and real
enough, almost no 'sit' needs to happen, i.e. *Porridge*, *Steptoe* to
make 'com': whatever the character does should be so 'in
character' that it makes us laugh out of recognition.

237

The Good Life (l. to r.) Penelope Keith (Margo), Richard Briers (Tom), Paul Eddington (Jerry) and Felicity Kendal (Barbara). © BBC Enterprises 1977

The Good Life

Margo: No, I won't 'Come on'! You make such a virtue of seeing the funny side of things. Well it isn't a virtue when it's me you keep seeing the funny side of.

Tom: But Margo. That's what Margos are for.

Margo: Well I'm sick of it! (*She stands up angrily*). And if you are set on playing the red-nosed comedian for the rest of your life, I suggest you find yourself another stooge!

Tom: But Margo, you're the best in the business.

Margo: Oh shut up!

(*Margo flounces out. Tom is highly amused but Barbara looks at him, thinking he has gone too far*)

(from *The Wind Break War* by John Esmonde and Bob Larbey in *Television Comedy Scripts*)

Su Pollard as Peggy in *Hi-de-Hi* © BBC Enterprises

This recognition is essential, and it has to be accepted that while Peggy appeals to a common feeling of hopelessness in people, other sitcoms relate to the characters and predicaments of a more specific social situation and cannot possibly be to everyone's personal taste. This is partly why the quality of sitcom is so often hotly disputed. Denise Coffey:

> For a lot of people who are comfortable and middle-aged it's a hoot to see Terry and June.

Although it is unhealthy if women are always portrayed as meek, stupid underdogs, it has to be accepted that at times women are as prone to meekness and folly as men. The desire to portray women as permanent towers of strength and resolve is no closer to reality than portraying them as permanent underdogs. Moreover, such idealisation is not a source of humour. Jan Ravens talked about a Royal Court benefit show in which many women wanted to break the comic stereotypes of the meek woman. But total role reversal cannot work:

> I heard an interview with one of the actors involved and she said 'It was great because we were funny and we were funny because we were strong.' I thought, 'well, how can you possibly be funny if you're strong?' It just doesn't go with any kind of role of comedy that I know. How can someone be strong and efficient and brave and courageous, how can that person be funny? The funny person is the one that gets it wrong, the pompous one, the pretentious one, not the person who's always right and brave and strong.

Human vulnerability is a strong source of humour. Women's vulnerability is sometimes exacerbated by social conditions and sexist treatment. Can it be that comedy confuses reality and prejudice, so that the natural characteristic of being vulnerable some of the time colludes with the preoccupation that women are vulnerable all of the time, and so a stereotype is formed? The problem arises not solely from the treatment of character but from the nature of the genre. Humour, as we have suggested, is often created out of pretension. For the humour to be maintained characters can never achieve their ideals, and are always reminded of what they really are. Writer Barry Took:

> All successful comedies really have some trap in which people must exist – like marriage. [The perfect sitcom] is a little enclosed world where you have to live by rules.
> (from *Television* by Francis Wheen)

Such limited scenarios can be seen as a contributory factor to the limitations of the genre but attempts to write less conventionally do not always succeed. Andy Medhurst and Lucy Tuck on Carla Lane's *Solo*:

> Gemma gets what she wants, and the satisfying of female desire breaks out of the most fundamental sitcom conventions because it invalidates such a vast area of the traditional sources of humour (if women start being competent, what are men going to laugh at?).
> (*The Gender Game* in BFI dossier *Television Sitcom*)

Where comedy brings out positive qualities and shows people trying to change and equivocate, it tends to be gentler and to border on drama. But when it portrays sociological monsters who are totally entrenched in their prejudices, the humour is broad and, ironically, so is the popularity. Alf Garnett in *'Til Death Us Do Part* is a prime example. Johnny Speight, who wrote the series:

> I personally despised, hated, loathed him for a long, long time . . .
> The funny thing was, though, that as I wrote him and Warren
> (Mitchell) performed him, we grew to love him.
> (from *Television* by Francis Wheen)

It has to be accepted that we do not necessarily laugh at political ideals. Johnny Speight's attempt at satirising a racist and reactionary partially failed because the audience loved him precisely for his fascist views. Some producers nevertheless believe in the power of sitcom to broach political questions. Television producer Norman Lear took *'Til Death Us Do Part* and *Steptoe and Son* to America and also produced *Mary Hartman, Mary Hartman*, *All That Glitters* and *Soap*, 'three of the most satirical, sexy and provocative comedy shows the US have ever seen' (*Guardian*). In the MacTaggart Lecture at the Edinburgh International Television Festival in 1979 he said that subjects which had previously been taboo in situation comedy must be broached. Without a perspective on reality, sitcom would be reduced to mindless escapism:

> Throughout the 50s and 60s American television was surfeited
> with a steady diet of television comedies, dozens upon dozens of
> them, in which the most serious problem was – the roast ruined
> and the boss was coming to dinner – or mother had dented the
> fender and the kids had to keep the father from finding out.
> Fifteen or twenty hours a week of that kind of programming was,
> in my opinion, and by omission, shouting the loudest message in
> the world. It was saying to the country: you have no race
> problems; there is no economic concern in the nation; we are not
> in trouble in Vietnam; everyone does have an equal crack at
> medical attention; there are no problems with the poor and
> elderly or the uneducated – and all mothers and fathers and
> children live in absolute harmony – the loudest noise in the house
> being the popping and cracking of the breakfast cereal in the
> morning.

Women and women's issues are affected by this cultural taboo, and so are groups which include racial minorities. *No Problem* is one of the few sitcoms, along with *Love Thy Neighbour*, *The Fosters* and *Tandoori Nights*, to be centred around a black or Asian cast. It was created by members of Black Theatre Co-operative, a theatre company whose aim is to present work of interest to the black community. Judith Jacobs, who has been with BTC since 1981 and played Sensimilia in *No Problem*, explained the work process by which the series was written:

Humphrey Barclay, who's head of comedy at London Weekend, approached us because he'd seen our work before and wanted us to devise our own comedy. So we had a four-week workshop period where eight actors from the company were chosen. *No Problem* was one of a series of ideas we thought of, it was the one the actors felt happiest with. It was actually Shope Shodeinde's idea we chose.

The collective, improvised theatre approach brought a greater democracy to the idea and this was obviously maintained through to production. Judith Jacobs:

I think the fact we had black actors devising it and not writers coming in who knew nothing about black people and saying 'This is how it should be' was important. We devised it, we made a conscious effort to make it young, British black people living now, here, and to make it comedy. So, taking a real-life situation and making it slightly different, like Bellamy living in the garden. You know people who love animals a lot, and if they just went a little bit further they might move out into the garden. And Toshiba – everyone lives with their brothers who play music day in day out – that's acceptable. My sister who was cleaning the house, she's acceptable. Shope's character, Terri, the model whose biggest thing was advertising her fingernails – we know people like that. There may not be a lot of people like that, but they are there. And then you had my character of Sensimilia who was a motorbike mechanic, which was very different because a lot of people think, 'Oh, black girls don't ride motorbikes.' Bullshit!

It is clear from previous comments, and from the work process and results of *No Problem*, that situation comedy imaginatively draws on 'type'. *No Problem* was a positive departure because Black Theatre Co-operative members devised and chose the characters they wished to present, rather than having to accept a racist stereotype created by a hierarchy out of touch with the black community. The argument holds for women's representation on television. They must be allowed opportunities to develop, expand and to have control over their work, but this control is not easily achieved. Sheila Hancock described the impossible series of events which resulted from her own attempt to develop her public image. She had appeared in many BBC sitcoms such as *The Rag Trade* and *Bedsit Girl*, and she wanted a change:

As I got a bit older, I asked them if I could do something a little more demanding, (and certainly after having read *The Female*

Judith Jacobs and her daughter Aisha

Eunuch, my whole attitude changed greatly). I did a show called *Simply Sheila* (1968) which was a bit more sophisticated in that I used some revue material which had been used in the theatre, which was a bit more advanced to what was being done then on the telly in the field of light entertainment and revue. It was not a bad success considering it was on late at night on BBC2.

Sheila Hancock
This lady's a genius, I think. She's an intuitive actress. There's no way she could time a laugh wrong. She was a brilliant technical actress and she also had a built-in director's kit going on in her brain as well. (Dennis Main Wilson)

Her next project, realised only after a good deal of negotiation, was *Now Seriously it's Sheila Hancock* (1972) which she worked on with Barry Took. She approached a different subject each week, centring the discussion on an anchor interview with guests who included John Mortimer, Peter Hall, Germaine Greer and Kenneth Allsop:

> It was a very imaginative breakthrough programme and the mail from it was huge, particularly from women.
> (Sheila Hancock)

Like *Simply Sheila*, it had respectable figures but the audience response was not echoed by those at the top:

> All the way through, the people at the BBC, and some of them are still there, were appalled because I was breaking my image – being lovely, lovable, tizzy Sheila, and there was one particularly dreadful row about a sketch I'd done in a revue called *Vacancy* by a bloke called Ken Hoare, and it was about prejudice. There was this mad landlady who was just prejudiced about everything, absolutely everything. She was like a witch, and I wanted to do this and they said 'No' and I said 'What do you mean, no?' and they said 'No really, that is going too far, it's too unpleasant, it'll break your image' and I said 'I'm doing it' and I went to the head of BBC2 and I eventually went to the Controller and they said 'All right, you can do it, but if when we see it we don't like it, it won't be broadcast', and they saw it and they let it through. But I never again worked for the BBC Light Entertainment department. They were doing it, they thought, for my good; they thought I was good at doing funny ladies and little tizzy things. Like most men in authority they were so out of touch with what was happening to women in the rest of the world, they didn't understand. I think, sincerely, they thought I'd gone a bit strange. They really thought I'd gone a bit mad and they couldn't cope with me anymore.

If the higher echelons of the BBC are out of touch and inflexible, then it is hardly surprising that women have found it difficult to make progress in the organisation or its output. A solution is for women to become directors, producers and to fill positions of authority within the BBC, and indeed, throughout television. Production involves a rare combination of financial and artistic interest and skill. One of the few women in light entertainment production, Denise O'Donoghue, now Associate Producer of *Who Dares Wins*, began her career as a management consultant in the city:

Production allows you to do things that you've never done before . . . it allowed me to have feet in both camps – production budgeting and vetting scripts, choosing and casting.

Sadly, women directors in Light Entertainment are not yet commonplace: at present there are only two female directors of situation comedy in television. Susan Belbin has just become a BBC director and, prior to her appointment, Mandie Fletcher was the only woman director in the department. Mandie Fletcher believes that comedy is still a male preserve and told us that the preconception in the BBC is '. . . women can't play sports or swear. Neither can they be funny. They were the last bastions.'

Apart from the isolation of being the only woman in the department, Mandie Fletcher finds that she has 'been patronised more than you will ever imagine' and this treatment is frustrating. The working conditions of situation comedy may seem irrelevant to its production, but they are not. If male television producers still expect women to behave in a predictably 'feminine' manner, this attitude will be reflected in their work:

At the beginning people were waiting for something to happen, they were waiting for you to crack. They want you to cry: they know how to deal with it.

The belief that she will be 'feminine' and weak discourages Mandie Fletcher from conforming to the expectation, but she wishes that this were not necessary.

I hope in ten years' time women's femininity will be able to come through and you won't have to play the men's game.

Mandie Fletcher is at pains to cast women imaginatively; she finds that women relax and therefore perform well when they are being auditioned by her. She is sensitive to sexism in scripts. She has directed traditional situation comedies such as *Three Up, Two Down*, but she has also tackled the more unconventional: *Black Adder* and *The Fainthearted Feminist*.

The Fainthearted Feminist (1984) provides an example of an attempt to move away from BBC conventions, to break accepted female stereotypes and to innovate. The series was written by Jill Tweedie and adapted from her column in the *Guardian*, also collected in book form, *Letters from a Fainthearted Feminist*. As a newcomer to the BBC, Jill Tweedie was struck by its male chauvinism:

And the men in comedy there are cavemen. They really are. It's a

Lynne Redgrave in *The Fainthearted Feminist.* © BBC Enterprises 1984

weird thing and I really cannot understand why the men in the comedy department are like that . . . you open the door and it's – ugh! Gorillas!

The freedom of the director was infringed by the conservatism of the BBC hierarchy:

Mandie Fletcher made a decision when we were rehearsing which was to do with something as earth-shattering as somebody's height of heel – I think it was Lynn Redgrave because she's pretty tall – and she got a note from the comedy hierarchy and it was headed 'insubordination'. Insubordination! I mean I haven't heard that word since Lindsay Anderson's prep school films. Can you believe it?

The Fainthearted Feminist is set in North London and revolves around the attempts of Martha, a housewife and mother, to reconcile the demands of a conventional husband and home with her feminist enlightenment and the example of her radical friend Mary. The series attempted to show something of the disorganised shambles some people live in, rather than a neat domestic ideal.

247

When a set was being built, Jill Tweedie requested that it should be 'not too glossy' but 'a bit squalid' and one of the men in the comedy department said: 'I don't think places like that exist'. When Jill Tweedie replied that they certainly did exist, and that her house was a bit like that, he replied: '*My* wife runs a very tight ship.'

These problems arose not only because the men in the BBC hierarchy did not know or could not accept domestic disorder but also because they could not accept that this unglorified realism should be presented on television. There was a similar resistance to presenting women as they naturally look and not, again, as a glamorous ideal: attempts to feature female actors without make-up were blocked. The insensitivity of the BBC to the nature of the production extended to hiring a warm-up comedian whose act consisted of sexist and racist jokes. These tensions arose not only because the series was unconventional: 'There was a huge difference because we were women. No doubt about it' (Jill Tweedie). Stalemate was reached. The conventional men of the BBC found it difficult to accept the *Fainthearted Feminist* team, and they, in turn, found the product totally unsatisfactory. Jill Tweedie wanted to withdraw her name from the series, but in the end she decided she had a responsibility to it. The series fell between two stools: it was neither unconventional nor conformist. By allowing a radical element to be given airtime, but not full rein, the BBC maintained control while appearing to be liberal: potential subversion was anaesthetised by incorporation. The French structuralist Roland Barthes writes:

> One immunises the contents of the collective imagination by means of a small innoculation of acknowledged evil: one thus protects it against the risk of a generalized subversion.

Not all comedy series have been thwarted in their attempts to innovate. *Monty Python's Flying Circus* and *The Young Ones* shocked and delighted because they broke certain rules of television comedy which had become ossified. Roger Wilmut on the Python legacy:

> What they did for (or rather to) television – to trample conventions underfoot, and to take the medium apart piece by piece gave it a thorough and beneficial shaking-up.
> (*From Fringe to Flying Circus*)

Ten years after Python, *The Young Ones* had a similar strategy: Co-writer Lise Mayer:

> It seemed to us that there are very few formats which are actually

originated for television – Game Shows and sitcom are about the only two, I think. We used the basic format of a sitcom – the cut-aways enabled us to do sketches if we wanted, build them into the thrust of the narrative.

It is interesting that these two major television comedy series almost entirely featured men and that, moreover, their writers felt that this was a natural result of their comic imaginations and not something that could necessarily be altered. Lise Mayer:

I went through quite a long stage of thinking: 'this is awful, there aren't many female characters in it,' but in the end there are two things you can do. You can try and write in, given the fact that it's based on five men, as many female parts as you can. The other thing you can do is just be as funny as possible – I think it's the only way to write comedy – and not worry about your audience at all. As soon as you start tailoring what you're doing for no reason towards an audience, then you're compromising yourself professionally.

Carol Cleveland spoke about the dearth of women in *Monty Python*:

I'm sorry that I didn't do more. The boys were forever apologising. They said that they just weren't very good at writing parts for women.

Both series were non-naturalistic and highly dependent on fantasy and surrealism. While women are numerous in the traditional family sitcom, they are almost absent from these fine examples of imaginative television. Does this imply that women have no place in fantastical comedy which often produces exceptional results?

This question is illuminated by comments made by Marti Caine. When we asked her whether there would ever be more women comedians she said:

. . . there won't be – ever. Not in my lifetime. Because there are still males and there are still females and we're brainwashed into accepting we're two separate genders by our parents, lovingly and unknowingly, and by our schoolteachers and by pubs and magazines and television adverts and everything that you see in general reminds you constantly that there are men and that there are women – there aren't individuals, there aren't just people. Sex, or gender, should be a third or fourth consideration – and that won't happen for a long, long time.

Marti Caine then developed an argument against the likelihood

Marti Caine

of the number of women comedians increasing. She went on to explain why she thought that women weren't, on the whole, comic:

> Women are definitely the stronger of the species, they're the serious ones, they're the ones who guide the family, they're the ones who control everything, whilst making it appear that the man's doing everything. Because women are strong, they don't have enough time to look around and absorb everything and transmit it into comedy.

Marti Caine believes that the traditional comic point of view is male, because it derives from irresponsibility and childishness:

> It's usually the weak characters who are comics. You see, strength depends on self-discipline. Self-discipline depends on being single-minded and blinkered, almost. You've got to look straight ahead, you can't look to the left or to the right. Now the idiot or the baby or the immature will walk around, looking about and observing and copying and mimicking and that's what a comic does. So if you're self-disciplined and strong and serious about everything there's no way you're going to be a comic.

This is a revealing argument. Marti Caine is not a feminist ('I'm not a feminist at all – I love chauvinistic men'); she sees a clear distinction between the sexes and doesn't believe that women will ever equal men in the domain of professional comedy. This could be interpreted as a negative view because a feminist aims to achieve equality. But many feminists also argue that women are different from men and should treasure their differences.

Marti Caine's ideas about women's strength echo the latter argument. Women may choose not to be comedians because the comic point of view is irresponsible and out of keeping with the approach to life demanded of them.

The argument is not, however, as simple as this. It may be flattering to believe that women are the stronger of the species, but Marti Caine's explanation of their strength implies that they develop their attributes out of necessity because men do not take equal responsibility. This is not necessarily a role that all women want. If women are hampered by practical and domestic responsibilities, releasing the comic imagination, literally 'being silly' in the way that the Python team and The Young Ones are, is a luxury that they cannot afford. It is ironic that men have a lot of the real power in society, and can act the fool.

The Women's Movement has inspired a huge upsurge in women's writing. An element of this new literature has been fantastical. Similar developments are apparent in women's theatre where all-female companies including Cunning Stunts, Scarlet Harlets and Little Women have produced original comedy work. These forms have partly emerged out of the need to find imaginative alternatives to a male-dominated society but they have also served as a springboard for women's fantasy.

This kind of work has not yet been adequately transferred into television comedy. This could be because women's theatre companies have wanted greater control over their work than television companies have been prepared to offer; it could be that television's commissioning editors have undervalued and ignored this area of work. It seems that the powers that be in television often opt for the known and tried formula, however poor the quality. New ideas are not approached with the imagination it would take to make them work.

The television sketch-show is as capable of conservative and radical extremes as sitcom. Women's roles within it reflect this. The vast majority of sketch-shows feature men – Stanley Baxter, Benny Hill, Morecambe and Wise, Russ Abbott, Frankie Howerd, and so on. It is in this milieu that women are most often used for their 'glamour' or 'old-bagness' (Maureen Lipman). Eve Ferret is appalled at the quality of most sketchwork.

> It's rubbish. Rubbish. We're not well served. You have to make the best of a bad job.

Some women are less critical of the work they are given. Bella Emberg has played the stooge, the large lady, to many male comedians including Benny Hill, Les Dawson, Frankie Howerd, Stanley Baxter and Russ Abbott. She enjoys her role:

> I'm very happy playing second fiddle. I don't mind. As long as it makes people laugh, that's the main thing. If that works, it's all that matters.

Even in sketch-shows where women are not stooges, they are always in the minority: *Alfresco* had four men and two women (Siobhan Redmond and Emma Thompson), *Who Dares Wins* four men and one woman (Julia Hills) and *Naked Video* has five men and two women (Helen Lederer and Elaine C. Smith).

Despite these limitations certain women have made their mark. Eleanor Bron was a vital element in satirical television series of the 1960s, Denise Coffey is well known for her work on the popular children's programme *Do Not Adjust Your Set* and Sheila Steafel made her mark in *The Frost Report*. More recently Marti Caine (*The Marti Caine Show* and *Marti Caine*) and Faith Brown

Denise Coffey

(*The Faith Brown Awards* and *The Faith Brown Chat Show*) have emerged as two of the few women to host their own series. Both Marti Caine and Faith Brown have worked at the 'glossy' end of the variety market. The talented young impressionist Jessica Martin has swiftly made a name for herself in such varied television shows as *Spitting Image*, *And There's More*, *The Laughter Show* and *Bobby Davro on the Box*.

Jessica Martin as Angie from *Eastenders*

Pamela Stephenson

Pamela Stephenson made her name in the more political arena of *Not the Nine O'Clock News*. John Lloyd, who produced the programme, explained its approach:

> In *Not the Nine O'Clock News* we reflect the more outrageous, violent and tasteless elements in life. We do things about taboo subjects, like people eating each other after a plane crash. (*Television Today*)

Tracey Ullman in *Three of a Kind*. © BBC Enterprises 1981

Pamela Stephenson emerged as a comic performer who could combine glamour and talent. Julie Welch:

> A comic performer of genius, she has overcome the disadvantage of being too beautiful to be funny by dint of her outstanding powers of mimicry, her use of voice, dress and gesture accomplishing her descent into the ridiculous.
> (*The Observer*)

Pamela Stephenson is one of the widest known and most commercially successful women in comedy. She has combined her performance skills, her appearance and her image as a 'media personality' to become a very public figure. Tracey Ullman is similarly successful. She has additionally captured the pop star's market and is now known to the American public, where she has branched into films (*Plenty*) and is, at the time of writing, working on her own series for American television. Like Pamela Stephenson, it is Tracey Ullman's skilful characterisation and voice work (combined with a 'girl next door' appeal) that have earned her respect. She first came to public attention in *A Kick Up the Eighties*

Maura McBitch, from *Three of a Kind*
Performed by Tracey Ullman
Written by Ruby Wax

(Edinburgh accent)
Hello girls, it's Maura McBitch here. I've been run off my Gucci's today, don't ask. This morning began at a fancy-dress charity in aid of 'Save the Aligator handbag'. We all had to come as our favourite hors d'oeuvre. I went as a stuffed artichoke of course. In the parking lot I bumped into Rod Stewart dressed as a large portion of taramasalata; Jackie Onassis had come as a lot of Greek bread. After a hideous mixup in the lobby the three of us went in together as a Ratatouille in a basket. I spotted Britt Ekland, naked except for a cocktail cherry in her navel, posing as a grapefruit. Gals, she was looking for a man who'd come as a spoon. Salad Niçoise, Victor Lowndes, asked to leave, threw himself onto the chandelier and hung by his anchovies. Are we not 'un petit' old for this behaviour, Victor, mmm? Afterwards I whirled off to Flambes, London's most exclusive health club. It's so select they don't take fat people. Then, as usual I met my oldest friend Margaret Trudeau having her unsightlies pruned yet again. My dears, you could crochet that woman. Margaret told me that Liz Taylor had her face sewn back so often, she's facing the other way. Then, 'bonne surprise!' who should wobble in but my oldest friend, Joan Collins. We waited for a few minutes until her behind arrived, then the two of us sat on it and talked yoghurt.

---

and *Three of a Kind* and has most recently appeared on British television in *Girls on Top*.

The pattern of television work is comparable to that of character acting. Individual women have emerged, but have been relatively rare. Their success and fame must be weighed against the experience of many women who have been given limited and unimaginative roles and whose attempts to develop those roles have been thwarted by political and practical limitations.

Is this discrepancy between fame and frustration inevitable or can it be resolved? One solution is for women to get themselves into positions where they have greater artistic control. Victoria Wood is one of the few women in Light Entertainment who has a high level of control over her work.

Girls on Top: on sofa, from left to right – infantile Jennifer (Jennifer Saunders) whose jokes include:
  'Knock Knock!' Who's there? Amanda who? Amanda Ripley. Oh no.'

bossy Amanda (Dawn French), whose posters for sensible living include: 'NEED A LIGHT? YES! SO DO LOTS OF PEOPLE IN SOUTH AMERICA. So please save fuel and turn off that light before you leave the room.'

and actress Shelley (Ruby Wax) whose roles include:
  'Screaming woman, wearing dacron' in an industrial film about allergies caused by synthetic fibers.
    'Screaming camper' in an industrial film about blowing out matches when in a tent.
    'Screaming unseatbelted driver' in an industrial film about driving without a seatbelt while eating a hamburger.

and behind them, their equally eccentric landlady, Lady Carlton (Joan Greenwood)
(Quotations from *Girls on Top*, Grafton Books)

Victoria Wood and **Julie Walters** in *Wood and Walters*. © BBC Enterprises 1984

This has been enhanced by the fact that she learnt about television relatively early in her career:

> And I had an instant affinity with it. I loved it. I love it now. It was the first thing I ever did. I mean before that I think I'd done maybe two pub shows and I'd sung a couple of songs and done a couple of gags out of a book by Les Dawson (I changed the names) but I'd not performed at all apart from school plays and at the Youth Theatre.

Dawn French and Jennifer Saunders enjoy a similar control inherited from their work as part of the Comic Strip and have now developed in *Girls on Top* and in their own series.

Artistic control is not the only key to success; it must be matched by high-quality material and performance. The media have entered a curious era in which 'stars' are created at an early age. This is healthy in that idea and approach are contemporary and fresh, but it also puts a huge pressure on comedians to keep up their early promise.

The pressures of youth can be coupled with the pressures of being a woman. Because there have been relatively few women in comedy, each woman who is successful is under pressure 'not to let the side down'. It is to be hoped that one day a situation of equality will be achieved where it is permissible, and not an argument against the sex, for a woman merely to be average.

We hope that eventually there will be enough prominent women performers for gender to no longer be an issue: women will not have to be cited as 'women' performers because they will be the rule rather than the exception. Sheila Hancock:

> I think Victoria Wood is such a breakthrough . . . she's
> wonderful . . . she's a real beacon . . . I look at them and think:
> 'They're doing what I tried to do in my pathetic little way in *Now
> Seriously, it's Sheila Hancock.'*

Conclusion

Really, I just want everybody to have a good time. That's what I want
them to do. I want to be worth the money, whatever that takes.
(Victoria Wood)

We feel that we should be able to draw some hard and fast
conclusions from our study of women in comedy, but it is a subject
where absolutes rest uneasily. So we will let the text speak for itself,
and simply draw together the various strands of our research and
discovery.

We have made the point that because women have for centuries
been considered second-class citizens, the public development of
their personal humour has been arrested, and they have been
bypassed by the documentation of comedy history. However, as
women reclaim areas of artistic expression, their visibility makes
them more in demand, and the areas of film, television and live
comedy are no exception. Despite this interest, women are often
held back from achieving their full potential by personal factors as
well as by the inflexibility of existing structures of employment. By
talking to women who have experienced difficulties first-hand, we
hope we have gone some way to showing how they may be
overcome. We have discovered that a new perspective is generally
needed within the current light entertainment set-up before women
can feel totally at ease, so that they can be funny on their own
terms. More women are needed in areas of writing, directing and
producing comedy, and although we are not suggesting that women
in positions of power will necessarily employ or encourage other
women, at the very last they will redress the current male bias.
Women cannot afford to be confined by their chosen medium
through lack of control of its workings.

Our aim has been to bring comic women to the fore, and to show
that a tradition, however, submerged, does exist. Funny women,
witty women are everywhere. We hope that this will become

261

Conclusion

increasingly apparent. It can be argued that you're either funny or you're not; we've simply put forward the case for allowing women to find out for themselves.

Historical chart

Year	Monarch	Prime Minister	Events	Comedy and the Arts
1889	Victoria	Salisbury (Con)	1st movie camera (kinetoscope) invented by Thomas Edison	Revue as theatrical form appears
1893			Independent Labour Party formed	
1900			Keir Hardie becomes first Labour MP	
1901	Edward VII		Marconi sends first wireless message across Atlantic	
1902		Balfour (Con)		
1903			Emmeline Pankhurst forms Women's Social and Political Union	

Year	Monarch	Prime Minister	Events	Comedy and the Arts
1905		Campbell Bannerman (Lib)		
1906				First British cinema opened
1907			Women vote for and are elected to local councils	Jessie Matthews born. Music hall strike
1908		Asquith (Lib)	Women's Freedom League formed	Actresses' Franchise League set up
1909			First suffragette hunger strike	
1910	George V	Asquith (Lib)	40% women use contraception	
1911			Lloyd George introduces National Insurance. Working women and Divorce published by Malthusian League	
1912			Christabel Pankhurst begins arson campaign	First Royal Command performance. Marie Lloyd holds an alternative 'command' performance
1914			War declared	
1915		Asquith (Coalition)	Emmeline Pankhurst organises demonstration for 'Women's Right to Serve'. W.I. set up	Music hall tours to drum up volunteers

Year	Monarch	Prime Minister	Events	Comedy and the Arts
1916		Lloyd George (Coalition)	Compulsory military service Strikes.	
1918			War ends. Fisher Education Act. Maternity and Child Welfare Act. Fourth Reform Act – women over 30 enfranchised	
1919			Lady Astor first woman M.P. Marie Stopes publishes *Unmarried Love*	
1921			Unemployment at 2 million. Marie Stopes opens first birth control clinic	
1922		Bonar Law (Con)	Infanticide Act relaxes law for mothers of new born children	BBC (company) formed. First regular radio broadcasts. Marie Lloyd dies
1923		Baldwin (Con)		
1924		Macdonald (Lab) Baldwin (Con)		Michael Balcon sets up Gainsborough Pictures
1925				First radio comedy series goes out
1926			General Strike	BBC (corporation) formed

Year	Monarch	Prime Minister	Events	Comedy and the Arts
1928			Flapper vote: all women over 21 enfranchised. Housing Act launches slum clearance	Caroline Lejeune becomes *Observer* film critic
1929		Macdonald (Labour)	Wall Street Crash	Sound movies begin
1930			National Union of Societies for Equal Citizenship and National Birth Council set up. Amy Johnson's flight	*Love on the Dole* published. Gertrude Lawrence appears in *Private Lives*, London
1931		MacDonald (Nat)	Anomalies Act (anti-unemployment benefit for married women). Women's League of Health and Beauty set up	*Sally in our Alley*, Gracie Field's first screen role
1932			Contraceptive jelly invented. Women's magazines grow	First woman admitted to Footlights revue. Eric Maschewitz made Head of Radio Variety
1935		Baldwin (Con)		
1936	Edward VIII George VI	Baldwin	Edward VIII abdicates. Housing Act gives councils wider power	First BBC television transmission
1937		Chamberlain (Nat)	Factories Act limits hours of work	

Year	Monarch	Prime Minister	Events	Comedy and the Arts
1938			Women industrial workers average £1.63 a week. Divorce petitions filed reach 9,970. Trade Unions include 926,000 women	
1939			World War II	BBC television, cinemas and theatres closed down for defence reasons. ITMA on radio. ENSA formed. Vera Lynn and Gracie Fields become stars. Balcon is head of Ealing Studios. Dilys Powell becomes *Sunday Times* film critic
1940		Churchill (Coalition)	Conscription for single women 19-24	
1941			Co-operative guilds for women set up. Labour party women's sections grow	
1943			37% of women over 14 in work	Farjeon's revue: *Sweet and Low*. Joyce Grenfell on radio in *How* programmes
1944			Butler Education Act. Half a million women in armed forces	Revue: *Sweeter and Lower*
1945		Atlee	End of war. Launch of Welfare State	Joan Littlewood founds Theatre Workshop. Film: *Blithe Spirit*. Theatre: *Joyce Grenfell Requests the Pleasure* (Fortune)
1946			Cinema audiences reach a peak – third of population go once a week	Revue: *Sweetest and Lowest*. Television starts again

Year	Monarch	Prime Minister	Events	Comedy and the Arts
1948			National Health Service	Radio: *Take it from Here*. Nellie Wallace dies (b. 1870)
1949			Clothes rationing ends	Films: *Passport to Pimlico*, *Whisky Galore*, *Kind Hearts and Coronets*
1950		Atlee (Lab)	Emergence of 'Teddy boy'	Radio: *The Glums*, *Ray's a Laugh* and Dance Hall
1951		Churchill (Con)		Radio: *The Goons*
1952	Elizabeth II			Vesta Tilley and Gertrude Lawrence die
1953				Theatre Royal Stratford East set up. Radio: *Educating Archie*. Film: *Genevieve*
1954				Radio: *Life with the Lyons*. Films: *The Belles of St Trinians*, *Doctor in the House*
1955		Eden (Con)		Independent Television set up. Film: *The Ladykillers*. Book: Nabokov's *Lolita*
1956			Suez crisis	Theatre: *Look Back in Anger*. Hancock's *Hour* first televised
1957		Macmillan (Con)		*Benny Hill Show* first televised

Year	Monarch	Prime Minister	Events	Comedy and the Arts
1958				Film: First Carry On – Carry On Sergeant. Black and White Minstrel Show starts
1959			Mental Health Act. Lady Chatterley's Lover publication trial	Theatre: The Last Laugh, Fings Ain't Wot They Used t'be, The Birthday Party. Books: Take a Girl Like You. Films: A Taste of Honey, Look Back in Anger, Room at the Top. Radio: Just Fancy
1960			End of National Service	TV: Coronation Street. Film: Saturday night and Sunday Morning. Peter Hall at RSC (Stratford)
1961				Revue: Beyond the Fringe. TV: The Rag Trade.
1962			Britain has highest number of employed women in Europe. The Pill first prescribed on NHS	Film: Sparrers Can't Sing. Television: That Was the Week That Was.
1963		Douglas Home (Con)	The Profumo Affair	Films: This Sporting Life, The Collector, The Servant.
1964		Wilson (Lab)		Traverse Theatre set up. Theatre: Marat Sade. Theatre of Cruelty. Radio Caroline set up. Film: A Hard Day's Night. TV: Not so much a programme.

Year	Monarch	Prime Minister	Events	Comedy and the Arts
1965				Film: *Help!* Radio: *I'm sorry I'll read that again*
1966			Abolition of Hanging. 2,250,000 women in Trades Unions	TV: *BBC3*, *'Til Death us do part* Films: *Alfie*, *Georgy Girl*
1967			Abortion Act. NHS Family Planning Act. Sexual Offences Act allows adults homosexual acts in private	TV: *Not in Front of the Children* Films: *Smashing Time*, *The Accident*
1968				TV: *What is this thing called, love?* Films: *If*, *I Want It Now*, *The Prime of Miss Jean Brodie* Theatrical censorship abolished
1969				TV: *The Liver birds*, *Monty Python's Flying Circus* Films: *On Her Majesty's Secret Service*, *The Waterfall*
1970		Heath (Con)	Equal Pay Act. *The Female Eunuch* published	
1971			Voting age lowered to 18	TV: *And Now for Something Completely Different*

Year	Monarch	Prime Minister	Events	Comedy and the Arts
1972				TV: *Beyond a Joke* Film: *A Touch of Class*
1973				Film: *O Lucky Man*
1974		Wilson (Lab)	Winter of Discontent. Unisex clothes on the increase. Women watch more TV than men. Most women have had sexual experience before the age of 16	National Theatre starts to be built
1975			Wilson retires.	Book: *Sweet William* (Beryl Bainbridge) TV: *Faulty Towers*
1976		Callaghan (Lab)	Television is Britain's biggest leisure activity	Books: *Praxis* (Fay Weldon), *The Passion of New Eve* (Angela Carter)
1977			All but 2% of births in hospital	
1978				TV: *Butterflies* Film: *California Suite* Radio: *Hitchhiker's Guide to the Galaxy* Book: *Switchback* (Molly Parkin)
1979		Thatcher (Con)		TV: *Not the Nine O'Clock News* Films: *The Life of Brian*, *That Sinking Feeling*. Book: *The Obstacle Race* (Germaine Greer). Theatre: Spare Tyre and Siren founded

Year	Monarch	Prime Minister	Events	Comedy and the Arts
1980				First woman president of Footlights. Films: *Gregory's Girl*, *Carry On Emmanuelle* (last *Carry On*) TV: *Hi-de-Hi* Women's Playhouse Trust founded
1981			Race riots	TV: *Solo*, *Revolting Women*, *Three of a Kind*. Theatre: Sensible Footwear founded Radio: *Radio Active* Jessie Matthews dies
1982			Falklands War	Film: *Five go mad in Dorset*
1983		Thatcher (Con)		TV: *No Problem* Films: *Local Hero*, *The Meaning of Life* Theatre: Charabanc founded
1984			Unemployment tops 3 million for first time. Divorce petitions filed reach 178,940. Miners' strike	TV: *The Fainthearted Feminist*, *Leaving* Film: *Educating Rita* Government Film Act Book: *Sex and Destiny* (Greer)
1985				TV: *Victoria Wood as seen on TV* Film: *A Private Function* British Film Year

Year	Monarch	Prime Minister	Events	Comedy and the Arts
1986			Wapping Dispute	Films: *My Beautiful Laundrette, Letter to Brezhnev, Supergrass, Absolute Beginners* Theatre: *When We Are Married, No Son of Mine, Thee Thy Thou Thine*

Interviews

We wish to thank the following people for giving us interviews:

Adele Anderson, Annabel Arden, Helen Atkinson Wood, Beverley Bell, Connie Booth, Jackie Bratton, Eleanor Bron, Faith Brown, Marti Caine, Jennie Campbell, Charabanc Theatre Company, Carol Cleveland, Denise Coffey, Pat Coombs, Frances de la Tour, Claire Dowie, Jenny Eclair, Bella Emberg, Rose English, Eve Ferret, Flamin' Hamsters, Mandie Fletcher, Dawn French, Fringe Benefits, Abi Grant, David Grant, Germaine Greer, Sheila Hancock, Irene Handl, Kit Hollerbach, Nerys Hughes, Sheila Hyde, Krissie Illing, Judith Jacobs, Dillie Keane, Kneehigh Theatre Company, Ellie Laine, Bryony Lavery, Jenny Lecoat, Helen Lederer, Peta Lily, Sue Limb, Maureen Lipman, Lip Service, Dennis Main Wilson, Miriam Margolyes, Jessica Martin, Pauline Melville, Lise Mayer, The Millies, Rona Munro, Denise O'Donoghue, Sue Parrish, Vicky Pile, Su Pollard, Jan Ravens, Marjorie Rea, Beryl Reid, Christina Reid, Alison Renshaw, Patricia Routledge, Sensible Footwear, Siren Theatre Company, Spare Tyre, Elaine C. Smith, Andrea Solomons, Alison Steadman, Sheila Steafel, Maggie Steed, Rebecca Stevens, Jennifer Saunders, Emma Thompson, Janette Tough, Jane Traies, Jill Tweedie, Betty Warren, Elsie Waters, Leila Webster, June Whitfield, Barbara Windsor, Victoria Wood

Photographic credits

Chris Adams for Krissie Illing
Sarah Ainslie for Rose English
Annabel Arden for *No Son of Mine*
Laurie Asprey for Emma Thompson
Associated Press for Joan Littlewood
Michael Barnett for Eleanor Bron
BBC for *The Rag Trade*, *The Liver Birds*, *The Fainthearted Feminist*, *Hi-de-Hi*, *Fawlty Towers*, *Wood and Walters*, *The Good Life*, *Butterflies*, Hylda Baker, Bebe Daniels, June Whitfield, *Revolting Women*, *3 of a Kind*
Bryanston Films Ltd for *A Taste of Honey*
Lisa Butterfield for Parker and Klein
Marti Caine for Marti Caine
Cannon Screen Entertainment Ltd for *The Ladykillers*, *The Belles of St Trinians*, *Whisky Galore*, *Morgan*, *Carry on Screaming* and *Carry on Nurse*
Peter Cartwright for Christine Pilgrim
Central Independent Television plc for *Girls on Top*
Columbia Pictures for *California Suite*
Dee Conway for Peta Lily
Dino de Laurentis for *A Touch of Class*
Paul Fulton for Claire Dowie
© 1986 Goldcrest Films and Television Limited and Virgin Vision Limited for Eve Ferret
Gordon Graham for Marjorie Rea
Grand National/The Kobal Collection for Cicely Courtenidge
Martin Haswell for Spare Tyre Theatre Company
John Haynes for Patricia Routledge
Christopher Hill for Charabanc Theatre Company
Peter Hughes for Lilla Miller
Gordon Hull for Germaine Greer
Jim Hutchinson, *Daily Mail* photographer, for Helen Atkinson Wood
Kerstin Rodgers for French and Saunders
Kettledrum Productions for Carol Cleveland
Ellie Laine for Ellie Laine
London Weekend Television for Maureen Lipman
Ian McKell for Rebecca Stevens
The Raymond Mander and Joe Mitchenson Theatre Collection for Florrie Forde,

Photographic credits

Jenny Hill, Marie Lloyd, Bessie Bellwood, Vesta Tilley, Gert and Daisy, Nellie Wallace, Beatrice Lillie (Angus McBean), Gertrude Lawrence, Hermione Gingold and Hermione Baddeley (Angus McBean), Joyce Grenfell, Jessie Matthews, Gracie Fields

The Millies for The Millies

Brian Moody for Victoria Wood

Tim O'Sullivan for Fascinating Aïda

Palace Picture/Channel Four for Margi Clarke

D. Paul for Pauline Daniels

Jill Posener for Miriam Margolyes

Roy Pottinger for Beverley Bell

Stills from the films *Genevieve*, *Blithe Spirit*, *Carry on Camping* and *Carry on Doctor* by courtesy of The Rank Organisation plc

Michael Sanders for Judith Jacobs

Peter Simpkin for Jan Ravens and Sheila Hancock

Nick Skinner for Beryl Reid

Jean-Bernard Souliez for Pauline Melville

Sphere Books for Lise Mayer and The Young Ones

Television South for Jessica Martin

Martin Thompson for Jenny Eclair

Universal Pictures for Patricia Hayes. Copyright © by Universal Pictures, a Division of Universal City Studios, Inc. Courtesy of MCA Publishing Rights, a Division of MCA Inc.

Extract credits

Beverley Bell for stand-up routine extract
Alan Bennett and London Weekend Television for *The South Bank Show*
Bob Block and Ronnie Hanbury for *Life with the Lyons*
Cannon Films for *Sing as we go* and *The Ladykillers*
Connie Booth and John Cleese for *Fawlty Towers*
The BBC for *The Wordsmiths of Gorsemere, In One Ear, Weekending, Round the Horne, Hancock's Half Hour, Life with the Lyons, Educating Archie, The Glums, ITMA*
Eleanor Bron and John Fortune for *Is your marriage really necessary?*
Frank Clarke and Channel Four for *Letter to Brezhnev*
Pauline Daniels for joke
Angus Deayton and Jimmy Mulville for *Joanna Jaundice*
Dino de Laurentis for *A Touch of Class*
John Docherty and Moray Hunter for *Pancake Sketch*
Claire Dowie for joke
Jenny Eclair for joke
Rose English for *Thee Thy Thou Thine*
Marty Feldman and Barry Took for *Round the Horne*
Dawn French and Jennifer Saunders for *Friendly Advice*
Dawn French, Jennifer Saunders, Ruby Wax and Grafton Books for *Girls on Top*
Samuel French Ltd for *Hermione Gingold Wrote These*
Ray Galton and Alan Simpson for *Hancock's Half Hour*
Abi Grant and Spitting Image Productions Ltd for *Cell net Car Phones*
Trevor Griffiths and Faber and Faber for *Comedians*
Irene Handl for *Shadows in the Grass*
Handmade Films for *A Private Function*
Kit Hollerbach for joke
Ted Kavanagh for *ITMA*
Ellie Laine for joke
Carla Lane for *The Liver Birds*
Jenny Lecoat for *The Willy Song*
Helen Lederer for stand-up routine extract
Sue Limb for *The Wordsmiths of Gorsemere*
Liz Lochhead for *True Confessions* from *True Confessions and New Cliches*
Macmillan for Joyce Grenfell's *Flowers* in *George – don't do that*
Pauline Melville for stand-up routine extract

Extract credits

Lilla Miller for Cornish story
Frank Muir and Denis Norden for *The Glums*
Rona Munro and Methuen London for *Piper's cave* from *Plays by Women, Volume 5*
Karen Parker and Debby Klein for routine
Vicky Pile for *Get Yourself a Trauma*
Christine Pilgrim for stand-up routine extract
Rank Films for *Carry on Girls*. Extract from the script of *Carry on Girls* by courtesy of Gerald Thomas and Peter Rogers
Marjorie Rea for joke
Andrea Solomons for *Medallion Man*
Rebecca Stevens for joke
Elsie Waters for *Gert and Daisy, a Piano and How*
Ruby Wax for *Maura McBitch*
Victoria Wood and Methuen, London for Kitty's monologue from *Up to you, Porky*
David Jackson Young and Eddy Kanfor-Dumas for *Orgasm Sketch*

Useful addresses

Campaign for Real Equality in Equity
C/O 183 Albert Road
London N22 4AQ

Equity Women's Committee
C/O Christine Payne
British Equity Actor's Association
8, Harley Street
London W1N 2AB
01-636 6367

London Screenwriters' Workshop
20 Jeffreys Street
London NW1 9PR
01-482 0527

Standing Conference of Women Directors and Administrators
C/O Madeleine Hutchins
Chaldon Court North
Church Lane
Chaldon
Caterham
Surrey.
CR3 5AL
0883-45011

Women's Film Television and Video Network
79, Wardour Street
London W1V 3PH
01-434 2076

Women in Entertainment
7, Thorpe Close
London W10 5XL
01-969 2292 / 969 3742

Useful addresses

Women's Playhouse Trust
46/48 Osnaburgh Street
London NW1 2GH
01-388 3957

Bibliography

BOOKS

Anderson, J. *History of Movie Comedy*, Deans International, 1985.
Auty, M. and Roddick, N. (Eds), *British Cinema Now*, BFI, 1985.
Bergson, H., *Le Rire*, Presses Universitaires de France, 1940.
Blatchford, R. (ed.), *Television Comedy Scripts*, Longman, 1983: includes Esmonde, J., and Larbey, B., 'The Wind-Break War' (*The Good Life*) and Lane, C., 'Oh the Shame of it' (*The Liver Birds*)
Bratton, J., *Music Hall: Performance and Style*, OUP, 1986.
Bratton, J., 'The Vital Spark', Unpublished.
BBC yearbooks 1931-1986.
BFI, *Film and Television Yearbook*, 1985.
Bron, E., *Life and Other Punctures*, Andre Deutsch, 1978.
Bron, E., *The Pillow Book of Eleanor Bron, or an Actress Despairs*, Jonathan Cape, 1985.
Brough, P., *Educating Archie*, Stanley Paul, 1955.
Busby, R., *British Music Hall, an Illustrated Who's Who*, Paul Elek, 1976.
Chance Newton, H., *Idols of the Halls, being my Music Hall Memories*, Heath Cranton, 1928.
Cleese, J., and Booth C., *Fawlty Towers*, Contact Publications, 1977.
Cook, J. (ed.), *Television Sitcom*, BFI Dossier 17, BFI, 1982, includes Medhurst, Andy and Tuck, Lucy 'The Gender Game' and Lovell, Terry 'A Genre of Social Disruption'.
de Frece, Lady, *Recollections of Vesta Tilley*, Hutchinson, 1934.
Dyer, R., *Stars*, BFI, 1985.
Eliot, T.S., *Selected Essays*, Faber and Faber (3rd edition), 1951.
Farson, D., *Marie Lloyd and Music Hall*, Tom Stacey, 1972.
Fiddy, D. (ed.), *Television Yearbook*, Virgin Books, 1985.
Fisher, J., *Funny Way to be a Hero*, Frederick Muller, Granada Publishing, 1973.
French, D., Saunders, J. and Wax, R., *Girls on Top*, Grafton Books, 1986.
Fuller, K., and Jackson, P. (eds), *Three of a Kind*, BBC Books, 1983.
Gammond, P., *Your own, Your very own. A Music Hall Scrapbook*, compiled by Peter Gammond, Ian Allen, 1971.
Gardener, V., *Sketches from the Actresses' Franchise League*, Nottingham Drama Texts, 20th Century, 1985.

Bibliography

Garrett, J.M., *Sixty Years of British Music Hall*, Chappell in Association with André Deutsch, 1976.

Goldstein, J., and McGhee, P. (eds), *The Psychology of Humour*, includes La Fave, L., 'Humour Judgements as a function of Reference Groups and Identification Classes', NY Academic Press, 1972.

Greer, G., *The Female Eunuch*, MacGibbon & Kee, 1970.

Greer, G., *The Obstacle Race*, Secker & Warburg, 1979.

Greer, G., *Sex and Destiny*, Secker & Warburg, 1984.

Grenfell, J., *George – Don't Do That*, Macmillan, 1977.

Grenfell, J., *Joyce Grenfell Requests the Pleasure*, Macmillan, 1978.

Grenfell, J., *Stately as a Galleon*, Macmillan, 1978.

Grenfell, J., and Moore, K., *An Invisible Friendship*, Macmillan, 1981.

Griffiths, T., *Comedians*, Faber, 1976.

Guinness, A., *Blessings in Disguise*, Hamish Hamilton, 1985.

Hayes, C., *Not Waving*, Faber, 1984.

Hewison, R., *Footlights! 100 Years of Cambridge Comedy*, Methuen, 1983.

Holledge, J., *Innocent Flowers*, Virago, 1981.

Johnson, T., *Unsuitable for Adults*, Faber, 1985.

Kirk, K., and Heath, E., *Men in Frocks*, Gay Men's Press, 1984.

Ledger, C., *The Virgin Guide to London's Best Restaurants*, Virgin, 1986.

Leigh, M., *Abigail's Party*, Penguin Plays, 1983.

Legman, G., *Rationale of the Dirty Joke: An Analysis of Sexual Humour*, vol.2, Panther, 1972.

Lochhead, L., *True Confessions and New Cliches*, Polygon Books, 1985.

MacInnes, C., *Sweet Saturday Night*, MacGibbon & Kee, 1967.

McCloud, C., 'Silvia Something and the Boxers', Thesis on Women's Humour, Dip HE Dartington College of Arts, 1984, unpublished.

Maitland, S., *Vesta Tilley*, Virago Press, 1986.

Maltin, L., *The Great Movie Comedians – Charlie Chaplin to Woody Allen*, New York: Crown Publishers, 1978.

Marwick, A., *The Pelican History of Social Britain, British Society since 1945*, Penguin, 1982.

Morley, S., *Gertrude Lawrence*, Weidenfeld & Nicholson, 1981.

Muir, F., and Brett, S. (eds), *Frank Muir Presents the Book of Comedy Sketches*, Elmtree Books, 1982.

Noble, P., *Films of the Year, 1955-56*, Express Books, 1956.

Norden, D., Harper, S., and Gilbert, N., *Coming to you live!*, Methuen, 1985.

Norman, F., *Why Fings Went West*, Lemon Tree Press, 1975.

Northern Irish Women Writers, *The Female Line*, Northern Ireland Women's Rights Movement, 1985.

Parker, D., *Radio: the Great Years*, David & Charles, 1977.

Pedder, E. (ed.), *Who's Who on Television* (3rd edition), Independent Television Books Ltd, 1985).

Perry, G., *Forever Ealing*, Pavillion, Michael Joseph, 1981.

Perry, G., *Life of Python*, Pavillion, Michael Joseph, 1986.

Pickard, R., *A Companion to the Movies*, Muller, 1979.

Plante, D., *Difficult Women*, Futura, 1979.

Quinlan, D., *British Sound Films: The Studio Years, 1929-1959*, Batsford, 1984.

Quinlan, D., *The Illustrated History of Film Character Actors*, Batsford, 1985.

Raving Beauties, *In the Pink*, The Women's Press, 1983.

Reid, B., *So Much Love*, Hutchinson, 1984.

Remmant, M., *Plays by Women*, vol. 5 (includes *Piper's Cave* by Rona Munro), Methuen, 1986.

Rivers, J., *The Life and Hard Times of Heidi Abromowitz*, Comet, 1985.

Robinson, D., *World Cinema 1895-1980*, Eyre Methuen, 1981.

Rogers, D., *The Avengers*, ITV Books and Michael Joseph, 1983.

Rowe, M., *Spare Rib Reader*, Penguin, 1982.

Russell Taylor, J., *A Dictionary of the Theatre*, Penguin, 1966.

Rutherford, M., *An Autobiography*, W.H. Allen, 1972.

Seyler, A., *The Craft of Comedy*, J.G. Muller, 1943.

Showcall 1986, Carson and Comerford, 1986

Sloan, T., *Television Light Entertainment*, BBC Lunchtime Lectures, 8th series, 1969.

Stevenson, J., *The Pelican Social History of Britain. British Society 1914-45.* Penguin, 1984.

Steward, S., and Garrett, S., *Signed, Sealed and Delivered*, Pluto, 1984.

Thomson, D., *The Pelican History of England. England in the Twentieth Century*, Penguin, 1965.

Thomson, D., *A Bibliographical Dictionary of the Cinema*, Secker & Warburg, 1975.

Todd, S. (ed.), *Women and Theatre: Calling the Shots*, Faber, 1984.

Took, B., *Laughter in the Air*, Robson Books, BBC, 1976.

Tracey, S., *Who's Who on Radio*, World's Work, 1983.

Turner, B. and Fulton, M., *The Playgoer's Companion*, Virgin Books, 1983.

Tynan, K., *A View of the English Stage, 1944-63*, Davis-Poynter, 1975.

Uglow, J. (ed.) *The Macmillan Dictionary of Women's Biography*, Macmillan, 1982.

Wandor, Micheline, *Understudies: Theatre and sexual politics*, Eyre Methuen, 1981.

Wheen, F., *Television*, Century, 1985.

Wilmut, R., *From Fringe to Flying Circus*, Eyre Methuen, 1980.

Winegarten, R. (ed.) *Selections on the status of women in American society*, University of Texas, Dallas, 1978 (includes Gravely, N., 'Sexist humour as a form of social control or – unfortunately – the joke is usually on us').

Women in Entertainment, Members' Dictionary, 1985.

Wood, V., *The Victoria Wood Songbook*, Methuen, 1984.

Wood, V., *Up to you Porky*, Methuen, 1985.

Woolf, V., *A Room of One's Own*, Penguin, 1945.

SURVEYS

Conference of Women Theatre Directors and Adminstrators, *The Status of Women in the British Theatre, 1982-83.*

The Women's Film Television and Video Network, *Channel 4 Television and Equal Opportunities.*

Bibliography

ARTICLES

Bardsley, B., 'Victoria Wood', *Women's Review*, no.7, May 1986.

Barker, F., Review of Glenda Jackson in *A Touch of Class*, *Evening News*, 24.5.73.

Barker, R., McConville, B. and Gerrard, N., 'At the Frontiers of Feminism', *The Guardian*, 22.4.86.

Barnes, G., 'Not On Your Ellie' (on Ellie Laine), *Daily Mirror*, 10.2.86.

Bishop, K., 'Anti-Everything' (on 'No Son of Mine'), *Nine To Five*, 3.2.86.

Booth, C., 'Stuck in Deep Walters' (on Julie Walters), *LAM*, 25.2.86.

Broadcast Reporter, 'Cloak of Secrecy as Agran Quits Thames' (on Linda Agran), *Broadcast*, 21.3.86.

Brompton, S., 'Sweet F.A.' (on Fascinating Aïda), *Cosmopolitan*, June 1985.

Butterworth, J., 'Funny Girls' (on Wood and Walters, Pauline Daniels, Helen Atkinson Wood), *MS London*, 27.1.86.

C.R.E.E. Election Manifesto.

Carroll, S., 'Your shirt must be pure silk, it's still got a worm inside' (on Ellie Laine), *The Sun*, 15.4.86.

Clarke, J., 'Love, Liberation and Liverpool' (on Margi Clarke,), *Spare Rib*, May 1986.

Cooper, C., 'Making Whoopi' (on Whoopi Goldberg), *The Face*, March 1986.

Cosgrove, S., 'Bombshell' (on Margi Clarke, Diana Dors), *NME*, 11.1.86.

Dixon, C., Review of Katie Johnson in *The Ladykillers*, *Daily Telegraph*, 10.12.55.

Driver, C., 'How to play an almighty joke' (on *No Son of Mine*), *The Guardian*, 9.8.85

Edwardes, J., Review of *No Son of Mine*, *Time Out*, 12.2.86.

Fiddick, P., Report of the Edinburgh International Television Festival, *The Guardian*, 13.3.78.

Freedland, M., 'Make 'Em Laugh' (on *Who Dares Wins*), *TV Times*, 23-29.11.85.

Goodwin, C., and Milae, T., 'Working with Joan' (on Joan Littlewood), *Encore*, July-August 1960.

Harcourt Smith, S., Review of Margaret Rutherford in *Blithe Spirit*, *Daily Mail*, 16.4.45.

Hinyman, M., Review of Maggie Smith in *California Suite*, *Daily Mail*, 20.3.79.

Howell, G., 'Laughter: The New Liberator' (on Linda Agran, Dawn French, Caroline Holden, Helen Lederer, Maureen Lipman, Posy Simmonds and Paula Youens), *Sunday Times Magazine*, 19.1.86.

Hughes, G., 'Me and My Bump, Pamela Speaks Out' (on Pamela Stephenson), *Woman's Own*, 14.6.86.

Hulse, T., 'Funny Peculiar' (on Julie Walters), *Blitz*, April 1985.

Irwin, K., 'Funny Girls' (Top ten funny women), *Daily Mirror*, 24.2.86.

Jackson, A., 'If You Knew Peggy/Su' (on Su Pollard), *NME*, 25.2.86.

Jerome, K.J., review of Bessie Bellwood, *Idler Magazine*, 1892.

Johnson, M., Review of Glenda Jackson in *A Touch of Class*, *Los Angeles Times*, 27.8.72.

Kendall. E., 'Irene Handl, A Room of My Own', *Observer Magazine*, 13.10.85.

London Screenwriters' Workshop Newsletters, ed. Barbara Cox.

Margolyes, M., 'Top Ten Books', *Women's Review*, no. 5.

May, P., 'Red Wedge Tour' (on Sensible Footwear), *LAM*, 25.2.86.

Mooney, B., 'All Joking Apart' (on Christine Ellerbeck, Jenny Lecoat, Rebecca Stevens), *Observer*, 22.7.84.

Morley, S., 'Solid Gold Gingold' (on Hermione Gingold), *The Times*, 12.4.75.

Morley, S., 'Keeping Up The Baddeley Style' (on Hermione Baddeley), *The Times*, 1.10.81.

Nixon, A., *Broadcast*, February 1984.

Obituaries, *The Times*, 15.10.70, Dame Edith Evans, *The Times*, 23.5.72, Margaret Rutherford, *The Times*, 5.5.86, Hylda Baker.

Paton, M., 'Funny Girls' (on Susie Blake, Su Pollard, Victoria Wood), *Daily Express*, 24.2.86.

Paton, M., 'Comedy's a Serious Business' (on Julia Hills, Maureen Lipman, Carla Mendonça), *Daily Express*, 25.2.86.

Paton, M., 'Bold Bawdy and Beautiful' (on Emma Thompson and Helen Lederer), *Daily Express*, 26.2.86.

Paton, M., 'Beware, These Hamsters Bite!' (on The Flamin' Hamsters), *Daily Express*, 1.3.86.

Pukas, P., 'Pam Has a Change' (Pamela Stephenson), *South London Press*, 22.4.86.

Ratcliffe, M., 'A Saucy Night at Spithead' (Review of Maureen Lipman in *Wonderful Town*), *Observer*, 27.4.86.

Smith, J., 'Miss Ellie – Britain's Own Joan Rivers' (on Ellie Laine), *Sunday People*, 26.1.86.

Shivas, S., 'Oh Ellie!' (on Ellie Laine), *Daily Record*, 26.2.86.

Starburst, no. 67. vol. 5, no.4, March 1984 (on Diana Rigg).

Television Today Reporter, Interview with John Lloyd, *Television Today*, 24.1.80.

Twomey, C. (On Krissie Illing, Nickleodeon), *LAM*, 11.2.86.

Welch. J., 'Funny Girls' (on Pamela Stephenson), *The Observer*, 13.6.85.

Wiseman, T., Review of Dora Bryan in *A Taste of Honey*, *Sunday Express*, 17.9.61

Wood, V., 'Sing Something Silly' (Victoria Wood song lyrics), *Cosmopolitan*, October 1984.

Woods, W., 'Still Following in Father's Footsteps' (Review of *Vesta Tilley* by Sara Maitland), *The Guardian*, 23.4.86.

Index

A Fine Romance, 235
A Hard Day's Night, 157
A Kick up the Eighties (SVT), 206, 256
A Little Bit of Fluff, 132
A Little Bit on the Side, 67
A Private Function, 161, 163
A Question of Silence, 167
A Taste of Honey, 155, *156*
A Touch of Class, *158*, 159, 160
Abbott, Russ, 252
Abigail's Party, 109
Absolute Beginners, 164, 171, *173*
Actresses' Franchise League, 180
Adams, Douglas, 73, 188
Agony, *111*
Agran, Linda, 167, 224
Albee, Edward, 20
Aldwych Farce, 133
Alfie, 157
Alfresco, 190, 252
All that Glitters, 241
Allen, Keith, 25, 84, 164
Allen, Tony, 25
Allen, Woody, 224
Allsop, Kenneth 245
*And Now For Something Completely
    Different* (BBC), 158, 205
And There's More (Central TV), 253
Anderson, Adele, 86, 183, *184*
Anderson, Lindsay, 247
Andrews, Archie, 65
Anybody here seen thingy?, *234*
Anything May, 189
Animal House, 224
Archer, Paul Mayhew, 70
Arden, Annabel, *92*, 93, 100
Arts Council, 119
Askey, Arthur, 53
Asquith, Anthony, 131
Asquith, Robin, 152
A Taste of Honey, 155, *156*
Aunt Sally, 133
Ayckbourn, Alan, 109

Bachelor Father, 229
Baddeley, Angela, 97

Baddeley, Hermione, 97, 98, 99, 141, 147
Baker, Hylda, 88, 111, *115*, 155
Balcon, Michael, 131, 136, 138, 139, 141,
    172
Balfour, Betty, 131
Ball, Lucille, 111, 130
Bandwagon, 53
Banks, Monty, 138
Bara, Theda, 133
Barclay, Humphrey, 188, 242
Barclay, Jim, 25
Bardot, Brigitte, 148
Barker, Ronnie, 87, 204
Barlow, Deirdre, 44
Barnett, Jeni *209*
Barthes, Roland, 248
Baxter, Stanley, 252
Bedsit Girl, 242
Beech, Anne, *232*
Beerbohm, Max, 5
Behn, Aphra, 180
Belbin, Susan, 246
Bell, Beverley, 44, *45*
Bellamy, David, 87
Bellwood, Bessie, 15, 16, *17*
Bennett, Alan, 114, 161, 163, 220, 224
Bentine, Michael, 69
Beryl and the Perils, 119
Bevan, Tim, 164
Bewitched, 224
Beyond a Joke, 194
Beyond the Fringe, 187
Bicycling, 186
Bilko, 224
Bird, John, 188, 189, 191
Bird, Philip, *209*
Black Adder (BBC TV), 246
Black on Black, 44
Black Theatre Co-operative, 241, 242
Blessings in Disguise, 89
Bless This House, 229
Blithe Spirit, 144, *146*
Bloom, Claire, 125
Bluett, Kitty, 63
Bobby Davro on the Box (TVS), 253
Bogarde, Dirk, 147

Bombastes Furioso, 188
Bond, James Bond, and Bond films, 157, 159, 161
Booth, Celia Gore, 92
Booth, Connie, 206, 235, 237
Born in Flames, 167
Bottle Boys, 171, 252
Bragg, Melvyn, 114
Bresslaw, Bernard, 150
Briers, Richard, *238*
Bright Eyes, 132
Britton, Mark, 122
British Broadcasting Corporation, 52, 53, 55, 58, 63, 65, 70, 71, 72, 80, 81, 83, 84, 199, 206, 208, 226, 228, 243, 245, 246, 247, 248
British Cinema Now, 167
British Film Foundation, 166
Broadcasting House, 69
Bron, Eleanor, 1, 105, 157, 188, 189, 190, 191, 192, *193*, 194, 224, 227
Brookes, Maggie, 167
Brough, Peter, 65, 66
Broughton, Linda, *209*
Brown, Faith, 128, 224, 252-3
Brown, Steve, 82
Bryan, Dora, 102, 114, 144, 155, *156*
Buhr, 'Miss', 196
Burke, Patricia, 69
Burns, Nica, 183
Burnt Bridges, 119
Butt, Alfred, 187
Butterflies, 230, *231*
Bygraves, Max, 65

Cabaret Upstairs, 83
Caine, Marti, 11, 13, 14, 20, 21, 129, 249, *250*, 251, 252-3
Caine, Michael, 161, 170
California Suite, 161, *162*
Campaign for Real Equality in Equity, 119
Campbell, Jennie, *51*, 80, 81, 225
Campbell, Ken, 220
Cannon, Esma, 152, 230, 231, *232*
Capital Radio, 83, 84
Capra, Frank, 133
Capra, Jean, 53
Car Trouble, 171
Carne, Judy, 230, *232*
Carrott's Lib, 70
Carry On films, *54*, 63, 147, 148, 150, 151, *152*, 153, *154*, 155, 158, 165, 233
Carry on Admiral, 150
Carry on Camping, 152
Carry on Doctor, 54
Carry on Emmanuelle, 158
Carry on Girls, 153
Carry on Nurse, 150
Carry on Screaming, *154*
Carry on Sergeant, *150*
Carry on Teacher, 150

Cellar Tapes, 78, 190
Cellnet Car Phones, 212
Champagne, 132
Channel Four, 164, 166, 226
Chant, Mrs Ormiston, 44
Chaplin, Charles, 131, 224
Chapman, Graham, 188
Charabanc Theatre Company, *118*, 219, 225
Chariots of Fire, 167
Charlot, André, 187
Cheer Boys Cheer, 138
Cheers, 224
Christie, Agatha, 144
Christie, Julie, 157
Churchill, Winston, 47
Cinderella, 98
Cinema of Women, 166
Circles, 166
Clarke, Frank, 169
Clarke, Margi, *168*, 169, 170
Cleese, John, 161, 188, 190, 206, 235, 236, 237
Cleveland, Carol, 204, *205*, 249
Cliff Hanger Theatre Company, 35
Clockwise, 161
Coffey, Denise, *51*, 73, 78, 116, 124, 178, 224, 225, 239, *253*
Cogan, Alma, 111
Cole, George, 225
Coliseum, The, 44, 89
Collins, Pauline, 229
Comedians, 31
Comedy Store, 15, 37, 84, 171, 182
Come into the Garden, Maud, 47
Comfort and Joy, 164
Comic Strip, 15, 76, 83, 158, 165, 166
Compagnie Philippe Gaulier, 91
Confessions films, 152, 161
Congreve, William, 119
Connolly, Billy, 1, 224
Connery, Sean, 157
Connors, Kenneth, 63
Constanduros, Mabel, 53, 60
Consuela, 164
Cook, Peter, 187, 188, 191
Copperfield, David, 213
Corbett, Harry, 157
Corbett, Ronnie, 204
Counting the Ways, 20
Coupland, Diana, 229
Courtenidge, Cicely, 133, *134*, 188
Courtenidge, Robert, 188
Cover Girls, 202
Covington, Julie, 188
Coward, Noel, 95, 144, 187
Craig, Wendy, 229, *231*, 237
Crewe, Cathy, 199
Cunning Stunts, 252
Cutts, Marilyn, *184*

Dad's Army, 230

Index

Dale, Jim, 151
Daniels, Bebe, 53, 65, 67, 68, 132
Daniels, Pauline, *12*, 13
Davies, Betty Ann, 147
Dawson, Les, 182, 224, 252, 259
Day, Diana, 69
Day, Doris, 130
Day, Robin, 87
Deayton, Angus, 75
de Cassalis, Jean, 60
de Courville, André, 187
de la Tour, Frances, 224, 237
Dench, Judi, 88, 235
Deneker, Susan, 78
Desert Island Discs, 78
Desmond, Florence, 2
Diana, 157
Did you hear the One about the Irishman?, 219
Dimensions, 105
Dobell, Linda, 209
Dobson, Anita, 2
Doctor in the House, 147
Donmar Warehouse, 183
Do Not Adjust Your Set, 252
Dors, Diana, 171
Dowie, Claire, *38*, 51
'Down at the Old Bull and Bush', 2
Draper, Ruth, 106
Dunant, Sarah, 198
Durbin, Deanna, 130

Ealing Comedies, Ealing Studios, 131, 138, 139, 144, 172, 224
Eastenders, 2, 254
Eaton, Shirley, 147, 148, 151
Eclair, Jenny, *36*, 128
Eddington, Paul, *238*
Edinburgh Festival Fringe, 187
Edinburgh International Television Festival, 241
Edmonds, Noel, 9
Edmonson, Adrian, 84, 164, 165, *207*
Edna, the Inebriate Woman, 63
Educating Archie, 65, 66
Educating Rita, 170, 171
Electric Voodoo, 190, 201
Eliot, George, 50
Eliot, T.S., 40, 43
Elizabeth R, 160
Elton, Ben, 1, 206
Emmanuelle, 161
Empire, Liverpool, 47, 109
English, Rose, 93, 96, 97
Entertainments National Service Association, 55
Equity Women's Committee, 119
Estenson, Elizabeth, 233
Evans, Edith, 88
Evergreen, 134
Eyre, Richard, 167, 188

Fairbanks, Tasha, 215
Farjeon, Herbert, 59, 105, 187
Farson, Daniel, 6, 8
Fascinating Aïda, 98, 102, 183, *184*
Fat is a Feminist Issue, 120
Father Dear Father, 229
Fawlty Towers, 190, 206, 235, *236*, 237
Feldman, Marty, 71
Female Trouble, 215
Ferret, Eve, 87, 171, 172, *173*, 252
Field, Sid, 112
Fielding, Fenella, *154*, 155
Fielding, Henry, 69
Fields, Gracie, 54, 55, 136, *137*, 138
Fings Ain't Wot They Used t'Be, 125
Finney, Albert, 155, 159
Firecrackers, 230
First a Girl, 134
Fisher, John, 89
Five go Mad in Dorset, 164
Five go Mad on Mescalin, 164
Flamin' Hamsters, 51
Fleming, Ian, 157
Fletcher, Mandie, 50, 246, 247
Flowers, 106
Footlights, 75, 188, 189, 190, 195, 196, 197, 198, 199, 202, 204
Forde, Florrie, 2, *3*
Forsyth, Bill, 161, 163, 164
Fortune, John, 188, 191, 192
Fox, Maggie, 26
Fox, Samantha, 172
Francis, Jan, 235
Fraser, Liz, 151
Frayn, Michael, 188
Frears, Stephen, 164
Free Cinema, 172
French, Dawn, 15, *18*, 19, 26, 58, 84, 148, 164, 165, 169, 214, 258, 259
French and Saunders *see* French, Dawn *and* Saunders, Jennifer
Frost, David, 194
Fugue, 216
Funny Way to Be a Hero, xii, 89, 115

Gainsborough Films and Gainsborough Pictures, 131, 136
Galton, Ray, 69, 70, 211, 228
Galton and Simpson *see* Galton, Ray, *and* Simpson, Alan
Game for a Laugh, 171
Gandhi, 166
Garden, Graeme, 188
Gardner, Carol, 69
Gascoigne, Bamber, 188
Gaulier, Philippe, 91
Gaumont British, 136
Gaumont Film Company, 130
Gaumont, Léon, 130
Geldof, Bob, 2
Genevieve, 148, *149*

George, Susan, 157
Georgy Girl, 157
Gert and Daisy *see* Waters, Doris and Elsie
Gertrude Stein and a Companion, 73
Get Some In, 230
Get yourself a trauma, 210
Gibbons, Walter, 131
Gilliam, Terry, 204
Gingold, Hermione, 53, 97, 98, 99, 141, 186
Girls on Top, 148, 214, 257, *258*, 259
Grandma Buggins, 53
Grant, Abi, 87, 176, 212
Gravely, Norma J., 21, 22
Great Rock and Roll Swindle, 164
Greater London Council, 119
Green book, 84
Greenwood, Joan *140*, 148, *258*
Greer, Germaine, 34, 129, 177, 188, 195,
   196, *197*, 198, 245
Gregory's Girl, 162, 164
Grenfell, Joyce, 1, *59*, 65, 69, 88, 94, 102,
   105, 106, *107*, 108, 111, 147, 148, 185,
   186, 224
Griffith, David Wark, 131
Griffiths, Trevor, 31, 49
Grogan, Claire, 163
Gold in the Streets, 118
Good Morning Britain, 9, 44
Gordon, Bette, 167
Gordon, Richard, 147
Guinness, Alec, 89, 139, 141, 224

Hale, Sonnie, 134
Hall, Peter, 245
Hampshire, Susan, 198
Hancock, Sheila, 122-3, 125, 230, 231, *232*,
   242-3, *244*, 245, 260
Hancock's Half Hour, 63, 179, 211
Hancock, Tony, 61, 65, 69, 70, 224, 228,
   229, 235
Handl, Irene, 6, 71, 141, 144, *145*, 147,
   152, 185, 186, 233
Handley, Tommy, 53
Happy Families, 82
Happy Since I met You, 220
Harben, Joan, 53
Hard Corps, 119
Hardy, Oliver, 224
Harris, Anita, 151
Hawkins, Carol, 153
Hawks, Howard, 133
Hawn, Goldie, 130, 233
Hayes, Catherine, 15
Hayes, Patricia, 63, 114, 144
Hayman, Carol, 219
Heal, Joan, 69, 70
Healey, Denis, 224
Help!, 157
Henderson, Maggie, 188
Henry Hall's Guest Night, 60, 65
Henry, Lenny, 70, 176

Hepburn, Dee, 162
Hepburn, Katherine, 130, 148
Heseltine, Michael, 25, 43
Hewison, Robert, 188
Hickson, Joan, 148
Hi-de-Hi, 100, 116, 227, *239*
Hi Gang, 53
Hill, Benny, 2, 252
Hill, Jenny, *4*, 5, 16
Hills, Julia, 252
Hippodrome, 4
Hird, Thora, 114, 144, 152, 155, 233
Hitchcock, Alfred, 131
Hitch-hiker's Guide to the Galaxy, 73
Hoare, Ken, 245
'Hold your hand out, you naughty boy', 2
Hollerbach, Kit, *37*, 86, 199
Holliday, Judy, 130, 224
Horne, Kenneth, 71
Horne, Lena, 150
Houston, Renée, 147
How, 60
Howerd, Frankie, 252
Hudd, Roy, 204
Hughes, Nerys, 225, 233, *234*, 235
Hulbert, Jack, 133, *134*, 188
Humphries, Barry, 195
Hyde, Sheila, 128, 201

IBA, *see* Independent Broadcasting Authority
I love Lucy, 224, 233
I Married a Bachelor, 229
Idle, Eric, 188, 197, 198
Idler Magazine, 15
Illing, Krissie, 122, *123*
In at the Death, 220
Injury Time, 75
Independent Broadcasting Authority, 226
Independent Television, 226
In One Ear, 72, 82
In Whose Image, 120
I'm sorry I'll read that again, 72
Intimate Revue, 59, 187
ITMA *see It's that Man again*
'It's a long way to Tipperary', 2
It's love again, 134
It's that Man again, 53, 54, 55, 58
ITV *see* Independent Television

Jackson, Glenda, 122, *158*, 159, 160
Jack's the Boy, 133
Jacobs, Judith, 241, 242, *243*
Jacques, Hattie, 53, *54*, 55, 65, 150, 151,
   233
James, Clive, 224
James, Polly, 214, 233, *234*
James, Sid, 69, 153
Johnson, Katie, 141, *143*, 144
Johnson, Sandy, 164
Johnson, Terry, 16
*Jolly Good Luck to the Girl Who Loves a
   Soldier*, 131

Index

Jones, Ann, 189
Jones, Griff Rhys, 188
Jones, Marie, 225
Jones, Peter, 232
Jones, Sarah, 120
Jones, Terry, 204
Jongleurs, 26
Jonson, Ben, 152
Joyce Grenfell Requests the Pleasure, 105
Joyce, Yootha, 229
Joyriders, 219
Just Fancy, 69
Just Good Friends, 235

Karen, Anna, 153
Karlin, Miriam, 69, 122, 230, 231, *232*
Kavanagh, Ted, 53
Keane, Dillie, 98, 102, *184-5*
Keaton, Buster, 131
Keaton, Diane, 130
Keen, Diane, 184
Keith, Penelope, 237, *238*
Kelly's Eye, 76
Kempinska, Maria, 26
Kendall, Felicity, 184, 237, *238*
Kendall, Jo, 73, 188, 195
Kendall, Kay, 148, *149*
Kendall, Marie, 8
Kensit, Patsy, 172
Kerr, Bill, 69
Kind Hearts and Coronets, 139, 148
Kitty:One, 221-2
Klein, Debby, 46, *47*
Kureishi, Hanif, 166

La Cage aux Folles, 224
Ladies First, 120
La Fave, 21
Laine, Ellie, 9, *10*, 11, 13, 21, 22, 28, 48
Lambert, Verity, 167
Lancaster, Burt, 163
Lane, Carla, 214, 234, 240
Lapotaire, Jane, 122
Last Laugh, 189
Last of the Summer Wine, 227
Laugh In, 151
Laughing at Love, 188
Laughter in the Air, 60, 68
Laurel and Hardy, *see* Laurel, Stan *and* Hardy, Oliver
Laurel, Stan, 224
Lavery, Bryony, 180, 215-16
Lawrence, Gertrude, *95*, 187
Lay Up Your Ends, 118
Lazenby, George, 157
Lear, Norman, 241
Leaving, 230
Lecoat, Jenny, 26, *27*, 28, 30, 31, 34, 50, 86, 128, 185
Lecoq, Jacques, 91
Leddy, Caroline, 202, *203*

Lederer, Helen, 26, 31, 32, *33*, 82, 87, 181, 252
Lee, Anna, 188
Leigh, Mike, 109, 161
Letter to Brezhnev, *168*, 169, 170
Levin, Bernard, 108, 194
Life with the Lyons, 53, 65, 66, 68
Light and Shade, 105
Lillie, Beatrice, 53, 91, 93, *94*, 97, 98, 187
Lily, Peta (And Peta Lily Mime Theatre), 100, *101*
Limb, Sue, 52, 71, 80, 188, 198, 199
Lindsay, Robert, 224
Lipman, Maureen, 58, 88, *110*, 111, 114, 224, 227, 237, 252
Lip Service, 26, 181
Lister, Moira, 69
Little Review, 105
Little Theatre, 105
Little Women, 119, 252
Littlewood, Joan, 124, 125, *126*, 150, 232
Liverpool Festival of Comedy, 13
Liverpool Playhouse, 30
Lloyd, Harold, 109
Lloyd, John, 70, 188, 229, 255
Lloyd, Marie, xi, 2, 5, 6, 7, 8, 9, 13, 20, 30, 40, 43, 47, 48, 89, 180
Local Hero, 163
Lochhead, Liz, 217
Loftus, Cissie, 2
London Weekend Television, 242
Look Back in Anger, 155
Loose Connections, 167
Love From Judy, 61
Love Thy Neighbour, 241
Lucky Bag – The Victoria Wood Songbook, 220
Lucy *see I Love Lucy*
Lumiere and Son, 93
Lynn, Jonathon, 188
Lyons, B, 53

McCauley, Maureen, *118*
McDowell, Malcolm, 160
McInnes, Colin, 8, 9, 20
Mackendrick, Alexander, 141
McKenzie, Julia, 88, 225
McNee, Patrick, 194
McPhail, Donna, 202, *203*
Maitland, Sarah, 28, 131
Making Faces, 194
Manning, Bernard, 1, 14, 22, 48
Mantle, Clive, 82
Marconi, 52
Margolyes, Miriam, xiii, 73, *74*, 86, 128, 177, 188, 190, 195, 225
Marks, Alfred, 65
Marsden, Betty, 71
Marshall, Arthur, 225
Martin, Jessica, 253, *254*
Martin, Millicent, 194

Martin, Steve, 224
Mary Hartman, Mary Hartman, 241
Mary, Queen of Scots, 160
Maschewitz, Eric, 53
Matthews, Jessie, 133, 134, *135*, 136, 138, 187
May, Elaine, 192, 224
Mayall, Rik, 84, 164, 206, *207*
Mayer, Lise, 50, 176, 206, 207, 224, 249
Me and My Girl, 190, 224
Medallion Man, 213
Medhurst, Andy, 240
Melly, Andrée, 69
Melville, Pauline, 22, 23, 25, 26, 34, 48
Mess Mates, 230
Methuen, Eleanor, 18
MGM, 134
Midler, Bette, 87, 224
Miller, Jonathan, 88, 224
Miller, Lilla (Mrs Sosewarne), 39, 40, *41*
Milligan, Spike,
Minder, 167
Miss Jones and on, 230
Mitchell, War, 66
Monday Night Eight, 60
Monstrous ment, 119, 215
Monty Pyths Flying Circus, (Python) 72, 100, 1580, 204, *205*, 206, 224, 248, 249
Monty Pyn and the Holy Grail, 158
Moore, ck, 87
Moore, en, *191*
Moreca Eric, 224, 252
More Fe Trouble, 215
Morrisby, 102
MorrisDiana, 53
MortinJohn, 224, 245
Mothekes Three, 229
Mounggy, 229
Mrs ington's Daughters, 119
Muir k, 60
MulDorothy, 189
MulJimmy, 75
Murona, 216, 217, 219
Murboy, 147
Mut the Gallop, 147
Mulost Foul, 147
Muhe Said, 147
M, Richard, 53
M Maeve, 202
Mall, 53, 69
utiful Laundrette, 167, 170
 Herbert, 195
d Woman, 229
e Next Door, 229

Video, 217, 252
al Film Finance Corporation, 166
al Theatre, 20, 122, 124
al Theatre of Brent, 215
a Happy Ending, 220

New Mates, 236
News Huddlines, 63, 72
Nicholls, Dandy, 152
Nicholls, Joy, 60
Nichols and May, *see* Nichols, Mike *and* May, Elaine
Nichols, Mike, 192, 224
Nichelodeon, 122
Nightingale, Florence, 5
Nippy Sweeties, 217
Nixon, Alan, 83, 84
Noble, Katina, 120, *121*
No More Women, 188
No Problem (LWT), 241, 242
Norden, Denis, 60
Normand, Mabel, 130, 132
No Son of Mine, 91, 92, 93, 100
Not in Front of the Children, 229, 237
Nothing Else Matters, 132
Not so much a programme, more a way of life, 189
Not the Nine O'Clock News (BBC 2), 206, 208, 216, 229, 255
Now Seriously, It's Sheila Hancock (BBC), 245
Now Something Else (BBC 2), 70
Novello, Ivor, 131
Number 73 (TVS) 201
Nunn, Trevor, 188
Nuts In May, 109

Oddie, Bill, 188
O'Donoghue, Denise, 245
Oh! What a lovely war, 150, 151
Oklahoma, 97
Oliver, Vic, 69
O Lucky Man, 160
On a Clear Day, 151
On Her Majesty's Secret Service, 157
On the Buses, 153
Orbach, Susie, 120
Our Lizzie, 52
Out of Control, 120
Outside Edge, 110

'Pack Up Your Troubles', 2
Paddick, Hugh, 71, 72
Paines Plough, 216
Palin, Michael, 161, 163, 204, *205*
Palmer, Toni, 230, *232*
Parker, Karen, 46, 47
Parker, Dorothy, 50, 224
Passport to Pimlico, 139
Pathé Films, 132
Paul, Mr and Mrs Howard, 5
Payne, Cynthia, 171
Penny Plain, 105
Pepper, Harry, 55
Percival, Lance, 194
Perkins, Geoffrey, 75
Personal Services, 171

Index

Pickles, Wilfrid, 61
Pickford, Mary, 131
Pigg, Alexandra, 169, 170
Pile, Vicky, 51, 117, 208, 209, 210, 216, 224
Pilgrim, Christine, *24*, 25
Pinter, Harold, 187
Piper's Cave, 216
Pirate Radio Caroline, 72
Pirates Of Penzance, 102
Planer, Nigel, 84, 164, *207*
Platform, 202
Please Sir, 152
Plenty, 256
Pollard, Su, 88, 100, 116, 224, 227, 237, 239
Pollock, Eileen, 28
Pope, Philip, 75
Porridge, 237
Potter, Sally, 93, 167
Potter, Stephen, 59
Power, Nelly, 5
Priestley, J.B. 114, 221
Princess Diana, 44
Private Lives, 95
Pryor, Richard, 1
Pygmalion, 170
Pyke, Magnus, 87
Python *see Monty Python's Flying Circus*

Queen of Hearts, 138
Quick, Diana, 122

Radclyffe, Sarah, 164, 167
Radiation Newsreel, 211
Radio Active, 72, 75
Radio Luxembourg, 72
Radio Radiance, 53
Ramsden, Hilary, 121
Rank/Thorn-EMI, 167
Rantzen, Esther, 86
Ravens, Jan, 78, 80, 87, 188, 199, *200*
Ray's A Laugh, 63
Ray, Ted, 68, 69, 70
Rea, Marjorie, 39, 40, *42*
Rebellious Juke Box, 208
Redgrave, Lynn, 157, 247
Redmond, Siobhan, 252
Reid, Beryl, 1, 16, 20, 50, 62, 65, 66, 67, 102, 112, 117, 126, 144, 147, 187, 224, 225
Reid, Christina, 181, 219
Reith, J.C.W., 52, 53
Renshaw, Alison, 70, 210, 211, 216, 217
Retford, Ella, 8
Revolting Women, 208, *209*, 215
Richard Pryor Live at Sunset Strip, 132
Richardson, Peter, 164, 165, 166
Richardson, Tony, 157
Ridley, Wally, 66
Rigg, Diana, 157

Rise Above It, 98
Rising Damp, 237
Rivers, Joan, 11, 224
Rix, Jamie, 70, 82
Roach, Hal, 132
Roberts, Rachel, 159, 160
Rosenthal, Mr, senior and junior, 224
Rosewarne, Mrs *see* Miller, Lilla
Ross, Don, 6
Ross, Herbert, 161
Rossiter, Leonard, 224
Routledge, Patricia, 108, 109, 111, *113*, 114, 117, 187, 220, 224, 225, 226
Round The Horne, 71, 72
Royal Academy of Dramatic Arts (RADA), 61, 62
Royal Court, 239
Royal Shakespeare Company, 114, 122, 124
Rudner, Rita, 225
Russell-Smith, Joy, 68
Russell, Willy, 170
Rutherford, Margaret, 88, 144, *146*, 224
Rynn, Chris, *207*

Sadista Sisters, 119
Sally In Our Alley, 136
Samuelson, G.B., 131
Sanderson, Tessa, 44
Saturday Live, 190
Saturday Night and Sunday Morning, 155, 159
Saunders, Jennifer, 15, *18*, 19, 26, 84, 148, 164, 165, 167, 169, 214, 225, 259
Sayle, Alexei, 25, 84, 164, 224, 225
Scales, Prunella, 114, *236*
Scanlan, Carol, *118*
Scarlet Harlets, 119, 252
Scott, Linda, *92*, 93
Scott, Terry, 61
Searle, Ronald, 145
Secombe, Harry, 69
Secret Diary of Adrian Mole aged 13¾
Segal, George, 159, 160
Sellers, Peter, 63, 69
Sennett, Mack, 131, 132
Sensible Footwear, 119, 120, 121
Seven:Eighty Four (7:84), 34
Seyler, Athene, 108, 112, 114
Shadows on the Grass, 185
Shampoo, 161
Shaw, George Bernard, 116
She'll Be Wearing Pink Pyjamas, 171
Shine on Harvey Moon, 215
Shields, Ella, 5
Shipyard Sally, 138
Sigh No More, 105
Sim, Alistair, 145, *147*, 224
Simon, Neil, 161, 224
Simmonds, Jean, 150
Simms, Joan, 147, 148, 151

Simply Sheila (BBC 2), 245
Simpson, Alan, 69, 70, 211, 228
Simpson, N.F., 187
Sinclair, Gordon John, 162
Sing As We Go, 138
Siren, 119, 120-1, 215
Slings and Arrows, 98
Smashing Time, 157
Smith, Elaine, C., 252
Smith, George, 130
Smith, Liz, 163
Smith, Maggie, 160, 161, *162*, 163
Smythe, Rita, *232*
Soap, 230, 241
Solo, 230, 248
Solomons, Andrea, 70, 179, 213
Somebody's Darling, 132
Songs From the Show, 53
Spare Tyre, 112, 119, 120, *121*
Sparrers can't Sing, 150, 151
Speight, Johnny, 241
Spiers, Bob, 164
Spitting Image, 43, 70, 212, 229, 253
Sprigges, Elizabeth, 114
Squibbs, 132
St Trinians, 145, *147*
*Standing Committee of Women Theatre
    Directors*, 122
Starlight Hour, 65
Steadman, Alison, 73, 78, 161
Steafel, Sheila, 105, 252
Steed, Maggie, 26, 181, 215
Stephenson, Pamela, xi, 80, 172, 196, 215,
    255, 256
Steptoe and Son, 237, 241
Stevens, Michael Fenton, 75
Stevens, Rebecca, *35*, 86, 87
Stoll, Oswald, 44
Street-Porter, Janet, 86
Streets of London, 40
Summers, Dorothy, 53
Supergrass, 165
Superman III, 172
Sweet Saturday Night, 8
Sykes, Eric, 65

Take it from Here, 60, 61
Talent, 219
Tandoori Nights, 241
Tarrie a while, 56
Tarri, Suzette, 56, 69
Tati, Jacques, 224
Taylor, Myra, 214
Taxi, 224
Tea in a China Cup 229
Tebbit, Norman, 25
Temple, Julien, 164, 171
Terry and June, 63, 239
Terry, Ellen, 30
That Sinking Feeling, 162
That Was the Week That Was, 194, 204

The Avengers, 157, 194
The Bandung File, 44
The Beatles, 157
The Beggar's Opera, 151
The Belfast Home Help, 105
The Belles of St Trinians, 145, *147*
The Brat, 132
The Clitheroe Kid, 69
The Comic Strip, *see* Comic Strip
The Dustbinmen, 230
The English Family Robinson, 53
The Establishment, 105, 157, 191, 192
The Fainthearted Feminist, 218, 246, 247,
    248
The Faith Brown Awards, 253
The Faith Brown Chat Show, 253
The Fosters, 241
The Frost Report, 252
The Ghost Train, 133
The Glums, 61
The Gold Diggers, 93, 167
The Gold-Tipped Pfitzer, 185
The Good Companions, 134
The Good Life, 237, 238
The Goon Show, 69, 100
The Great Purple Dream, 185
The Hit, 164
The Hothouse, 157
The Killing Fields, 167
The Knack, 157
The Lady is a Tramp, 63
The Ladykillers, 141-4
The Late Late Breakfast Show, 9
The Laughter Show, 253
The Life of Brian, 158
The Liver Birds, 214, 233, *234*, 235
The Man in the White Suit, 148
The Marti Caine Show, 252
The Mary Tyler Moore Show, 224
The Meaning of Life, 158
The Millies, 202, *203*
The Natural Order, 220
The Other Cinema, 166
The Outer Limits, 84
The Prime of Miss Jean Brodie, 161
The Producers, 224
The Rag Trade, 69, 230, 231, *232*, 242
The Refuge, 219
The Sioux, 185
The Stud, 161
The Vagabond King, 53
The Way of the World, 117
The White Coons Concert Party, 53
The Willy Song, 26
The Wind-break War, 238
The Wordsmiths of Gorsemere, 73-5
The Young Ones, 76, 206, *207*, 224, 251
Thatcher, Margaret, Thatcherism, 44, 119
Theatre Royal and Theatre Workshop
    Stratford East, 124, 125, 150, 232
This Sporting Life, 155

Index

This Way Out, 195
Thompson, Emma, 78, 188, 190, *191*, 252
Three of a Kind, 257
Three plus one on Four, 78
Three up, two down, 246
Three Women, 100
'Till Death Us do Part, 241
Tilley, Vesta, 2, 5, 28, 29, 44, 131, 181
Toksvig, Sandi, 188, 201
Tom Jones, 157
Tomlin, Lily, 224
Took, Barry, 60, 71, 245
Townsend, Sue, 218
Traverse Theatre, 216
True Confessions, 217
Tuppence Coloured, 105
Tushingham, Rita, 155, 157
Tutti Frutti, 190
Tweedie, Jill, 128, 177, 218, 246, 248
Twentieth Century Coyote, 84

Ullman, Tracey, xi, 212-15, *256*, 257
Under your Hat, 134
Unnatural Acts, 70
Unwin, Jo, 86, 202, *203*
Up for Grabs, 191
Up Housewives and at 'em, 55
Upstairs Downstairs, 97
Up to You, Porky, 220
US Forces Network, 228

Variety, 167
Variety Bandbox, 60, 65, 68
Varney, Reg, 232
Victoria, Queen, 5
Victoria, Vesta, 89
Victoria Wood – as Seen on TV, 219
Vranch, Richard, 202, *203*

Wallace, Nellie, 89, *90*, 91, 186
Walters, Julie, 62, 170, 171, 194, 220, 224, 225, *259*
Watch the Woman, 30, 209
Waters, Doris, 55, 56, *57*, 58, 59, 69
Waters, Elsie, 55, 56, *57*, 58, 59, 69, 225
Waters, Naomi, 188
Wax, Ruby, 148, 257, *258*
Webster, Leila, *104*, 105, 117, 119
Weekending, 70
Weir, Mollie, 53
Welch, Julie, 256
We're in business, 71
West, Mae, 9, 130
Wharmby, Denise, 184

What did you say this thing was called, love?, 192
Wheen, Francis, 229
When we are married, 114
Where was Spring?, 192, 194
Whisky Galore, 139, *140*, 148
Whitehall Theatre, 114
Whitehouse, Mary, 44
Whitelaw, William, 224
Whitfield, June, 60, 61, *62*, 63, 225, 229
Who dares Wins, 245, 252
Whole Parts, *101*
WI Meeting, 105
Widows, 167
Wilder, Gene, 171, 224
Williams, Kenneth, 69, 71, *152*
Williams, Robin, 224
Williamson, James, 130
Wilmut, Roger, 194
Wilson, Dennis Main, 70, 230, 232
Wilson, Snoo, 220
Wilton, Nick, 82
Wilton, Rob, 69
Windsor, Barbara, 6, 14, 116, 125, 127, 130, 148, 150, 151, *152*, 153, 155, 230, *232*, 233
Winter, Brenda, *118*
Wireless Willie, 52
Wise, Ernie, 252
Wogan, 43
Wolf, Ronnie, 66
Woman's Hour, 201
Women in Love, 160
Women's Film and Television Network, 167
Women's Playhouse Trust, 122
Women's Therapy Centre, 120
Women's Theatre Group, 119
Women Writers' Suffrage League, 180
Wonderful Town, 111
Workers' Playtime, 56, 60, 65
Worsley, Bill, 65
Wood, Helen Atkinson, 50, 75, 76, 77, 86, 87, 128, 225
Wood, Victoria, 5, 14, 51, 73, 86, 87, 102, *103*, 183, 185, 219, 220, 221, 222, 223, 224, 225, 257, *259*, 260
Wood and Walters, 220
Wood Green Empire, 132
Wyndhams Theatre, 125

York, Susannah, 157
Young, David Jackson, 78
Yule, Fred, 63

Zounds, 189